Feminist Research for 21st-century Childhoods

Feminist Thought in Childhood Research

Series editors: Jayne Osgood and Veronica Pacini-Ketchabaw

Drawing on feminist scholarship, this boundary-pushing series explores the use of creative, experimental, new materialist and post-humanist research methodologies that address various aspects of childhood. *Feminist Thought in Childhood Research* foregrounds examples of research practices within feminist childhood studies that engage with post-humanism, science studies, affect theory, animal studies, new materialisms and other post-foundational perspectives that seek to decentre human experience. Books in the series offer lived examples of feminist research praxis and politics in childhood studies. The series includes authored and edited collections – from early career and established scholars – addressing past, present and future childhood research issues from a global context.

Also available in the series

Feminists Researching Gendered Childhoods: Generative Entanglements,
edited by Jayne Osgood and Kerry H. Robinson

Feminist Research for 21st-century Childhoods

Common Worlds Methods

Edited by

B. Denise Hodgins

BLOOMSBURY ACADEMIC
LONDON • NEW YORK • OXFORD • NEW DELHI • SYDNEY

BLOOMSBURY ACADEMIC
Bloomsbury Publishing Plc
50 Bedford Square, London, WC1B 3DP, UK
1385 Broadway, New York, NY 10018, USA

BLOOMSBURY, BLOOMSBURY ACADEMIC and the Diana logo are trademarks of
Bloomsbury Publishing Plc

First published in Great Britain 2019

Copyright © B. Denise Hodgins and Contributors, 2019

B. Denise Hodgins and Contributors have asserted their right under the Copyright,
Designs and Patents Act, 1988, to be identified as Authors of this work.

Series design by Anna Berzovan
Cover image: © Sylvia Kind

All rights reserved. No part of this publication may be reproduced or
transmitted in any form or by any means, electronic or mechanical,
including photocopying, recording, or any information storage or retrieval
system, without prior permission in writing from the publishers.

Bloomsbury Publishing Plc does not have any control over, or
responsibility for, any third-party websites referred to or in this book. All
internet addresses given in this book were correct at the time of going
to press. The author and publisher regret any inconvenience caused if
addresses have changed or sites have ceased to exist, but can
accept no responsibility for any such changes.

A catalogue record for this book is available from the British Library.

A catalog record for this book is available from the Library of Congress.

ISBN:	HB:	978-1-3500-5657-2
	ePDF:	978-1-3500-5659-6
	eBook:	978-1-3500-5658-9

Series: Feminist Thought in Childhood Research

Typeset by Integra Software Services Pvt. Ltd.

To find out more about our authors and books visit www.bloomsbury.com
and sign up for our newsletters.

Contents

List of Figures	vii
Notes on Contributors	viii
Series Editors' Introduction	xv
Acknowledgments	xvii

Common Worlding Research: An Introduction *B. Denise Hodgins*   1

Part One   Relations with Materials

1 Claying: Attending to Earth's Caring Relations
  Veronica Pacini-Ketchabaw and Kelly Boucher   25
2 Fabricating: Fabric Fluidities and Studio Encounters
  Sylvia Kind and Adrienne Argent   35
3 Sticking: Children and the Lively Matter of Sticks
  Tonya Rooney   43
4 Literacying: Literacy Desiring in Writers' Studio
  Candace R. Kuby   53
5 Intergenerationaling: Children, Elders and Materials
  Making Waves *Rachel Heydon and Elisabeth Davies*   63
6 Muscling: Doing Physiologies with Pedagogies in
  Education Research *Nicole Land*   73

Part Two   Relations with Other Species

7 Crowing: Coevolving Relationships *Kathleen Kummen*   85
8 Shimmering: Animating Multispecies Relations with
  Wurundjeri Country *Mindy Blaise and Catherine Hamm*   93
9 Tracking: Cultivating the "Arts of Awareness" in Early
  Childhood *Narda Nelson*   101
10 Rabbiting: Troubling the Legacies of Invasion *Affrica Taylor*   111

Part Three   Relations with Place

11 Gathering: An A/r/tographic Practice *Vanessa Clark*   121

12	Mashing: A Practice That Makes Vision Felt *Nikki Rotas*	131
13	Playing: Inefficiently Mapping Human and Inhuman Play in Urban Commonplaces *Linda M. Knight*	139
14	GoProing: Becoming Participant-Researcher *Susannah Clement*	149
15	Presencing: Decolonial Attunements to Children's Place Relations *Fikile Nxumalo*	159

Part Four   Relations with Retheorizings

16	Caring: Method as Affect, Obligation and Action *B. Denise Hodgins*	171
17	Learningliving: Aesthetics of Meaning Making *Randa Khattar and Karyn Callaghan*	179
18	Colaboring: Within Collaboration Degenerative Processes *Cristina D. Vintimilla and Iris Berger*	187
19	Childing: A Different Sense of Time *Karin Murris and Cara Borcherds*	197

Index   209

List of Figures

1.1	Clay-plastic movement. Photo credit: Kelly Boucher	26
1.2	Digging. Photo credit: Sylvia Kind	29
1.3	Assembling. Photo credit: Sylvia Kind	30
2.1	The fabric studio	36
2.2	The fabricated hockey game	40
3.1	Sticking with the lake, Canberra, Australia	46
4.1	Game board	55
6.1	How do muscles matter with tree trunks and tumbling?	74
6.2	How do we notice (with) muscles?	77
6.3	How do we make muscles perceptible, differently?	78
8.1	Creek-egretta-child-yabbie relations. Author's photograph	96
9.1	Something happened here	102
9.2	Past, present and ongoing connections	103
9.3	Reading for refusal	106
11.1	Portfolio layer	126
11.2	Map of walk	127
11.3	Gathering of photographs	128
13.1	Mapping. Pencil on tracing film. 2016. Artist: Linda Knight	143
13.2	Mapping. Pencil on tracing film. 2016. Artist: Linda Knight	144
19.1	Karin in the university classroom	200
19.2	Intra-action patterns: educator-students-newspaper-bird puppets-glass-tree-wind-waterbottles-tables-light	202
19.3	Diffracting two images	203
19.4	Diffracting with the educator (top) and the educator's disappearance (bottom)	205

Notes on Contributors

Adrienne Argent works as both an early childhood educator and a faculty member within the Capilano University Children's Centre and the university's ECCE degree program. She holds a BA in child and youth care and a MEd in early childhood education. Inspired by the schools in Reggio Emilia, Adrienne has a special interest in pedagogical documentation, collaborative encounters, and the vibrant and intra-active role that materials can play in infant and toddler spaces. Adrienne also enjoys immersing herself in place-based pedagogical inquiry that is situated within the west coast landscape.

Iris Berger has been involved in the field of early childhood education as a classroom teacher, researcher, community organizer, policy consultant and university lecturer since the mid-1990s. Her passion for early childhood education as a distinct and ever-engaging realm of/for research-pedagogy began when she worked with 2-, 3- and 4-year-olds in the model classrooms at the UBC Child Study Centre under the auspices of the Faculty of Education. At the center of her professional and academic inquiry lies the abiding notion that matters pertaining to education and childhood are entangled with the question of ethics and politics. To this end, Dr. Berger has developed a special interest in rethinking leadership in early childhood education and in making the complexity of the pedagogical relations in the early years visible through practices such as pedagogical documentation.

Mindy Blaise is an Australian American settler woman and a professor of education at Edith Cowan University, Western Australia. She is also a founding member of the Common Worlds Research Collective and Feminist Educators against Sexism (#FEAS). Her teaching and research are committed to troubling the developmental, racist, (hetero)sexist and imperialist knowledge base that dominates early childhood education.

Cara Borcherds is a graduate of the School of Education, University of Cape Town, with a postgraduate certificate in education (foundation phase). With a background in the fine arts, online marketing and business management (currently managing director of a small niche tourism business in Papua New

Guinea called Scuba Ventures), her teaching practice is grounded in an embodied and aesthetic philosophy. Cara makes extensive use of the arts as a bridge to thinking, expression, social interaction and making meaning in her own and others' learning. She plans to embark on a full-time career as a teacher and to continue exploring and developing the use of the technical image/digital media and augmented reality in her own and others' pedagogical documentation.

Kelly Boucher is an academic teaching scholar in early childhood at Victoria University, Melbourne. She is an arts specialist with broad and varied experience teaching in the arts and education sectors. Her research interests include children's relations with materials in early childhood, arts-based collaborative inquiry, sustainability, architecture and children as designers of place.

Karyn Callaghan has been a professor in college and university ECE programs for over thirty years and founded and coordinated the Artists at the Centre project. She is president of the Ontario Reggio Association and a board member of the North American Reggio Emilia Alliance and represents Canada on the Reggio Children International Network. Karyn has been a keynote speaker at conferences across North America and in Asia and Australia, and she consulted with Ontario's Ministry of Education as it developed its pedagogy for early years document *How Does Learning Happen?* A book entitled *Documenting Children's Meaning: Engaging in Design and Creativity with Children and Families*, coauthored by Karyn, Carol Anne Wien and artist Jason Avery, has been published by Davis Publications.

Vanessa Clark is an artist-teacher in the School of Education and Childhood Studies at Capilano University on the unceded and ancestral territories of the Coast Salish people. She collaborates with educators and children in her role as a pedagogical facilitator, and she bridges contemporary art and pedagogy in early childhood care and education. Her recent pedagogical and aesthetic interests are in situated, relational studio practices in early childhood education.

Susannah Clement is a human geographer whose research interests can be best described as taking a material feminist approach to explore the gendered politics, spatialities and mobilities of everyday family life. Her doctoral dissertation *Walking and Family Lives*, completed in 2018 at Australian Centre for Cultural Environmental Research and School of Geography and Sustainable Communities, University of Wollongong, Australia, explores the walking practices and experiences of families with children. She has recently published papers in *Gender, Place, and Culture* and *Children's Geographies*.

Elisabeth Davies works in research support in the Faculty of Information and Media Studies and the Faculty of Education at Western University. Her research and teaching interests include information practices, documents and time, and metadata management.

Catherine Hamm is a white settler woman who lives and works with Wurundjeri Country, now known as Melbourne, Australia. She is a senior lecturer at La Trobe University and a member of the Common Worlds Research Collective. Catherine's connections to the Victorian Aboriginal community strengthen her commitment to respectfully foreground local, Aboriginal worldviews of place as part of everyday practice in early childhood education.

Rachel Heydon is a professor in the Faculty of Education, Western University, where she specializes in early childhood literacies and curriculum. Her SSHRC-funded research focuses on intergenerational literacies and arts, which she has written about in books such as *Learning at the Ends of Life* (published by University of Toronto Press), *Why Multimodal Literacy Matters* (with Susan O'Neill, published by Sense) and the forthcoming *Advancing Interdisciplinary Research in Singing: Volume III Singing and Well-being* (with Daisy Fancourt and Annabel Cohen, published by Routledge). Rachel is the Canadian regional editor of the forthcoming *Bloomsbury Education and Childhood Studies* and executive editor of *Journal of Curriculum Studies*.

B. Denise Hodgins is the executive director of the Early Childhood Pedagogy Network in British Columbia, Canada, a founding member of the Early Childhood Pedagogies Collaboratory, and a member of the Common Worlds Research Collective. Her research interests include gender and care as material-discursive phenomena and the implications that postfoundational theories and methodologies have for early childhood research and pedagogy. She explores these in her book *Gender and Care with Young Children: A Feminist Material Approach to Early Childhood Education* (to be published by Routledge in 2019), chapters in edited books on critical perspectives in ECE/CYC, and published articles in *International Journal of Child, Youth, and Family Studies*; *Journal of Childhood Studies* (formerly *Canadian Children*); and *International Journal of Spirituality*.

Randa Khattar is an adjunct professor at Western University and Charles Sturt University, and the Executive Director of the Secretariat for the Centres of Excellence for Early Years and Child Care in Ontario. She has been teaching in andragogical contexts for the past 15 years. Her research, which is anchored within an interdisciplinary constellation of postfoundational, complexity, and eco-feminist theories and located within the Common Worlds Research Collective, uses creative paradigms to problematize developmental childhood discourses. She has published and presented internationally and serves in elected positions as the Ontario provincial director for the Canadian Association for Young Children (CAYC) and publication coordinator on the board of the Ontario Reggio Association. In 2018 she became coeditor of the *Journal of Childhood Studies*, a peer-reviewed international journal.

Sylvia Kind is a faculty instructor in early childhood education at Capilano University and an atelierista at the Capilano University Children's Centre. She has a particular affinity for the pedagogical values and approach of the schools in Reggio Emilia and their commitment to relational and artistic ways of knowing. Her work is motivated by an interest in young children's studio practices, lively material improvisations and collective experimentations and in developing understandings of studio research in early childhood contexts. She coauthored the book *Encounters with Materials in Early Childhood Education* and has written several journal articles and book chapters on studio work in early childhood.

Linda M. Knight is in the School of Early Childhood and Inclusive Education at Queensland University of Technology and specializes in community education in urban settings. Her international and award-winning reputation in arts-based methodologies in education-focused research includes the use of iPads in developing literacy and creativity in young children, using drawing to improve oral communication between educators and children, examining diverse urban citizenships through the mapping of urban (play)spaces, and using artificial intelligence and coding to examine algorithmic diversity in early childhood. Linda has exhibited internationally, and her work is held in private collections around the globe.

Candace R. Kuby is an associate professor of early childhood education at the University of Missouri. Her research interests are twofold: (1) the ethico-onto-epistemologies of literacy desiring(s) when young children work with materials to create multimodal, digital and hybrid texts, and (2) approaches to qualitative inquiry drawing on poststructural and posthumanist theories and the teaching of qualitative inquiry. Candace is coauthor of *Go Be a Writer! Expanding the Curricular Boundaries of Literacy Learning* with Tara Gutshall Rucker (2016, Teachers College Press), author of *Critical Literacy in the Early*

Childhood Classroom: Unpacking Histories, Unlearning Privilege (2013, Teachers College Press), and coeditor of *Disrupting Qualitative Inquiry: Possibilities and Tensions in Educational Research* with Ruth Nicole Brown and Rozana Carducci (2014, Peter Lang). Journals in which her scholarship appears include *Literacy, Qualitative Inquiry, International Journal of Qualitative Studies in Education, Journal of Early Childhood Literacy* and *Language Arts*.

Kathleen Kummen is an instructor in the early childhood care and education program and chair of innovation and inquiry in childhood studies at Capilano University on the unceded territorial lands of the Squamish and Tsleil-Waututh First Nations. Kathleen is interested in the real lifeworlds that 21st-century children inherit and how these lifeworlds are shaped by the legacies of environmental damage, imperial expansion, colonial dispossession and global inequalities. She is particularly interested in developing pedagogies that support student educators in attending to the everyday, complex and contradictory lives of 21st-century children. Kathleen is a founding member of the Early Childhood Pedagogies Collaboratory and a member of the Common Worlds Research Collective.

Nicole Land is an assistant professor in the School of Early Childhood Studies at Ryerson University. Anchored within a transdisciplinary perspective, Nicole's research interrogates the complexities of children's experiences amid cultural discourses of health, fitness, physical activity, and obesity. Nicole is particularly interested in reconfiguring how childhood studies might utilize physiological sciences to foster innovative, critical and politically attuned pedagogies that grapple with how children's learning unfolds with fat, muscles and movement.

Karin Murris is a professor of pedagogy and philosophy at the School of Education, University of Cape Town. Grounded in philosophy as an academic discipline, her main research interests are in early childhood education, literacies, school ethics, posthumanism, postqualitative research methods and de/colonizing pedagogies such as philosophy with children and Reggio Emilia. She is program convener of the postgraduate certificate in education foundation phase, teaches master's courses and supervises PhD students. Karin is principal investigator of the Decolonising Early Childhood Discourses: Critical Posthumanism in Higher Education research project funded by the South African government for three years (2016–2018). Her publications include *Teaching Philosophy with Picture Books* (1992), *The Posthuman Child: Educational Transformation through Philosophy with Picturebooks* (2016), and (with Joanna Haynes) *Literacies,*

Literature, and Learning: Reading Classrooms Differently (2018), *Picturebooks, Pedagogy, and Philosophy* (2012), and *Storywise: Thinking through Stories* (2002). She is also coeditor of the *Routledge International Handbook of Philosophy for Children* (2017).

Narda Nelson is a pedagogist at University of Victoria Child Care Services and a member of the Common Worlds Research Collective and the Early Childhood Pedagogies Collaboratory. Drawing on her master's in child and youth care and her background in gender studies, Narda takes an interdisciplinary approach to early childhood research with a particular focus on reimagining ethical futures with animals, plants, landscape forms and waste flows in early childhoods.

Fikile Nxumalo is an assistant professor of early childhood education at the University of Texas at Austin, where she is also affiliated faculty with African and African Diaspora Studies and Native American and Indigenous Studies. Fikile's research interests are centered on environmental and place-attuned early childhood studies that are situated within and responsive to young children's uneven inheritances of anthropogenic, anti-Black and settler colonial worldings. This scholarship, which is published in journals including *Environmental Education Research, Contemporary Issues in Early Childhood, International Journal of Qualitative Studies in Education* and *Environmental Humanities*, is rooted in perspectives from Indigenous and black feminisms.

Veronica Pacini-Ketchabaw is a professor of early childhood education in the Faculty of Education at Western University. Her current research, within the Common Worlds Research Collective, traces the common world relations of children with places, materials and other species.

Tonya Rooney is a lecturer in early childhood at the Australian Catholic University. Tonya's research focuses on children's relations with space, time and more-than-human worlds in contemporary society and more recently looks to the scenario of anthropogenic climate change and what this means for young children's lives and futures. Tonya is currently working on an early years environmental education research project with a particular emphasis on ethnographic walking methods and children's relations with the weather. She is the author of several articles, book chapters and a coedited book, *Surveillance Futures*, with Emmeline Taylor, published by Routledge in 2017.

Nikki Rotas is an assistant professor in the Department of Interdisciplinary and Inclusive Education at Rowan University. Her research intersects ecology, embodiment, and theories of movement and affect in relation to educational research. She is also a visual methodologist with expertise in the use of wearable technologies in schools and communities.

Affrica Taylor is an adjunct associate professor in the Centre for Creative and Cultural Studies at the University of Canberra and a founding member of the Common Worlds Research Collective. Her background in Indigenous Australian education and her doctoral studies in cultural geography have shaped her abiding interest in the relations among people, place and other species in settler colonial societies and in the need to decolonize these relations. She explores these relations in *Reconfiguring the Natures of Childhood: Unsettling the Colonial Places and Spaces of Early Childhood Education* (with Veronica Pacini-Ketchabaw) and *The Entangled Lives of Children and Animals: Cultural, Environmental, and Ethical Issues* (also with Veronica Pacini-Ketchabaw).

Cristina D. Vintimilla is an assistant professor in the Faculty of Education at York University and is also the pedagogista for the Ontario Centre of Excellence for Early Years and Child Care. She pursued her pedagogista studies at the University of Siena (Italy) and is currently the pedagogista at Capilano University Children's Centre. Her research interests address the ethical question of living well with others within pedagogical gatherings. She engages with this question by problematizing issues of subjectivity in relation to prescribed practices in education and by unsettling pedagogies that are based in human supremacy and instrumental-managerial logics. In her work as a pedagogista, she is also inspired by pedagogical work that considers the life of curriculum from tangible and intangible formations.

Series Editors' Introduction

The series Feminist Thought in Childhood Research considers experimental and creative modes of researching and practicing in childhood studies. Recognizing the complex neoliberal landscape and worrisome spaces of coloniality in the 21st century, the Feminist Thought in Childhood Research books provide a forum for cross-disciplinary, interdisciplinary and transdisciplinary conversations in childhood studies that engage feminist decolonial, anticolonial, more-than-human, new materialisms, post-humanist and other post-foundational perspectives that seek to reconfigure human experience. The series offers lively examples of feminist research praxis and politics that invite childhood studies scholars, students and educators to engage in collectively to imagine childhood otherwise.

Until now, childhood studies has been decidedly a human matter focused on the needs of individual children (Taylor, 2013). In the Anthropocene (Colebrooke, 2012, 2013), however, other approaches to childhood that address the profound, human-induced ecological challenges facing our own and other species are emerging. As Taylor (2013) reminds us, if we are going to grapple with the socio-ecological challenges we face today, childhood studies needs to pay attention to the *more*-than-human, the *non*human others that inhabit our worlds and the *in*human. Toward this end, Feminist Thought in Childhood Research series challenges the humanist, linear and moral narratives (Colebrook, 2013; Haraway, 2013) of much of childhood studies by engaging with feminisms. As a feminist series, the books explore the inheritances of how to live in the Anthropocene and think about it in ways that are in tension with the Anthropocene itself.

The second book in the series, *Feminist Research for 21st-century Childhoods*, makes a significant contribution to the field by foregrounding feminist theories and practices within early childhood studies and by realizing new materialist and post-humanist ambitions. It offers a rich compendium of provocative examples, which provide persuasive accounts of ways to overcome the theory-practice divide in research with young children in the Anthropocene. Denise Hodgins has successfully brought together a collection of storying practices that illustrate the liveliness of feminist new materialist doings. Each chapter is theoretically rich, and together the chapters offer thought-provoking accounts of how to undertake childhood studies *differently* in ways that are seriously playful and profoundly political. The authors recount a wide range of experimental, creative and worldly encounters with place, space, materialities, and human, nonhuman and more-than-human entanglements in order that we might think more intensely about our entangled response-ability as educators and researchers working with children. The situated accounts that the authors present stress the lasting and ongoing importance of Indigenous worldviews and embodied practices—a theme to run throughout the entire book is that place acts as a pedagogical contact zone. Within each of the stories offered is a concern for situated knowledges and a recognition of worldly entanglements and connections to the past, present and future; this is foundational to the Common Worlds Framework that underpins the entire book. As stressed in the introduction:

> The [Common Worlds] collective takes seriously the proposition that by resituating our lives within indivisible more-than-human common worlds. Research and education can (re)focus on the ways in which our past, present, and future lives are entangled with other beings, non-living entities, technologies, elements, discourses, forces, landforms and so forth. Each of the research stories in this collection follows this proposition, reaching beyond dominant childhood studies and environmental humanities, as well as thinking with Indigenous knowledges, histories, and territories, Deleuzian vitalism, and the arts.

The book is both generative and nourishing; to read each chapter is to get lost in otherworldly encounters with the everyday. Stories are told "from the floor" of early childhood practice which brings a lively, grounded quality to the methodological questions that are posed. The stories are affective and provoking; they insist that the reader get in the thick of the dilemmas that are encountered daily, and within microscopic moments, in order to thinkfeeldo early childhood differently. Each story is creative, experimental and performative, and importantly, works to present the reader with much to ponder. Traces, reverberations and hauntings from each chapter will linger and leave evocative invitations to stay with the trouble that has been presented.

The lived examples of undertaking feminist new materialist research in early childhood contexts presented in this volume illustrate the enormous potential available to break free from familiar and normative ways to generate knowledge. Postqualitative approaches are distinct but varied, complex and intricate. Each chapter powerfully conveys this and further goes on to offer the reader ways and means to grapple with the research(ing) stories told and what this might mean for their own practice. The book sets into motion conversations about what transversal methods and techniques, such as those presented throughout, can produce. The book is indeed about lively doings and what those lively doings do.

Acknowledgments

Stepping outside of familiar Euro-Western authorship traditions, as the editor of this volume, I want to open it by using this acknowledgments section to foreground a different ethic of gratitude which threads throughout the book, a gratitude that actively centers accountability and grapples with what it requires for research to adequately care and respond to the acknowledgments we offer.

I have compiled this collection as an uninvited settler on the unceded territories of the Lekwungen-speaking peoples, including the Songhees, Esquimalt and WSÁNEĆ Nations. That I get to live, work, write and raise my family on these lands is because these Nations were forcibly removed through acts of colonization, acts that impacted, and continue to impact, not only Indigenous peoples but animal and plant species, land, water, minerals, air. I offer my acknowledgment and gratitude with humility, knowing it does not erase the legacies and ongoing acts of colonization within this settler colonial state. An acknowledgment in and of itself is not enough, but it is an essential beginning.

The book's authors have provided me with the acknowledgments they would like to offer in relation to the research and writing of their chapter contributions. Some of the acknowledgments are in reference to a particular chapter, while others refer to more than one chapter because those chapters' inquiries took place within the same place. With respect and gratitude, it is acknowledged that the research and writing that made this book possible took place on and with:

The traditional territories of the Anishinaabe, Haudenosaunee, and Leni-Lunaape First Nations.
The traditional homelands of the Chickasaw, Illini, Ioway, Missouria, Osage, Otoe, and Quapaw, and lands that were also crossed by the Cherokee, Delaware, Kickapoo, Sac and Fox, and Shawnee peoples when they were forcefully removed from their homelands in what is now the eastern United States.
The unceded territories of the Coast Salish peoples, including the Tsleil-Waututh, Skwxwú7mesh, shíshálh, Lil'Wat, Musqueam and Stó:lō Nations.
Dharawal country, whose traditional owners are the Wadi Wadi people.

The traditional territories of the Haudenosaunee and Anishinaabe peoples, in particular the Mississaugas of the New Credit, territory that is covered by the Two Row Wampum Treaty and the Upper Canada Treaties.

The territory of the Huron-Wendat and Petun First Nations, the Seneca, and, most recently, the Mississaugas of the Credit River. The territory was the subject of the Dish with One Spoon Wampum Belt Covenant, an agreement between the Iroquois Confederacy and Confederacy of the Ojibwe and allied nations to peaceably share and care for the resources around the Great Lakes.

The Kulin Nation and, in particular, the Wurundjeri, Wadawurrung, and Dja Dja Wurrung peoples who are the traditional owners of the land.

The unceded Lekwungen-speaking peoples' territories, including the Songhees, Esquimalt, and WSÁNEĆ Nations.

Meanjin country, whose traditional owners are the Turrbal and Jagera peoples.

Ngunnawal country, whose peoples are the traditional owners of the land.

Land that was inhabited for thousands of years by hunter-gatherers known as the San and seminomadic gatherers collectively known as the Khoekhoen.

All research and education in the countries currently known as Australia, Canada, South Africa and the United States takes place on Indigenous lands. Indigenous peoples have lived on these lands in their sovereign nations since time immemorial. Through tremendous resistance and resilience, Indigenous relationships to these lands continue to this day.

I contend that it is an ethical responsibility of researchers, academics and educators to commit to the labor of becoming accountable to the complexities, demands, and active ethical and political answerabilities of living in settler colonial spaces. Centuries in the making, this ongoing collective work is a 21st-century necessity, one that is deeply entangled with other 21st-century challenging realities. While the collective work in this volume adopts an accountability to our complicity in ongoing settler colonialism, the researching stories shared do not overtly intervene in colonial structures of land ownership, resource extraction or forcible removal from place. As we provide imperfect examples of what it might take to enact our acknowledgment in the chapters to come, we work toward presenting non-Euro-Western ontologies, disrupting the universality or "objectiveness" of colonial paradigms, and thinking knowledges as multiple, constructed and contingent.

I would like to thank all of the authors who have entrusted me with their researching stories, and all of the children, families, educators, students and researchers whose engagement made these stories possible. I would also like to thank my colleagues for their unfailing encouragement and support and my family for their unconditional patience and love.

Permission to include portions of Chapter 15 by Fikile Nxumalo that were first published within her chapter "Forest Stories: Restorying Encounters with 'Natural' Places in Early Childhood Spaces" in the book *Unsettling the Colonial Places and Spaces of Early Childhood Education*, edited by Veronica Pacini-Ketchabaw and Affrica Taylor, was kindly granted by Taylor Francis Group LCC Books.

Common Worlding Research: An Introduction

B. Denise Hodgins

Children born in the 21st century are inheriting the inextricably entangled legacies of colonization, human-caused climate change, mass species extinction, rapid technological advancements, the "digital information age," and mass migration and displacement. Just as developmental and sociological perspectives birthed new forms of inquiry within childhood studies in 19th-century industrialization and 20th-century urban change, respectively, innovative methodologies within childhood studies are urgently needed to address, respond to and engage with the realities of 21st-century children. Conversations about reimagining humanist qualitative inquiry have generated numerous possibilities for thinking-doing research when once-deemed-stable identifiers (e.g., essentialisms, subjectivity, truths, categories) are rendered unstable, fluctuating, moving, always already becoming. Educators and researchers have long challenged traditional research methods from social justice and equity perspectives and increasingly call for a reassembling of the field to address 21st-century issues.[1] Feminist methodology expert Patti Lather, in her explorative wondering about postqualitative research, poses the question, "What 'narration of methodology' might move us away from the theories and practices whose grip on us we are trying to break?"[2] This book's purpose is to share childhood studies stories of/with/from feminist postqualitative inquiries to provoke such a (becoming) narration of methodology for 21st-century childhoods.

Purposefully marking this book as examples of postqualitative research for 21st-century childhoods is not to suggest that this century is clearly demarcated from earlier ones. There is no pure "new" (time, theory, method, circumstance, context) that is not always already entangled with past inheritances and future possibilities. Even our intentional departures from particular modes of thinking and practicing research remain connected to that which we aim to resist and are always in potentially uneven conversation with enduring Indigenous and non-Euro-Western ontologies that have been silenced by these same dominant research paradigms. This view indicates a feminist ontological rethinking of temporality,[3] and it thinks alongside Indigenous cosmologies.[4] Both perspectives challenge assumptions about the nature of time as linear and segmented, one growing in circulation in Euro-Western science and humanities discourses, the other living in Indigenous knowledges for millennia.

Naming the researching stories that make up this collection as *postqualitative* requires some introductory comment. Euro-Western scholarship arising in the later 20th century that critiqued foundational and structuralist conceptualizations inherited from the Enlightenment, often labeled as "the posts" (e.g., postmodern, poststructural, postcolonial, postemancipatory, postfoundational), led to some rethinking and reimagining of research methods and their ontological loyalties.[5] These critiques acknowledged multiple realities, voices and truths and aimed to "disrupt disciplinary, exclusionary canons by including the knowledge of the dispossessed."[6] It was a strongly epistemological project. Some of this work also challenged representational and objectivity logics that position data (the world, subjects, phenomena, truth, knowledge) as knowable, "out there" to be found and representable through language. It troubled binary logics that situate one side of the binary as superior to the other (e.g., man/nature, man/woman, white man/people of color, adult/child) and uphold divisions between human/nonhuman, nature/culture, rational/emotional, Self/Other, researcher/participant and so forth. In what is often called the ontological turn (or new materialisms or new empiricisms), a significant shift "from an epistemology of human consciousness to a relational ontology"[7] has become important for scholars and practitioners who trace the consequences of understanding agency beyond human(ism) terms where isolated and distinct categories are unthinkable. Through this ontological turn researchers have questioned the ways in which qualitative research is conducted and analyzed. Gilles Deleuze and Felix Guattari's work has been particularly influential to scholars writing within postqualitative feminist research.[8] Their philosophy, "with its focus on becoming, affect, relationality, creativity and multiplicity,"[9] has supported a rethinking and redoing of qualitative methodology as experimental and nonrepresentational. Such critiques and conceptualizations bring the "post" to qualitative to reimagine and reinvent qualitative inquiry beyond the grasp of Enlightenment humanism, including Man's Euro-Western superiority to and mastery of everything else in the world.

Understanding the world through entangled relations, including the inseparability of knowing, being and ethics, which Barad puts forward as onto-ethico-epistemology, is a central thread running through this collection of feminist postqualitative research stories. But this "new" viewpoint has actually been central to Indigenous knowledges for millennia.[10] Feminist scholar Kim TallBear, tribal citizen of the Sisseton-Wahpeton Oyate in South Dakota, writes: "Now that theorists in a range of fields are seeking to dismantle those [humanist] hierarchies, we should remember that not everyone needs to summon a new analytical framework or needs to renew a commitment to 'the validity of [so called] things.'"[11] Red River Métis and Otipemisiwak feminist scholar Zoe Todd notes that when scholars in such fields as science studies, environmental humanities and multispecies ethnography rethink their primarily Euro-Western theories and methods through a relational ontology "without being aware of competing or similar discourses happening outside of the rock-star arenas of Euro-Western thought,"[12] they perpetuate an ongoing erasure of Indigenous knowledges. Todd also points out the risk when non-Indigenous scholars draw on Indigenous thinking "without contending with the embodied expressions of stories, laws, and songs as bound with Indigenous-Place Thought (Watts 2013: 31) or Indigenous self-determination."[13] As Mohawk/Anishinaabe scholar Vanessa Watts contends, "Indigenous histories are still regarded as story and process—an abstracted tool of the West."[14] These tensions of mobilizing "novel" Euro-Western theories designed to unsettle the colonial canon and foregrounding the labor of Indigenous scholars who refuse to subscribe to Euro-Western epistemic systems must be recognized, particularly by a postqualitative collection declared as reimagining and reinventing research methods for the 21st-century worlds that children are inheriting. Continuing to operate with Euro-Western standpoints as the central, or only, worldview maintains an unethical and problematic cognitive imperialism that made settler colonialism possible in the first place.[15] Honoring, rather than erasing, Indigenous presence (past, present and future) and acting to purposefully, carefully, and with full acknowledgment of how Indigenous scholars and knowledges complexify and work concurrently with these conversations—not as historical/static/traditional knowledges but as "engagement with the thinking that *living* indigenous people do today"[16]—is a call postqualitative researchers must take seriously. What does it mean, as settlers, to build imperfect but accountable worlds with incommensurable but potentially collaborative worldviews? Unangax̂ scholar Eve Tuck puts the settler academy firmly at the center of this challenge, calling on the academy to unsettle itself, with the understanding that it doesn't get to set the terms or decide when it succeeds.[17] This collection provides examples of researchers grappling and engaging with this call by presencing non-Euro-

Western ontologies, disrupting the universality or "objectiveness" of colonial paradigms, and thinking knowledges as multiple, constructed and contingent.

Common worlds methods

As one component of larger efforts to disrupt Euro-Western research paradigms, the stories in the book enact methodological approaches that lie within a common worlds framework. Most of the contributing authors belong to the Common Worlds Research Collective, an interdisciplinary network of researchers who situate research and pedagogy as within lively common worlds.[18] This framework grapples with the complexities of being deeply embedded in neoliberal and settler colonial capitalism. It challenges dominant approaches to child studies scholarship positioned through Euro-Western developmental and anthropocentric frames by foregrounding a more-than-human relational ontology. The collective takes seriously the proposition that by resituating our lives within indivisible more-than-human common worlds, research and education can (re)focus on the ways in which our past, present and future lives are entangled with other beings, nonliving entities, technologies, elements, discourses, forces, landforms and so forth. Each of the research stories in this collection follows this proposition, reaching beyond dominant childhood studies and developmental frames by drawing differently on scholarship from feminist science studies and environmental humanities, as well as thinking with Indigenous knowledges, histories, and territories, Deleuzian vitalism, and the arts.

This resolutely feminist project is indebted to inheritances from those who worked to make visible (public) that the personal and private is always political, that the mundane matters, that power is not equitably distributed and lived, that we become through webs of relations, and that we (as researchers, as educators) are not above or outside the process of generating material-discursive conditions and possibilities.[19] What emerges are common worlds methods where researchers are understood as embedded within the entangled lifeworlds they seek to explore, researching to *learn with* rather than *learn about*. They are methods designed to *attune to*, reaching beyond the scope of traditional research tools (e.g., interviews, focus groups, observation, note-taking) that aim to find human experience through what is (re)told and (re)seen (i.e., the researcher's "findings"). This approach results in experimenting with methods that are receptive to and gesture toward the sensorial, the affective, the historical presences that haunt. They operate within blurred boundaries, where the methods, analysis and "so what?" of research are interwoven and where theory is not brought in and applied to research but lived throughout the process. Common worlds methods are exploratory, active methods that work to make visible in varying ways the ethics and politics of *what is put into play* through/with/in research practices.[20]

The nineteen research(ing) stories that follow are offered as provocations for dialogue about transversal methods in childhood studies. They wrestle with complex methodological understandings and practices within postqualitative research within particular settler colonial states: Australia, Canada, South Africa and the Unites States. Each chapter presents a technique the authors have put to work in their efforts to unsettle the interpretative power of Euro-Western developmental knowledges and anthropocentric frameworks to reimagine research amid the colonialist, social and environmental challenges we face today. The examples of research praxis and politics have been researched directly with children, educators and/or early childhood student-educators, and the authors bring a strong practice-grounded dialogue to their methodological questions. These questions have emerged within their respective inquiries, most of which have taken place not only within early childhood classrooms (indoors or outdoors) in Canada and Australia but also within early elementary school classrooms in the United States and Canada, in intergenerational art classrooms in Canada and within postsecondary teacher education classrooms in Canada and South Africa. The emphasis on practice-grounded research is not to suggest that we privilege practical knowledge over theoretical. Rather, it enacts the inextricable entanglement of theory and practice, of knowledge and action, of thinking and doing, within a feminist relational ontology.[21] Thinking with Michi Saagiig Nishnaabeg scholar Leanne Betasamosake Simpson, theory is generated and regenerated through doing; it is embodied; it is told through stories.[22]

Feminist early childhood scholar Hillevi Lenz Taguchi suggests that "the territory of qualitative inquiry is so heavily sedimented that it requires very hard collaborative work to deterritorialize its habitual ways of thinking and practicing in order for new and different researcher practices and subjectivities to emerge."[23] The inquiries the authors are engaging in provide examples of, rather than road maps to, this kind of hard collaborative work. Each chapter is a serious play with postqualitative methods, not *a priori* but emergent, intentional, uncertain research responses to specific places and politics. The stories are partial, incomplete, not neutral or apolitical, but mattering. They are offered as performative researching stories, animated through playing with language, voice, grammar and form, including moments from research in a fragmented, interfering way, layering narratives, weaving narratives, making visible the writer/researcher (questions), (re)presenting images and text as a means to provoke, evoke and affect. They are speculative stories. María Puig de la Bellacasa, leaning on Donna Haraway and Joan Haran, notes that "the speculative then connects to a feminist tradition for which this mode of thought about the possible is about provoking political and ethical imagination in the present."[24] With this view of the speculative, these stories invoke what Puig de la Bellacasa calls "an indecisive critical approach, one that doesn't seek refuge in the stances it takes, aware and appreciative of the vulnerability of any position on the 'as well as possible.'"[25]

Researching as well as possible, with the best of intentions, has a murderous history that cannot be ignored in our enthusiasm for "new" methodologies and practices in childhood studies.[26] We are accountable—or, with Haraway, response-able—for that which we inherit and (continue to) put into the world. We are implicated. It matters that this work is from places rooted in ongoing settler colonialism, racial injustice and environmental precarity. It matters which stories we tell.[27] How might we *think with* alternative narratives to encounter ethically, politically and otherwise, while recognizing that we are complicit and entangled in our efforts? The dialogue the book is designed to provoke invites the reader to consider, discuss and enact complex ethico-onto-epistemological questions in the wake of postqualitative methodology-to-come. Because "the actual design and practice of the fieldwork of the future are up for grabs,"[28] as Lather asserts, creating space for exploring the doings and dialogues of postqualitative experimentations is critical. This collection's common worlding experimentations are strategies toward unsettling Euro-Western and neoliberal frameworks for being in the world. In the field of childhood studies, where settler colonial and neoliberal logics have so much clout, such strategies are crucial.

Approaching the book's chapters

Following a common worlds framework, the collection is divided into four parts: "Relations with Materials," "Relations with Other Species," "Relations with Place" and "Relations with Retheorizings." The first part challenges deeply rooted cultural oppositions that lead us to think of humans as animate agents who act on passive, inanimate materials.[29] These six chapters' authors think with materials—clay, fabric, sticks, a child-made literacy game, art materials and digital portfolios, and muscles—as inextricably entangled with our lives and as agentic and generative in their own right, if we (humans) only learn to pay attention. They all draw on feminist science studies, as well as Indigenous knowledges (Chapter 1), the environmental humanities (Chapters 2, 3 and 6), Deleuzian vitalism (Chapters 2 and 4) and the arts (Chapters 1 and 2) to make visible some of the ways that materials touch legacies of settler global capitalism and shape education practices and policies.

First, Veronica Pacini-Ketchabaw and Kelly Boucher trace clay and its earth relations in situated contexts as matters of care.[30] Employing new materialist methods and leaning on the arts and Indigenous knowledges, the authors think with clay encounters in a classroom in Australia and a creek in Canada. Rather than seeking purities in early childhood education's clay practices, Pacini-Ketchabaw and Boucher map ways to care for the webs of connections that are always already ingrained in actual clay relations and with/in what they refer to as pedagogies of intimacy. Claying challenges neoliberal, capitalist, anthropocentric assumptions about materials and land and their corresponding productions of consumption. It also renders researchers and educators inseparable from and accountable to that with which we engage.

Chapter 2 provides another example that rethinks hegemonic early childhood material practices, this time presenting young children's experimentations with long lengths of translucent fabric in an early childhood art studio. Sylvia Kind and Adrienne Argent think with fabric to participate with its textile, tensile, textural and fluid qualities, to articulate studio practices as instances and processes of research, and to consider the kinds of relations that are shaped amid these studio-fabric encounters. With a Deleuze-inspired arts-based approach, the authors play with fabrication as moments of creating, curating and composing realities in the mappings, movements, entanglements and gatherings that take shape. Their chapter explores the particular material experimentations, negotiations and pedagogical orientations that allow the early childhood studio to emerge as an event-full place of research-creation.

Next, Tonya Rooney presents moments from a collaborative ethnographic research project that included regular walks with a group of preschool children along the foreshores of an urban lake in Canberra, Australia, to explore children's attraction to the sticks they find scattered across the landscape. Rooney experiments with Ahmed's conceptualization of "sticky" to reimagine children's relations with sticks as forging connection. The interaction suggests a binding together that coshapes an ongoing relation across time and place. Bringing

Instone's provocation to risk "attachment with all manner of unlike others"[31] into conversation with Ahmed's sticky notion, Rooney replays risky-sticks-with-children as mutual vulnerability.

In Chapter 4, Candace Kuby's more-than-human (re)imagining and (re)defining of writing and writing pedagogy moves constructions of literacy as a noun to knowing and living literacy as a verb, a becoming force. Kuby engages with pedagogical documentation—note-taking, photographs, video recordings—of emerging literacies within a grade 2 Writers' Studio in the United States to story the unfolding of an Egyptian pyramid board game children created. With Barad's agential realism and Deleuzian notions of desire, Kuby's offering of literacy desiring(s) focuses on the relationship between material-discursive bodies and challenges dominant child-centered approaches to writing pedagogies and research. Literacying produced newness—new ways of thinking/be(com)ing/doing/knowing literacies—through research as an entanglement of becoming-with children and materials.

Material-discursive entanglements of/in the classroom are also a central focus in Chapter 5 with Rachel Heydon and Elisabeth Davies's research that integrated digital tools into the curricula of intergenerational art classes in Ontario, Canada. With feminist materialism understandings, the authors extend traditional curriculum theory to attend to the more-than-human. In particular, the physicality of the various constituents, such as art supplies, iPads and human bodies, leads to a rethinking of classic curriculum theory by suggesting an additional curriculum commonplace: materials. Heydon and Davies's intergenerationaling methodology collapses the dichotomies of adult/child and animate/inanimate and challenges dominant constructions of what gets lived as "developmentally appropriate" curriculum.

In this part's final chapter, Nicole Land explores muscles' materiality in her response to the dominance of anthropocentric childhood obesity narratives in education. Integrating documentation from a project with early childhood educators and children in Victoria, Canada, Land puts forward muscling as a transdisciplinary methodology for attending to how muscles interject, move and matter in early childhood education curriculum and pedagogies. Muscling actively resists such narratives that locate muscles within a fit and healthy bounded human body, obscure uncommon muscle performances within neoliberal notions of physical development and canonize Euro-Western scientific hegemony as the preeminent epistemology for understanding muscles. Land's chapter invites an important alternative approach for moving beyond understandings of children, movement and muscles as static and knowable that dominate in shaping health and wellness policies in early childhood classrooms.

"Relations with Other Species" forms the second part of the collection, with four contributions that center the coshaping multispecies entanglements that take place within early childhood places. Like the chapters in "Relations with Materials," these research stories work against the premise that agency is exclusive to humans and that human interests are the paramount starting point and rationale for child studies research and related practices.[32] The authors engage deeply with environmental humanities and feminist science studies and think with Indigenous knowledges, history and place (Chapters 8–10) to situate contemporary relations with other species within the colonial, neoliberal, ecological conditions we live with and bequeath to children. This part of the collection illuminates methodological approaches with young children and educators who seek new ways of fostering ethical, recuperative and flourishing multispecies futures.

Kathleen Kummen opens the part with a collection of stories that emerged from a multispecies ethnography study in an early childhood education program on the west coast of Canada. In Chapter 7, Kummen contributes crowing as a researching method that attended to the imperfect and complex relationships in child care, relationships haunted by multiple legacies of inequity and social injustice. As Kummen demonstrates through her research narratives, thinking with crows moved children and educators from the center of the pedagogical conversations. With such moves, researchers and educators are called to pay attention to the relational and coshaping events that take place in children's common worlds. Crowing as method invites educators, researchers and children to investigate and engage with curricular moments as political agents so that classrooms are recognized as political and ethical sites for researching and living well with others.

Integrating moments from their weekly walks with young children and teachers in Wurundjeri Country in Australia, Mindy Blaise and Catherine Hamm consider what might be learned by paying attention to the pulses of multispecies relations and how these moments call children and teachers into relation. Inspired by Deborah Bird Rose's lively stories where she makes visible how *shimmer*, the Aboriginal ancestral power of life, arises in relationship and encounter,[33] Blaise and Hamm show how shimmering makes us curious and draws us to our connections within multispecies worlds and worldings, and in so doing, makes us accountable and responsible. By experimenting with the grammar of animacy and writing in ways that dissolve the hierarchies that typically situate human and more-than-human entities as separate, Blaise and Hamm tell "creek-egretta-child-yabbie relations" as a lively, animate story to entice readers into multispecies worlds.

In Chapter 9, Narda Nelson tells how tracking animals with educators, researchers and a group of young children emerged as a method to cultivate the "arts of awareness"[34] in troubling times by opening ourselves up to new understandings of our shared vulnerabilities with others. Nelson's tracking troubles romanticized child–animal relations that are often framed as curative avenues for responding to ecologically challenging times and, as Nelson cautions, must be understood as more than training innocent settler children's imaginations to go visiting on these colonized lands.

In this part's final chapter, Affrica Taylor recounts a series of rabbiting tales and reflections that explore how a group of non-Indigenous Australian preschool children grapple with the messy legacies of invasion that co-implicate their lives with those of wild European rabbits. The three tales Taylor layers within Chapter 10 trace a series of challenging child-rabbit encounters. Within these tracings, children's visceral and affective understanding of their connections with rabbits within the damaged common worlds they co-inherit and co-inhabit is made visible. Thinking through rabbiting provides an avenue to strengthen resolves to resist the prevailing and divisive settler colonial logics of separation, vilification and control.

The collection's third part, "Relations with Place," continues to take methodological and pedagogical queries beyond exclusively human, cultural or social framings by grounding place relations in the stories shared. Place as an inherently *pedagogical contact zone* is a theme that runs through the entire book. However, the authors of the five chapters in Part Three put forward distinct methodologies that acknowledge place as lively and generative and people-place relations as mutually formative and significant to a sense of belonging.[35] Leaning on the environmental humanities, as well as feminist science studies (Chapters 12, 13 and 15), Indigenous knowledges (Chapters 11 and 15), Deleuzian vitalism (Chapters 12, 13 and 14) and the arts (Chapters 11), the authors present innovative ways to inquire into the co-constitutive nature of children's, educators' and researchers' relations with place and to promote an ethics of place relations.

Starting this part is Vanessa Clark's enactment of a new a/r/tographic practice called gathering that brings contemporary art practices of working with found objects into material-discursive conversations with Indigenous knowledges, unceded and ancestral multinational territories of the Coast Salish peoples, and preservice early childhood education students to grapple with settler colonial inheritances in research and teaching. Clark's exploration to reassemble and open up inclusive practices within early childhood and postsecondary education is (re)presented in a fragmented and deliberately disorderly poetic style. Gathering as a methodology creates conditions for meetings of ideas, matters and objects that might (otherwise) be logically divided.

Chapter 12 takes the reader to an urban elementary school in Canada's largest city, Toronto, where grade 2 and 3 students wore small action cameras during research events related to the provincial science and technology curriculum. Thinking with Puig de la Bellacasa's concept of *touching visions*,[36] Nikki Rotas reenvisions the mobile camera, body and image as an entanglement of more-than-representational thought. Working with digital images that were recorded with the cameras, Rotas presents the student-initiated practice of "mashing" as a more-than-representational practice that attends to the affective dimensions of imaging (and/or data making), subjectivity making and movement in research. This chapter is a provocation to take up pedagogies with students to relationally see/live/feel environments and to question if and how moving images alter perceptions of the child in ways that disrupt marginalizing discourses of disengaged children in urban schools.

In Chapter 13, Linda Knight explores urban play spaces (including playgrounds) in Australia and theorizes play in relation to reconceptualizations about urban citizenships. Leaning on Barad's work, Knight shifts the question being asked from "Does play matter?" to "Does matter play?" and shares her drawn-on-site research mappings as a means to examine and comment on (play with) movement, matter and the ethics of urban planning and demarcation. Knight's maps are purposefully partial renderings that capture traces of lively playings in urban commonplaces: overlapping, simultaneous, multiple movements, forms, light and time. With mapping, Knight executes a gestural and speculative method that focuses on the affect and experience of place, a method that places the researcher deep within the milieu.

Also reimaging researcher tools and engagement is Susannah Clement's chapter GoProing, where she analyzes moments from her study about everyday walking practices of families with young children in Wollongong, a regional city on the east coast of New South Wales, Australia. Clement used GoPro cameras to record parents and children walking together to better understand what it feels like to walk in a car-dependent city. In Clement's analysis, the camera emerged as an agentic research tool that shaped participant engagement in the project, and as such it provokes particular ethical considerations. Clement offers GoProing as a performative research method that blurs the divides between participant and researcher, human and technology, and activity and place and where multiple participant and researcher subjectivities emerge.

In this part's final chapter, Fikile Nxumalo explores pedagogical encounters with a mountain forest on unceded Musqueam, Stó:lō, Squamish and Tsleil-Waututh territories. Using an approach of *refiguring presences*, Nxumalo interrupts innocent perspectives of place-based environmental early childhood education by bringing together decolonial and more-than-human orientations. As she explains, refiguring is understood as reanimating, rethinking and relating to the Indigenous presences so often erased in settler colonial curriculum, while presencing[37] actively stories Indigenous people back into present place and time. Nxumalo puts refiguring presences to work through an illustrative encounter between young children, a mountain forest and more-than-human co-inhabitants and, in doing so, demonstrates the importance of situating environmental education with young children within the settler colonial and anthropogenic places they co-inhabit with more-than-human others.

While all of the contributions in this volume think with and (re)conceptualize theory, the four chapters that make up the book's final part, "Relations with Retheorizings," engage with words, concepts and theory as the chapter's primary focus. These chapters' authors take up here a purposeful playing with language— deconstructing words, revisiting their etymological and philosophical roots, reconfiguring them for conceptual effect—in their methodological experimentation in early childhood and postsecondary classrooms. In their efforts to reconceptualize theory and put it to work methodologically, the authors draw on feminist science studies (Chapters 16, 18 and 19), the environmental humanities (Chapter 18) and the arts (Chapter 17).

B. Denise Hodgins begins this part with a chapter that utilizes Puig de la Bellacasa's conceptualization of care. Hodgins revisits traces of doll moments from an action research inquiry with young children and early childhood educators in a small Canadian city to rethink how caring was put to work in their collective project. She presents caring as method through three integral concepts: (1) care as being called into response, (2) care as always already an act of dis/connection and (3) care as a transformative ethos. What Hodgins makes visible through her narratives is that caring is not about finding the (final) answer but about opening up speculative possibilities. She argues that an onto-ethico-epistemological conceptualization of care may well serve both researchers' and educators' commitments to fostering equitable, livable worlds.

In Chapter 16, Randa Khattar and Karyn Callaghan consider the educational approaches taken within Reggio Emilia, Italy, and their own early childhood pedagogical practices in Ontario, Canada, to put forward the concept learningliving. Their chapter shares stories of public learning related to childhoods to illuminate this concept as a lively aesthetic movement capable of making meaning of meaning making. Challenging neoliberal capitalist approaches to education, they invoke Bill Readings' argument that institutions for learning have the potential to be sites of "doing justice to thought"[38] and suggest that a taste for aesthetic patterns that connect is needed in early childhood education. Their chapter proposes that such an appetite might draw educators, researchers, children and communities to experiment with pedagogies that unfold a radically different way of learningliving.

In Chapter 18, Cristina Vintimilla and Iris Berger bring their collaborative research projects with early childhood educators and students in two universities on Canada's west coast, as well as Vintimilla's work as a pedagogista,[39] to their exploration of the everyday material and discursive practices around collaboration. Through engaging with stories and the doings of language, Vintimilla and Berger decompose the commonly idealized notion of collaboration in early childhood education to expose its messy (co)laboring possibilities.

This section's final chapter tells the story of how a childhood studies course within a teacher education program in South Africa affected a student through images she made of her lecturer. Karin Murris (the lecturer) and Cara Borcherds (the student) play with Barad's diffractive methodology to retheorize child and childhood as *childing*: a notion of posthuman identity that is in/determinate, porous and with no fixed boundaries. Troubling age, development and progress, Murris and Borcherds put forward childing as a particularly forceful and intense experience of being in time that reaches beyond the usual associations with childhood and disrupts the typically hierarchical relationship between lecturer and student.

Together these nineteen researching stories offer an imaginary of what a postqualitative narration of methodology might be. It is not an attempt to declare what postqualitative research is, because it is and always will be ongoing. The thinkings and doings of research (re)presented through this volume have not attempted to resolve the messy, entangled, inequitable 21st-century common worlds we live in. They are calls to action: to rethink, redo and question how we are implicated in them, and to do the hard labor of experimenting with methods in order to create opportunities and conditions for exploring our collective and individual responsibilities to the worlds we inherit and bequeath. They are interventions in the field of childhood studies and the domain of qualitative research that reveal the limits implicit within our strategies. The chapters invite many questions that can extend this book, and I hope readers will carry these questions into research and practice: What modernist legacies—dualisms, presence, reflexivity, categorization—continue to haunt our postqualitative efforts in childhood studies? How do we resist the Euro-Western singular master narrative without substituting one narrative for another? In our efforts to shift the anthropocentric stronghold in childhood and education research, do we succeed in moving beyond human-centered terms and understandings? Where are our human limits with/in our posthuman thinking-doing efforts? What conversations do these transversal methods and techniques put into action, and are we, as researchers and educators, suitably prepared and adequately accountable? How do we work (with/in) postqualitative inquiries as always already becoming, speculative fabulations[40] rather than assured research designs? How do we persevere in our researching efforts when, in Patti Lather's words, "what (post)qualitative research offers is no match for what we want from it?"[41]

Other questions will undoubtedly emerge as you read these stories. As this collection's authors continue to work in our research worlds, these and other questions will niggle and brew, invigorate and trouble. And we research, story, carry on. With the questions. With the certainty of no final answers. With the responsibility to live the questions.[42] Our efforts are (partially) shared in this childhood studies research collection. They are little stories, purposefully short. They will not do or say everything. No story could. They are glimpses of possibilities. But we hope they are provocative stories that will spark other stories and enliven more experimentations in childhood research. They are offered with a common worlds ethic to incite researchers to cultivate methodologies that intentionally, carefully and resolutely work to refuse the dominance of Euro-Western neoliberal touchstones and experiment with speculative, multiple, situated enactments of postqualitative research-to-come.

Notes

1   For example, Patti Lather, "Methodology-21: What Do We Do in the Afterward?" *International Journal of Qualitative Studies in Education* 26, no. 6 (2013): 634–645; Nick Lee, Childhood and Biopolitics: Climate Change, Life Processes, and Human Futures (New York: Palgrave Macmillan, 2013); Veronica Pacini-Ketchabaw and

Affrica Taylor, eds., *Unsettling the Colonial Places and Spaces of Early Childhood Education* (New York: Routledge, 2015); Veronica Pacini-Ketchabaw and Affrica Taylor, *The Common Worlds of Children and Animals: Relational Ethics for Entangled Lives* (New York: Routledge, 2018); Hans Skott-Myhre, Veronica Pacini-Ketchabaw, and Kathy Skott-Myhre, eds., *Youth Work, Early Education, and Psychology: Liminal Encounters* (New York: Palgrave Macmillan, 2016); Margaret Somerville and Monica Green, *Children, Place and Sustainability* (Basingstoke, UK: Palgrave Macmillan, 2015); Elizabeth A. St. Pierre, Alecia Y. Jackson, and Lisa A. Mazzei, "New Empiricisms and New Materialisms: Conditions for New Inquiry," *Cultural Studies—Critical Methodologies* 16, no. 2 (2016): 99–110; Carol A. Taylor and Gabrielle Ivinson, "Material Feminisms: New Directions for Education," *Gender and Education* 25, no. 6 (2013): 665–670; Jennifer White, Scott Kouri, and Veronica Pacini-Ketchabaw, "Risking Attachments in Teaching Child and Youth Care Twenty-first-century Settler Colonial, Environmental, and Biotechnological Worlds," *International Journal of Social Pedagogy* 6, no. 1 (2017): 43–63.

2   Patti Lather, *Against Proper Objects: Toward the Diversely Qualitative*, Summer Institute in Qualitative Research, Manchester Metropolitan University, 6 July 2015, 13.

3   For example, Karen Barad, *Meeting the Universe Halfway: Quantum Physics and the Entanglement of Matter and Meaning* (Durham, NC: Duke University Press, 2007); Claire Colebrook, "Stratigraphic Time, Women's Time," *Australian Feminist Studies* 24, no. 59 (2009): 11–16; Elizabeth Grosz, *The Nick of Time: Politics, Evolution, and the Untimely* (Durham, NC: Duke University Press, 2004); Elizabeth Grosz, *Time Travels: Feminism, Nature, Power* (Durham, NC: Duke University Press, 2005); Elizabeth Grosz, "The Untimeliness of Feminist Theory," *Nordic Journal of Feminist and Gender Research* 18, no. 1 (2010): 48–51; Donna Haraway, *Staying with the Trouble: Making Kin in the Chthulucene* (Durham, NC: Duke University Press, 2016); María Puig de la Bellacasa, *Matters of Care in Technoscience: Speculative Ethics in More Than Human Worlds* (Minneapolis: University of Minnesota Press, 2017).

4   This list is by no means exhaustive, but for examples of Indigenous scholars who describe and illuminate through their stories Indigenous understandings of time, see Heather Davis and Zoe Todd, "On the Importance of a Date, Or Decolonizing the Anthropocene," *ACME: An International Journal for Critical Geographies* 16, no. 4 (2017): 761–780; Robin Wall Kimmerer, *Braiding Sweetgrass: Indigenous Wisdom, Scientific Knowledge, and the Teaching of Plants* (Minneapolis, MN: Milkwood Editions, 2013); Robin Wall Kimmerer, *Gathering Moss: A Natural and Cultural History of Mosses* (Corvallis, OR: OSU Press, 2003); Leanne Betasamosake Simpson, *Dancing on Our Turtle's Back: Stories of Nishnaabeg Re-creation, Resurgence, and a New Emergence* (Winnipeg, MB: Arbeiter Ring, 2011); Leanne Betasamosake Simpson, "Land as Pedagogy: Nishnaabeg Intelligence and Rebellious Transformation," *Decolonization: Indigeneity, Education, and Society*

3, no. 3 (2014): 1–25.; Vanessa Watts, "Indigenous Place-thought and Agency Amongst Humans and Non-humans (First Woman and Sky Woman Go on a World Tour!)," *Decolonization: Indigeneity, Education, and Society* 2, no. 1 (2013): 20–34; see also Jessica Gerard, Sophie Rudolph, and Arathi Sriprakash, "The Politics of Post-qualitative Inquiry: History and Power," *Qualitative Inquiry* 23, no. 5 (2017): 384–394.

5 For more about the shifts from qualitative to postqualitative research see Lather, "Methodology-21"; Lather, *Against Proper Objects*; Patti Lather, "Top Ten+ List: (Re)thinking Ontology in (Post)qualitative Research," *Cultural Studies—Critical Methodologies* 16, no. 2 (2016): 125–131; Patti Lather, *(Post)critical Methodologies: The Science Possible after the Critiques: The Selected Works of Patti Lather* (New York: Routledge, 2017); Patti Lather and Elizabeth Adams St. Pierre, "Post-qualitative Research," *International Journal of Qualitative Studies in Education* 26, no. 6 (2013): 629–633; Elizabeth Adams St. Pierre, "Post-qualitative Research: The Critique and the Coming After," in *SAGE Handbook of Qualitative Inquiry*, 4th ed., ed. Norman K. Denzin and Yvonne S. Lincoln (Thousand Oaks, CA: SAGE, 2011), 611–625; Elizabeth Adams St. Pierre, "The Posts Continue: Becoming," *International Journal of Qualitative Studies in Education* 26, no. 6 (2013): 646–657; Elizabeth Adams St. Pierre, "Writing Post-qualitative Inquiry," *Qualitative Inquiry* (2017): 1–6; St. Pierre, Jackson, and Mazzei, "New Empiricisms and New Materialisms."

6 St. Pierre, "The Posts Continue," 649.

7 Lather, "Top Ten+ List," 125.

8 For an overview of Deleuzian influence in shaping feminist postqualitative research, the scholars cited in note 6 are of particular importance. Also see this special issue journal: Lisa A. Mazzei and Kate McCoy, eds., "Thinking with Deleuze in Qualitative Research," *Qualitative Inquiry* 23, no. 5 (2010). Also see Rebecca Coleman and Jessica Ringrose, eds., *Deleuze and Research Methodologies* (Edinburgh, UK: Edinburgh University Press, 2013).

9 Coleman and Ringrose, *Deleuze and Research Methodologies*, 2.

10 For example, Kimmerer, *Braiding Sweetgrass*; Kimmerer, *Gathering Moss*; Kim TallBear, "Beyond the Life/Not-life Binary," in *Cryopolitics: Frozen Life in a Melting World*, ed. Joanna Radin and Emma Kowal (Cambridge, MA: The MIT Press, 2017), 179–202; Kim TallBear, "An Indigenous Reflection on Working beyond the Human/Not Human," *GLQ: A Journal of Lesbian and Gay Studies* 21, no. 2–3 (2015): 230–235; Zoe Todd, "An Indigenous Feminist's Take on the Ontological Turn: 'Ontology' Is Just Another Word for Colonialism," *Journal of Historical Sociology* 49, no. 1 (2016): 4–22; Watts, "Indigenous Place-thought and Agency."

11 TallBear, "Beyond the Life/Not-life Binary," 193.

12 Todd, "Ontology," 8.

13 Ibid., 9.

14 Watts, "Indigenous Place-thought and Agency," 28.
15 Marie Battiste, *Decolonizing Education: Nourishing the Learning Spirit* (Vancouver: UBC Press, 2013); Davis and Todd, "On the Importance of a Date"; Jennifer A. Hamilton, Banu Subramanium, and Angela Willey, "What Indians and Indians Can Teach Us about Colonization: Feminist Science and Technology Studies, Epistemological Imperialism, and the Politics of Difference," *Feminist Studies* 43, no. 3 (2017): 612–623; Kimmerer, *Braiding Sweetgrass*; TallBear, "Beyond the Life/Not-life Binary"; Eve Tuck and Wayne Yang, "Decolonization Is Not a Metaphor," *Decolonization: Indigeneity, Education, and Society* 1, no. 1 (2012): 1–40; Watts, "Indigenous Place-thought and Agency."
16 TallBear, "Beyond the Life/Not-life Binary," 193.
17 CBC Radio, "'Universities Don't Become Different by Wishing for It': Eve Tuck on the Challenge of Changing Academia," *Unreserved*, 26 February 2018.
18 Common Worlds Research Collective website, http://commonworlds.net/.
19 Haraway, *Staying with the Trouble*; Lather, *(Post)Critical Methodologies*; Puig de la Bellacasa, *Matters of Care in Technoscience*.
20 Researchers in this collection have engaged various tools for generating and analyzing data. They, in collaboration with educators and children, have observed and recorded research moments through note-taking, photographs and/or video or audio recordings, documents which then become tangible traces for reflection both individually and collectively (e.g., with participating educators, children, families, community members). This reflection will often be documented in some form as well (e.g., video/audio recorded, researcher field notes) for further reflection and analysis. It is how one engages these tools, who engages with them, and what it is we understand them to be producing that marks these research skills typically (described as fieldwork) as postqualitative.
21 St. Pierre, Jackson, and Mazzei, "New Empiricisms and New Materialisms."
22 Simpson, "Land as Pedagogy."
23 Hillevi Lenz Taguchi, "Images of Thinking in Feminist Materialisms: Ontological Divergences and the Production of Researcher Subjectivities," *International Journal of Qualitative Studies in Education* 26, no. 6 (2013): 715.
24 Puig de la Bellacasa, *Matters of Care in Technoscience*, 7.
25 Ibid.
26 For example, Linda Tuhiwai Smith, *Decolonizing Methodologies: Research and Indigenous Peoples*, 2nd ed. (London: Zed Books, 2012); Eve Tuck and Wayne Yang, "Unbecoming Claims: Pedagogies of Refusal in Qualitative Research," *Qualitative Inquiry* 20, no. 6 (2014): 811–818; Eve Tuck and Wayne Yang, "R-words: Refusing Research," in *Humanizing Research: Decolonizing Qualitative Inquiry with Youth and Communities*, ed. Django Paris and Maisha T. Winn (Thousand Oaks, CA: SAGE, 2014), 223–247.

27 Donna Haraway, *SF: Science Fiction, Speculative Fabulation, String Figures, So Far*, Pilgrim Award acceptance comments, 7 July 2011, http://people.ucsc.edu/~haraway/Files/PilgrimAcceptanceHaraway.pdf.
28 Lather, "Methodology-21," 638.
29 Common Worlds Research Collective, "Children's Relations with Materials," http://commonworlds.net/childrens-relations-with-materials/.
30 Puig de la Bellacasa, *Matters of Care in Technoscience*.
31 Lesley Instone, "Risking Attachment in the Anthropocene," in *Manifesto for Living in the Anthropocene*, ed. Katherine Gibson, Deborah Bird Rose, and Ruth Fincher (New York: Punctum Books, 2015), 36.
32 Common Worlds Research Collective, "Children's Relations with Other Species," http://commonworlds.net/childrens-relations-with-other-species/.
33 Deborah Bird Rose, "Shimmer: When All You Love Is Being Trashed," in *Arts of Living on a Damaged Planet: Ghosts and Monsters of the Anthropocene*, ed. Anna Lowenhaupt Tsing, Heather Anne Swanson, Elaine Gan, and Nils Bubandt (Minneapolis: University of Minnesota Press, 2017), G51–G63.
34 Anna L. Tsing, *The Mushroom at the End of the World: On the Possibility of Life in the Capitalist Ruins* (Princeton, NJ: Princeton University Press, 2015).
35 Common Worlds Research Collective, "Children's Relations with Place," http://commonworlds.net/childrens-relations-with-place/.
36 María Puig de la Bellacasa, "Touching Technologies, Touching Visions: The Reclaiming of Sensorial Experience and the Politics of Speculative Thinking," *Subjectivity* 28 (2009): 297.
37 Simpson, *Dancing on Our Turtle's Back*.
38 Bill Readings, *The University in Ruins* (Cambridge, MA: Harvard University Press, 1996), 161–165.
39 A pedagogista is someone who works collaboratively with all the protagonists within an educational endeavor to promote critical and dialogical encounters that consider the specificity of a pedagogical project as well as its relations with the broader philosophical vision and commitments of the early learning setting.
40 Haraway, *SF: Science Fiction*; Haraway, *Staying with the Trouble*.
41 Lather, *Against Proper Objects*, 13.
42 Adam Kleinman, "Intra-actions: Interview with Karen Barad," *Mouse* 34 (2012): 76–81.

Bibliography

Barad, Karen. *Meeting the Universe Halfway: Quantum Physics and the Entanglement of Matter and Meaning*. Durham, NC: Duke University Press, 2007.
Battiste, Marie. *Decolonizing Education: Nourishing the Learning Spirit*. Vancouver: UBC Press, 2013.

CBC Radio. "'Universities Don't Become Different by Wishing for It': Eve Tuck on the Challenge of Changing Academia." *Unreserved*, 26 February 2018. http://www.cbc.ca/radio/unreserved/decolonizing-the-classroom-is-there-space-for-indigenous-knowledge-in-academia-1.4544984/universities-don-t-become-different-just-by-wishing-for-it-eve-tuck-on-the-challenge-of-changing-academia-1.4547278.

Colebrook, Claire. "Stratigraphic Time, Women's Time." *Australian Feminist Studies* 24, no. 59 (2009): 11–16.

Coleman, Rebecca, and Jessica Ringrose, eds. *Deleuze and Research Methodologies*. Edinburgh: Edinburgh University Press, 2013.

Common Worlds Research Collective. "Children's Relations with Materials." http://commonworlds.net/childrens-relations-with-materials/.

Common Worlds Research Collective. "Children's Relations with Other Species." http://commonworlds.net/childrens-relations-with-other-species/.

Common Worlds Research Collective. "Children's Relations with Place." http://commonworlds.net/childrens-relations-with-place/.

Davis, Heather, and Zoe Todd. "On the Importance of a Date, or Decolonizing the Anthropocene." *ACME: An International Journal for Critical Geographies* 16, no. 4 (2017): 761–780.

Gerard, Jessica, Sophie Rudolph, and Arathi Sriprakash. "The Politics of Post-qualitative Inquiry: History and Power." *Qualitative Inquiry* 23, no. 5 (2017): 384–394. doi: 10.1177/1077800416672694.

Grosz, Elizabeth. *The Nick of Time: Politics, Evolution, and the Untimely*. Durham, NC: Duke University Press, 2004.

Grosz, Elizabeth. *Time Travels: Feminism, Nature, Power*. Durham, NC: Duke University Press, 2005.

Grosz, Elizabeth. "The Untimeliness of Feminist Theory." *Nordic Journal of Feminist and Gender Research* 18, no. 1 (2010): 48–51.

Hamilton, Jennifer A., Banu Subramanium, and Angela Willey. "What Indians and Indians Can Teach Us about Colonization: Feminist Science and Technology Studies, Epistemological Imperialism, and the Politics of Difference." *Feminist Studies* 43, no. 3 (2017): 612–623.

Haraway, Donna. *SF: Science Fiction, Speculative Fabulation, String Figures, So Far*. Pilgrim Award acceptance comments, 7 July 2011. http://people.ucsc.edu/~haraway/Files/PilgrimAcceptanceHaraway.pdf.

Haraway, Donna. *Staying with the Trouble: Making Kin in the Chthulucene*. Durham, NC: Duke University, 2016.

Haraway, Donna. *When Species Meet*. Minneapolis: University of Minnesota Press, 2008.

Hollett, Ty, and Christian Ehret. "Bean's World: (Mine)Crafting Affective Atmospheres for Game-play, Learning, and Care in a Children's Hospital." *New Media and Society* 17, no. 11 (2015): 1849–1866.

Instone, Lesley. "Risking Attachment in the Anthropocene." In *Manifesto for Living in the Anthropocene*, edited by Katherine Gibson, Deborah Bird Rose, and Ruth Fincher, 29–36. New York: Punctum Books, 2015.

Kimmerer, Robin Wall. *Braiding Sweetgrass: Indigenous Wisdom, Scientific Knowledge, and the Teaching of Plants*. Minneapolis: Milkwood Editions, 2013.

Kimmerer, Robin Wall. *Gathering Moss: A Natural and Cultural History of Mosses*. Corvallis, OR: OSU Press, 2003.

Kleinman, Adam. "Intra-actions: Interview with Karen Barad." *Mouse* 34 (2012): 76–81.

Lather, Patti. *Against Proper Objects: Toward the Diversely Qualitative*. Summer Institute in Qualitative Research. Manchester Metropolitan University, 6 July 2015.

Lather, Patti. "Methodology-21: What Do We Do in the Afterward?" *International Journal of Qualitative Studies in Education* 26, no. 6 (2013): 634–645.

Lather, Patti. *(Post)critical Methodologies: The Science Possible after the Critiques: The Selected Works of Patti Lather*. New York: Routledge, 2017.

Lather, Patti. "Top Ten+ List: (Re)thinking Ontology in (Post)qualitative Research." *Cultural Studies—Critical Methodologies* 16, no. 2 (2016): 125–131.

Lather, Patti, and Elizabeth Adams St. Pierre. "Post-qualitative Research." *International Journal of Qualitative Studies in Education* 26, no. 6 (2013): 629–633.

Lee, Nick. *Childhood and Biopolitics: Climate Change, Life Processes, and Human Futures*. New York: Palgrave Macmillan, 2013.

Lenz Taguchi, Hillevi. "Images of Thinking in Feminist Materialisms: Ontological Divergences and the Production of Researcher Subjectivities." *International Journal of Qualitative Studies in Education* 26, no. 6 (2013): 706–716.

Mazzei, Lisa A., and Kate McCoy, eds. "Thinking with Deleuze in Qualitative Research." *Qualitative Inquiry* 23, no. 5 (2010).

Pacini-Ketchabaw, Veronica, and Affrica Taylor. *The Common Worlds of Children and Animals: Relational Ethics for Entangled Lives*. New York: Routledge, 2018.

Pacini-Ketchabaw, Veronica, and Affrica Taylor, eds. *Unsettling the Colonial Places and Spaces of Early Childhood Education*. New York: Routledge, 2015.

Puig de la Bellacasa, María. *Matters of Care in Technoscience: Speculative Ethics in More than Human Worlds*. Minneapolis: University of Minnesota Press, 2017.

Puig de la Bellacasa, María. "Touching Technologies, Touching Visions: The Reclaiming of Sensorial Experience and the Politics of Speculative Thinking." *Subjectivity* 28 (2009): 297–315.

Rose, Deborah Bird. "Shimmer: When All You Love Is Being Trashed." In *Arts of Living on a Damaged Planet: Ghosts and Monsters of the Anthropocene*, edited by Anna Lowenhaupt Tsing, Heather Anne Swanson, Elaine Gan, and Nils Bubandt (Minneapolis: University of Minnesota Press, 2017), G51–G63.

Simpson, Leanne Betasamosake. *Dancing on Our Turtle's Back: Stories of Nishnaabeg Re-creation, Resurgence, and a New Emergence*. Winnipeg, MB: Arbeiter Ring, 2011.

Simpson, Leanne Betasamosake. "Land as Pedagogy: Nishnaabeg Intelligence and Rebellious Transformation." *Decolonization: Indigeneity, Education, and Society* 3, no. 3 (2014): 1–25.

Skott-Myhre, Hans, Veronica Pacini-Ketchabaw, and Kathy Skott-Myhre, eds. *Youth Work, Early Education, and Psychology: Liminal Encounters*. New York: Palgrave Macmillan, 2016.

Smith, Linda Tuhiwai. *Decolonizing Methodologies: Research and Indigenous Peoples.* 2nd ed. London: Zed Books, 2012.

Somerville, Margaret, and Monica Green. *Children, Place, and Sustainability.* Basingstoke, UK: Palgrave Macmillan, 2015.

St. Pierre, Elizabeth Adams. "Post-qualitative Research: The Critique and the Coming After." In *SAGE Handbook of Qualitative Inquiry.* 4th ed., edited by Norman K. Denzin and Yvonne S. Lincoln, 611–625. Thousand Oaks, CA: SAGE, 2011.

St. Pierre, Elizabeth Adams. "The Posts Continue: Becoming." *International Journal of Qualitative Studies in Education* 26, no. 6 (2013): 646–657. doi: 10.1080/09518398.2013.788754.

St. Pierre, Elizabeth Adams. "Writing Post-qualitative Inquiry." *Qualitative Inquiry* (2017): 1–6. doi: 10.1177/1077800417734567.

St. Pierre, Elizabeth A., Alecia Y. Jackson, and Lisa A. Mazzei. "New Empiricisms and New Materialisms: Conditions for New Inquiry." *Cultural Studies—Critical Methodologies* 16, no. 2 (2016): 99–110.

TallBear, Kim. "Beyond the Life/Not-life Binary." In *Cryopolitics: Frozen Life in a Melting World*, edited by Joanna Radin and Emma Kowal, 179–202. Cambridge, MA: The MIT Press, 2017.

TallBear, Kim. "An Indigenous Reflection on Working beyond the Human/Not Human." *GLQ: A Journal of Lesbian and Gay Studies* 21, nos. 2–3 (2015): 230–235. doi: 10.1215/10642684-2843323.

Taylor, Carol A., and Gabrielle Ivinson. "Material Feminisms: New Directions for Education." *Gender and Education* 25, no. 6 (2013): 665–670. doi: 10.1080/09540253.2013.834617.

Todd, Zoe. "An Indigenous Feminist's Take on the Ontological Turn: 'Ontology' Is Just Another Word for Colonialism." *Journal of Historical Sociology* 49, no. 1 (2016): 4–22. doi: 10.1111/johs.12124.

Tsing, Anna L. *The Mushroom at the End of the World: On the Possibility of Life in the Capitalist Ruins.* Princeton, NJ: Princeton University Press, 2015.

Tuck, Eve, and Wayne Yang. "Decolonization Is Not a Metaphor." *Decolonization: Indigeneity, Education, and Society* 1, no. 1 (2012): 1–40.

Tuck, Eve, and Wayne Yang. "R-words: Refusing Research." In *Humanizing Research: Decolonizing Qualitative Inquiry with Youth and Communities*, edited by Django Paris and Maisha T. Winn, 223–247. Thousand Oaks, CA: SAGE, 2014.

Tuck, Eve, and Wayne Yang. "Unbecoming Claims: Pedagogies of Refusal in Qualitative Research." *Qualitative Inquiry* 20, no. 6 (2014): 811–818.

Watts, Vanessa. "Indigenous Place-thought and Agency Amongst Humans and Non-humans (First Woman and Sky Woman Go on a World Tour!)." *Decolonization: Indigeneity, Education, and Society* 2, no. 1 (2013): 20–34.

White, Jennifer, Scott Kouri, and Veronica Pacini-Ketchabaw. "Risking Attachments in Teaching Child and Youth Care Twenty-first-century Settler Colonial, Environmental, and Biotechnological Worlds." *International Journal of Social Pedagogy* 6, no. 1 (2017): 43–63. doi: 10.14324/111.444.ijsp.2017.v6.1.004

Part One

Relations with Materials

1

Claying: Attending to Earth's Caring Relations

Veronica Pacini-Ketchabaw and
Kelly Boucher

clay
clay cares
clay has histories
clay remembers
clay was once stone
clay experiences weathering
clay = plasticity
clay = multiple minerals
clay gifts
clay

Claying with

Clay slabs sit on Wurundjeri Country, stacked onto lino floor and plastic. Child bodies launch onto the stack. Clay is grabbed, pulled and pinched. Flat surfaces become textured with each hand pinch and fingernail scrape. Clay moves onto hands and under fingernails, onto arms, floor, knees. Clay is hard, heavy, soft. Children huff, puff and grrrr as small chunks are pulled off with pressed fingers and clenched fists. Clay bodies and child bodies wrestle and merge in a clay-child mosh pit. Clay moves into the room. Clay smears: across the floor, across plastic, onto boots. Clay is tracked over carpet. Clay travels.

Clay slabs are stacked in a line on this preschool classroom's floor. Clay is solid, moist, sticky. Child bodies stomp across clay bodies—a clay wall leading to a tower. The stacked slabs receive boot squish and hand slap. Clay moves onto hand, knee, clothes and floor. Clay receives as bodies prod. Clay slabs are steps to climb, and clay offers child bodies extra height and a different place to stand. Ellie steps

Figure 1.1 Clay-plastic movement. Photo credit: Kelly Boucher.

across clay and onto the castle tower. Clay is solid yet soft under booted foot. Ellie wobbles; clay supports. Clay holds her up. Clay becomes a tower, and Ellie surveys the room, delighted with her new perspective. Rita circles Ellie, shouting "Get off our tower!" Clay supports Ellie. Clay is solid, heavy, forceful, and the child-body-tower is defiant. Clay stays. Rita moves to the front of the child-body-tower and starts grabbing at the base. Clay is pulled and scooped from the bottom of the slabs. Rita digs into clay. Clay moves onto hands and under fingernails. Other children are called over to dig into the base in order to topple the tower and the child body balancing on top.

Wurundjeri Country receives this Wadawurrung and Dja Dja Wurrung clay. This clay is dug out of pits in Central Victoria, Australia. White clay is blended from two sites: Wadawurrung country (near the town of Bacchus Marsh) and Dja Dja Wurrung country (near the regional city of Bendigo). The terracotta clay is also Dja Dja Wurrung country (from the town of Ballarat). This clay, gathered with heavy machinery and transported in tip trucks, has traveled from a place where it was once rock. This clay, weathered and broken down over millennia, became aggregate, sediment. This clay is country, soil. This clay is living—an ecology of earth, minerals, microbes, particles. This clay might contain illite/smectites, kaolinites, smectites, micas and more.[1] This clay is brought together, mixed with water and manufactured to a consistency suitable to form slabs. This clay is cut into blocks, wrapped in plastic and transported on trucks onto Wurundjeri Country, to Naam—now known as the city of Melbourne. This clay is bought from a pottery supply store and travels in the boot of Kelly's car, then onto a trolley and into the preschool classroom. This clay is unwrapped and stacked in a line on the floor. This clay has journeyed far. Although its place of origin/country is no longer recognizable within its plastic wrap, this clay has a place. Because this clay is situated, it offers, questions and demands of children and educators to take part, to be present and to "attend and attune to questions from the world."[2] In other words, it demands that we attend to its history and memory.

Being present to/in this clay's ecological memory enacts what Michi Saagiig Nishnaabeg scholar and artist Leanne Betasamosake Simpson speaks to as an "ecology of intimacy."[3] For Simpson, this ecology of intimacy embraces and reveals land relations that are premised on connectivity, love, relationship, respect, reciprocity and freedom. As settlers in territories apart, we (Veronica and Kelly) wonder how clay might become a gift from the land rather than a natural material or even a natural resource with hundreds of uses (for instance, in education, in health, in aesthetics, in soil sciences and so on). We also ponder how clay engages as a gift that always demands modes of "clay care."[4] Drawing on María Puig de la Bellacasa's writings on matters of care, clay care requires embracing and maintaining the multiple webs of relations already existent "in the everyday fabric of troubled worlds."[5] In other words, the challenge becomes how to care for clay that has traveled so far, been made seemingly placeless and participated in capital exchanges. How might children and educators enact modes of clay care, always foregrounded in actual clay relations, with/in pedagogies of intimacy?

Yet it is not only humans who care for clay. Clay also cares. Clay lives in ongoing relations. Clay engages in intimate pedagogies in its own rights. This, of course, does not mean that clay cares for us humans.[6] We might describe this intimacy using these words of clay scientist Swapna Mukherjee: "Clay minerals can remove the ions of pollutants and contaminants from solutions," allowing "them to play very important roles in many natural neutralising reactions and facilitate their applications in many pollution control measures."[7] For instance, clay minerals are often used for water purification and treatment,[8] and clays are often used as cleaning and polishing agents.[9] Alternatively, we might describe clay enacting caring through all its relations, or establishing life-sustaining connections, by drawing on feminist science studies scholars such as Puig de la Bellacasa.[10] Clay cares as it "appropriates a toxic terrain" such as polluted water, "making it again capable of nurturing."[11] Clay cares when, through its multispecies communities, it does "the work of recuperating previously neglected grounds."[12] How might we attend to clay care relations when care is lived beyond human worlds?

With clay

At Komoka creek in Anishinaabe, Haudenosaunee, and Leni-Lunaape territory, thousands of miles away from where child-clay bodies meet on Wurundjeri Country, we (Veronica with a group of educators and pedagogues) visit an assembly of clay aggregates. The creek, with its grayish clay floor, feeds what is now known as the North Thames River in southwestern Ontario. More than 13,000 years ago, the area where the creek and river flow was a glacier. During the height of colonial residential schools in Canada, the Komoka area was a booming railway town and fertile farming place. Now, at a time of ecological crisis, the province of Ontario has named this area a provincial park, continuing the violences of colonial practices on the territory.[13]

As we walk on the smooth clay floor on a warm autumn day, we feel between our toes, feet and ankles the cold, clear water running from the nearby spring. With two large plastic pails, a hiking knife and an array of small metal garden tools (one hand fork, two hand transplanters, three hand cultivators and four hand trowels), we dig into the Komoka creek clay floor. As we dig, we wonder how we might care differently for clays that do not arrive in the classroom wrapped in thick plastic

Figure 1.2 Digging. Photo credit: Sylvia Kind.

bags. *Might this clay remind us of its histories, of its minerals, of the war declared on the land on which we stand?*[14]

Like the children on Wurundjeri Country, we apply force to dig out a block of iron-bearing clay that after many tries gives in to the knife's sharp blade. Clay is rock. Carefully, we chisel the rock inside the pail as we add more and more water from the creek. Wet, cold fingers help to further disintegrate the now smallish pieces of clay. We are starting to know this clay, feel this clay, care for this clay differently. In making time for this clay's specific temporalities, our obligations expand to the multispecies community that this clay is. This clay surface has been here for much longer than we can even imagine. This clay has been formed through relations, including the "microorganisms in microbial mats" *that constantly* "metabolize and use materials from the surrounding air, water, sediments, and rocks."[15] *Drawing on Puig de la Bellacasa's writings,*[16] *by* "focusing on the temporal experiences" *of Komoka clay, we are beginning to disrupt current conceptions of clay that are depleted from the clay's own minerals and lively entanglements.*

We pour water into the pail to regenerate the fine chunks of clay. Fatima Andrade and colleagues explain that

> when water is added to dry clay, the first effect is an increase in cohesion, which tends to reach a maximum when water has nearly displaced all air from the pores between the particles .... Addition of water into the pores induces the formation of a fairly high yield-strength body.[17]

As "water acts as a lubricant," we begin to make sense of clay's plasticity.[18] Clay scientists define plasticity in clay mineral systems as "the property of a material which allows it to be repeatedly deformed without rupture when acted upon by a force sufficient to cause deformation and which allows it to retain its shape after the applied force has been removed."[19] In fact, it is clay's plasticity that allows the child bodies on Wurundjeri Country and our bodies on Anishinaabe, Haudenosaunee and Leni-Lunaape land to convert clay "into a given shape."[20]

Several shapes emerge from the regenerated clay: Balls that we throw and catch between us as we stand on the creek bed. Nests that mimic the nests that a group of young children had made the day before our visit to the creek.[21] *Other shapes that are not necessarily identifiable. Big shapes. Tiny shapes. Shapes that stand strong on tree branches. Shapes that crack and disappear.*

We gift these shapes back to the creek and the river.

Objects travel through the gesture of gifting. Public Share,[22] a collective of artists from Aotearoa, focuses on the notion of sharing and exchange via the everydayness of clay and the production of clay vessels, containers and objects. For example, as a response to the politics of urban development, a group of artists collected clay from Auckland's SH16 northwestern motorway construction site in Te Atatu, New Zealand, and used the sourced raw clay to produce a collection of vessels, mugs and plates. These items were then returned to the worksite. Not

Figure 1.3 Assembling. Photo credit: Sylvia Kind.

only were the mugs and plates used for morning tea break with sixty workers employed by the road contractor Fulton Hogan, but the vessels were also gifted to the workers to take home. These events are a gesture toward cooperative practice made meaningful via collaboration and the reflective conviviality of taking time out to share a cup of tea. Relevant to this chapter, these practices also bring "a different perspective of the tons of clay that they dig out of the ground"[23] into the world through the act of gifting.

Gifting is also a way of returning back to the earth, and this is precisely what Alterfact's experimental designers Lucile Sciallano and Ben Landau are doing in Melbourne, Australia.[24] Sciallano and Landau note that "they push the boundaries" of clay as a "traditionally plastic-based medium, and play with its connotations of utilitarianism and gimmickry, as it moves into a feasible reality."[25] For instance, in their project Terre à Terre (a French term meaning "down to earth"), the artists gathered clay from a small produce farm in northern Victoria in an attempt to find clay composites suitable for making slip-molded vessels. The team experimented with firing the vessels (plates, bowls and containers) at different temperatures to produce utilitarian objects that were robust enough for a few uses (a dinner event) yet able to be crushed and composted. In other words, the designers experiment with the idea of "staying with the trouble"[26] of gifting clay back to the earth after it has been manipulated through modern manufacturing processes.

We also find Alterfact's clay projects significant because they emphasize "practices and accounts of prefiguration as a way to think about how we go about crafting another world within the shell of the old."[27] Sciallano and Landau's studio practices investigate "the intersection between handbuilt and industrial processes"[28] of production to make something *new*. Clay projects are "a platform through which to explore current and future issues and translate them into experiences, installations and objects."[29] For example, in their Handbuilt/Machinebuilt project, the designers employ industrial processes, specifically 3D scanning and printing, to reproduce a hand-formed vessel. They manipulate the clay by hand, bringing in the force of the human body to create undulations in the clay, and then scan it and print it on a 3D printer. They emphasize that following these processes is not about disrupting craft practices. Rather, they stress the in-between tensions of the handbuilt and the machinebuilt to bring new ideas/worlds to life. In other words, the vessels' production challenges "'industrial' and 'handbuilt' as mutually exclusive categories"[30] and requires the viewer to appreciate both the handmaking and the 3D scanning and printing as coming together to create unrecognizable forms.

Perhaps it is the notion of engaging in prefiguration, crafting another world with our own inheritances, that clay is inviting us to engage in, both in Wurundjeri Country and at Komoka creek.

Situating through claying

In this brief chapter, we traced clay's matters of care. Situating clay in relations, we wondered how we might care for the clay wrapped in plastic and for the clay we mine from a creek. Rather than finding purities[31] in early childhood education's clay practices, we mapped ways to care for the webs of relations that are always already ingrained in *this* clay, despite us humans. Through the idea that clay exists outside of our human intentions, we gifted clay back to the earth.

We end with the questions that we continue to grapple with/in our research with children, educators and clay: How might we nurture already existing microbial clay relations? Knowing that clay does not depend on us, how might we attend to humans' responsibilities for clay? What opportunities does gifting clay back to the earth bring to early childhood education?

Notes

1. C.C. Harvey and Gerhard Lagaly, "Conventional Applications," in *Handbook of Clay Science*, vol. 1, ed. Faïza Bergaya, Benny K.G. Theng, and Gerhard Lagaly (Amsterdam: Elsevier, 2006), 501.
2. Pauliina Rautio, *Thinking about Life and Species Lines with Pietari and Otto (and Garlic Breath)*, keynote address given at the Antipodes Summer Institute of Qualitative Inquiry "Wild Thinking," 21–25 November 2016, Western Sydney University, Australia.
3. Leanne Betasamosake Simpson, *Decolonial Love: Centering Resurgent Indigenous Nationhood*, keynote presentation, "Canada on the Global Stage," McGill University, Montreal, 23 February 2016, https://www.youtube.com/watch?v=x9tN4hPlKzs.
4. Veronica Pacini-Ketchabaw, Sylvia Kind, and Laurie L.M. Kocher, *Encounters with Materials in Early Childhood Education* (New York: Routledge, 2016).
5. María Puig de la Bellacasa, *Matters of Care: Speculative Ethics in More Than Human Worlds* (Minneapolis: University of Minnesota Press, 2017), 11.
6. Isabelle Stengers, *In Catastrophic Times: Resisting the Coming Barbarism* (Paris: Meson Press, 2015).
7. Swapna Mukherjee, "Beneficial and Hazardous Aspects of Clays in Nature: A Brief Overview," in *The Science of Clays* (Dordrecht: Springer, 2013), 237.

8   Giora Rytwoa, Shlomo Nirb, and Uri Shualib, "Preface," *Applied Clay Sciences* 67–68 (2012): iv–v.
9   Ibid.
10 Puig de la Bellacasa, *Matters of Care*.
11 Ibid., 11.
12 Ibid.
13 Robert Jago, "Canada's National Parks Are Colonial Crime Scenes," *The Walrus*, June 30, 2017.
14 Simpson, *Decolonial Love*.
15 Kazue Tazaki, "Clays, Microorganisms, and Biomineralization," in *Handbook of Clay Science*, vol. 1, ed. Faïza Bergaya, Benny K.G. Theng, and Gerhard Lagaly (Amsterdam: Elsevier, 2006), 478.
16 Puig de la Bellacasa, *Matters of Care*.
17 Fatima A. Andrade, Hazim A. Al-Qureshi, and Dachamir Hotza, "Measuring the Plasticity of Clays: A Review," *Applied Clay Science* 51 (2011): 5.
18 Ibid.
19 Walter W. Perkins, *Ceramic Glossary* (Westerville, OH: American Ceramic Society, 1995), as cited in Andrade et al., "Measuring the Plasticity of Clays," 3.
20 Andrade et al., "Measuring the Plasticity of Clays," 3.
21 Veronica Pacini-Ketchabaw, "Nest and Egg Making," *Encounters with Materials* blog, 6 April 2017, http://encounterswithmaterials.com/2017/04/06/nest-egg-making/.
22 Public Share website: http://publicshare.co.nz/.
23 Public Share, *A Break in Proceedings: Irregular Allotments*, 1, http://d11vl39i71yqtx.cloudfront.net/wp-content/uploads/2015/01/a-break-in-proceedings.pdf.
24 Alterfact, "Terre à Terre," https://www.alterfact.net/terre-a-terre-1.
25 Alterfact. "About," 2, https://www.alterfact.net/about/.
26 Donna J. Haraway, *Staying with the Trouble: Making Kin in the Chthulucene* (Durham, NC: Duke University Press, 2016).
27 Alexis Shotwell, *Against Purity: Living Ethically in Compromised Times* (Minneapolis: University of Minnesota Press, 2016), 185.
28 Alterfact, "Handbuilt/Machinebuilt," 1, https://www.alterfact.net/handbuiltmachinebuilt.
29 Alterfact, "About," 1.
30 Alterfact, "Handbuilt/Machinebuilt," 5.
31 Shotwell, *Against Purity*.

Bibliography

Alterfact. "About." https://www.alterfact.net/about/.
Alterfact. "Handbuilt/Machinebuilt." https://www.alterfact.net/handbuiltmachinebuilt.

Alterfact. "Terre à Terre." https://www.alterfact.net/terre-a-terre-1.

Andrade, Fatima A., Hazim A. Al-Qureshi, and Dachamir Hotza. "Measuring the Plasticity of Clays: A Review." *Applied Clay Science* 51 (2011). https://www.sciencedirect.com/science/article/pii/S0169131710003601#bb0180.

Haraway, Donna J. *Staying with the Trouble: Making Kin in the Chthulucene*. Durham, NC: Duke University Press, 2016.

Harvey, C.C., and Gerhard Lagaly. "Conventional Applications." In *Handbook of Clay Science*, vol. 5, edited by Faïza Bergaya, Benny K.G. Theng, and Gerhard Lagaly, 451–490. Amsterdam: Elsevier, 2006.

Jago, Robert. "Canada's National Parks Are Colonial Crime Scenes." *The Walrus*, 30 June 2017. https://thewalrus.ca/canadas-national-parks-are-colonial-crime-scenes/.

Mukherjee, Swapna. "Beneficial and Hazardous Aspects of Clays in Nature: A Brief Overview." In *The Science of Clays*. Dordrecht: Springer, 2013.

Pacini-Ketchabaw, Veronica. "Nest and Egg Making." *Encounters with Materials* blog, 6 April 2017. http://encounterswithmaterials.com/2017/04/06/nest-egg-making/.

Pacini-Ketchabaw, Veronica, Sylvia Kind, and Laurie L.M. Kocher. *Encounters with Materials in Early Childhood Education*. New York: Routledge, 2016.

Public Share. *A Break in Proceedings: Irregular Allotments*. http://d11vl39i71yqtx.cloudfront.net/wp-content/uploads/2015/01/a-break-in-proceedings.pdf.

Puig de la Bellacasa, María. *Matters of Care: Speculative Ethics in More Than Human Worlds*. Minneapolis: University of Minnesota Press, 2017.

Rautio, Pauliina. *Thinking about Life and Species Lines with Pietari and Otto (and Garlic Breath)*. Keynote address given at the Antipodes Summer Institute of Qualitative Inquiry "Wild Thinking," 21–25 November 2016, Western Sydney University, Australia.

Rytwoa, Giora, Shlomo Nirb, and Uri Shualib. "Preface." Special Issue on Clay and Water Treatment. *Applied Clay Sciences* 67–68 (2012): iv–v.

Shotwell, Alexis. *Against Purity: Living Ethically in Compromised Times*. Minneapolis: University of Minnesota Press, 2016.

Simpson, Leanne Betasamosake. *Decolonial Love: Centering Resurgent Indigenous Nationhood*. Keynote presentation, "Canada on the Global Stage," McGill University, Montreal, 23 February 2016. https://www.youtube.com/watch?v=x9tN4hPlKzs.

Stengers, Isabelle. *In Catastrophic Times: Resisting the Coming Barbarism*. Paris: Meson Press, 2015.

Tazaki, Kazue. "Clays, Microorganisms, and Biomineralization." In *Handbook of Clay Science*, vol. 5, edited by Faïza Bergaya, Benny K.G. Theng, and Gerhard Lagaly, 613–653. Amsterdam: Elsevier, 2006.

2

Fabricating: Fabric Fluidities and Studio Encounters

Sylvia Kind and Adrienne Argent

Long lengths of translucent fabric hang throughout the studio. Greens, blues and grays, the colors of the west coast, are interspersed with soft pinks, purples, reds and oranges in hues of salmon, coral, ruby and lavender. In the colors and delicate translucent quality of the fabric, we can feel the resonances of the coming summer. It's been an especially long, dark and wet west coast winter. For most of the winter and spring, clouds have hung dense and low in the sky, hiding the sun, coloring the world in muted hues of grays and blues, lending a certain heaviness and slowness to the days. But in the studio today, the sunlight filters through the large windows, catches the colors and enlivens the fabric, its surfaces shimmering in the sunlight. With the emerging sun and the lengthening days, a sense of lightness in the air and a colorfulness returning prevails as patches of cherry blossoms, rhododendrons, tulips and azaleas come into bloom and dot the landscape. Even the trees we can see through the studio windows are livelier in their greens. This fabric has a particular quality of lightness as well, floating as it catches the air, lying over bodies and structures but not quite settling or enveloping. It hovers with a lightness of touch, like a caress, luring us closer. The lengths of fabric sway slightly like breath, awaiting the soon-to-be-arriving children.

The studio is a fabricated space; that is, it is a carefully composed, curated and created space. It is not merely a background to children's experimentations or a container for art explorations but an emergent space itself always in the making. As a curated space, the studio brings different elements into relation with each other so that they touch, provoke, intra-act and encounter each other and create previously unrealized possibilities.[1] This, as Hans-Ulrich Obrist describes, is the task of curating. It is not simply about arranging an artistic space or filling it with

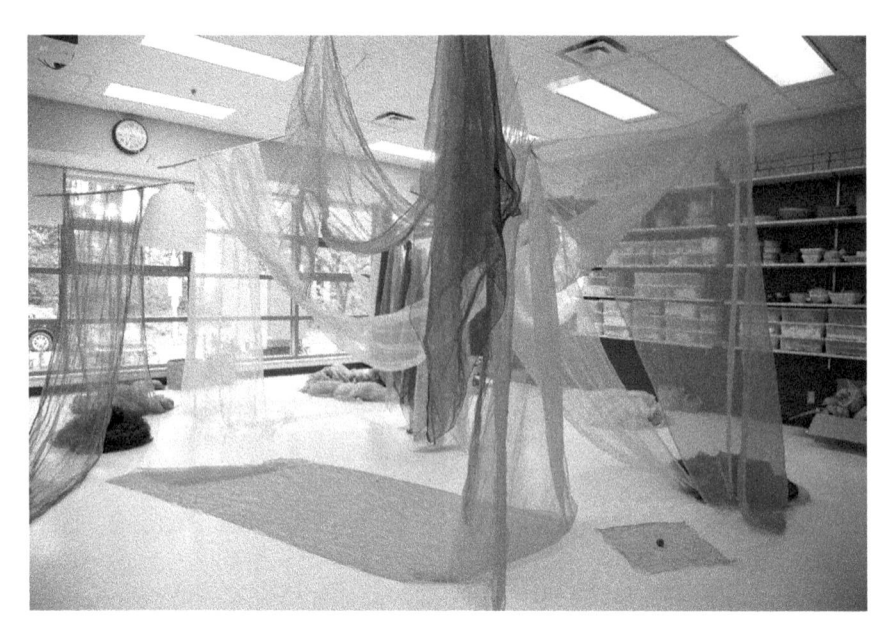

Figure 2.1 The fabric studio.

art materials, rather composing it so that there is an "invitation to realize projects not possible under existing conditions."[2] Thus, the work becomes an experiment, a desire to produce difference and a search for "unexplored horizons."[3] The studio becomes a productive *experience*, where something new is continuously produced, made and activated. It becomes a lively space of materials, bodies, ideas and processes that play with, speak to and intra-act with each other.[4] Intra-activity, according to Hillevi Lenz Taguchi, is the dynamic exchange of forces that take place *between* these elements.

Careful thought is put into how we might engage with this fabric's life and what is put into play. We resist instrumental aims, as if we decide ahead of time what ideas will be explored, what the fabric and materials will be used for, what purposes they will serve or what children will *do*. Rather, we think of the studio as an evolving composition that seeks to enhance the life of fabric, play with its movements and learn its ways as it interacts with bodies, beings, ideas and things. The studio also holds memories of other art encounters, for example, the work of Kimsooja, a South-Korean-born conceptual artist who works in video, performative and textile installations. In *Unfolding*, a retrospective of her work at the Vancouver Art Gallery, we had encountered an installation of a room filled with long panels of fabric hanging as if from a series of clotheslines. The vibrantly colored cloth swayed and brushed against our bodies as we walked through; richly patterned pinks, yellows and reds reflected and multiplied along the mirror-lined walls. As we lingered in the space, it was impossible not to touch and be touched by the fabric. We became caught up in the rhythms and flows of movements, colors, sounds, and sensations and the life of fabric, its affect remaining and even multiplying in the days following our visit.

The play of things

In the studio, the long panels of translucent fabric sway gently in the play of the morning light, the colors echoing with large baskets of remnants and fabric bundles arranged throughout the room. Small knit and felted body-like forms, a selection of *Small Exaggerations*, Sylvia's in-process artworks, line the low window ledge and gather in groupings under fabric-tent structures. Green felted pods in the colors of the west coast forest, wooden clothespins, metal clips, drawing boards and easels, chalk pastels, stools, densely knit square pillows, large skeins of green wool attached to a partially knit large wool cocoon, long, thin rolled paper tubes, twisted fragments of soft wire, one yellow felted heart, and a small round red wool ball laid out on a small salmon-colored scarf all sing together. Each element is a provocateur and participant.[5] Sylvia slips a long panel of apricot-orange fabric over her shoulders and, in the lightness of its weave and weight and in a particular affinity with the vibrant hue, feels an urge to fly. Adrienne reaches toward the fabric and in the touch joins with its tendency to slide, slip, twist and fall, and is mesmerized by the shifting hues as its gauzy reflective quality plays tricks on her eyes and never quite settles into a certainty of color. As the children enter, they remove their socks and shoes, which Sylvia echoes as well. The fabric seems to call for barefeet and intimate engagement, and in the touch of skin on fabric, something is proposed. Erin Manning describes touch as a gesture of turning toward or reaching toward, a movement, a tenuous, ephemeral exposure of oneself to the other, to the other that might emerge in the exchange.[6] Potentiality, that is, who one might be or what things might become, is at the heart of this gesture. Touch invents, Manning writes, "by drawing the other into relation."[7] To touch fabric is to be touched, to be affected, to be moved.

As the children enter, there is a rush of movement. Fabric and bodies become entangled as children immerse themselves in the vibrant folds of fabric. Rolling, covering, twisting, tying, knotting and wrapping, the children are reconfigured into pulsating fabric bundles. Fabric and children run, fly, dance and flow throughout the room. The fabric makes visible the children's lines of movement and exchanges. And while the fabric draws us all together in tangles of connections, the nonconforming and slippery nature of the fabric activates a particular quality of being together. The fabric takes shape, but only temporarily, because it cannot, on its own, hold a form. For a while, it becomes wings and enacts a possibility, but once released from hands, it slips to the ground and lies waiting in loose and colorful puddles. Its slipperiness lends itself to doings and undoings and to fluid and loose configurations and reconfigurations. Bodies in the studio respond to and echo the fabric's material qualities as the fabric instigates flowing and fluid-like gatherings. We begin to attune to the intra-activity and co-compositional movements of bodies and materials. Children, educators, atelierista,[8] fabric and materials are in moving correspondence together, and we give attention to what is being made and produced in the middle of this.

Making

It is quite typical in early childhood to think of artistic production, or making, as process and product, or as an individual and interior process, as if an artwork's evolution is a progression from idea to form. For instance, a child might have a nascent idea, something he or she wishes to explore or communicate, and the materials are used to give shape to this desire, as if it is a movement from interior to exterior with ideas being made visible and materials used for representative purposes. A work's origins are situated in a child's or maker's mind, preconceived and human centered. But here, in the studio, as expressed by Simon O'Sullivan, we are "less involved in making sense of the world and more involved in exploring the possibilities of being in—and becoming with—the world."[9] Thus, we pay attention to the movements, pulses, tempo, rates of flow and regions of intensity—to that which is activated and set in motion and to the webs of relation. We play with a loose interpretation of fabrication in the hope of opening dynamic, collective and improvisational understandings of making that consider things *in the making*, in the liveliness of their choreographies, co-compositions and emergences. This hope reflects Tim Ingold's proposition of thinking *through* doing[10] and Erin Manning and Brian Massumi's thought in the act.[11] "Making" or "fabricating" takes shape as choreography and movement and as "a process of correspondence; not the imposition of preconceived form on raw material substance, but the drawing out or bringing forth of potential immanent in a world of becoming."[12]

Everything has the potential to connect; thus, in the studio, there are multiple lines of intersecting and intra-acting movements, not just a singular or individual process from idea to form but an entanglement of things "in the making." The fabric plays with the child, with the space, with the materials, with the light, with the changing seasons and the lifting of the winter's darkness, with the trees outside, with the educators, with an artist's provocations, and with traces of children's own enchantments. We encounter a complicated process of noticing, attending to, enhancing and entering this play.

Fluid gatherings

A fascination with hockey weaves its way into the fabric studio. This fast, aggressively played sport suggests particular bodily performances and conjures up visions of cold ice, sharp skate blades, hard protective gear, and fast, precise movements. In the studio, the fabric intra-acts with this game and proposes other hockey enactments and performances, becoming fluid, dance like and soft. As fabric encounters hockey and hockey games are fabricated, we observe an emerging "hockeyness" from the fabric. We are invited in to children's fabrication of hockey through processes of wrapping, tying and knotting together the brightly colored swaths of cloth onto the children's bodies. Jerseys, helmets and kneepads are configured, but because of its slippery nature, the fabric refuses to take hold and conform to the shape of the children's small bodies, kneecaps, shoulders and heads. There is constant wrapping and unwrapping as the fabric releases, slips away and falls in long trails behind running bodies, creating pauses and interruptions. Ben calls out, "I need a helmet" as he places a vivid orange piece of fabric into Adrienne's hand. Her hands wrap the fabric around his head, trying to find a way to make it secure, awkwardly winding, tucking, untucking and loosely knotting the fabric around his forehead. As the sun streams through the window, it alights his soft, loose, orange head adornment and sets this bundle of fabric on his head ablaze. Taken aback by this beauty, we are puzzled by it. The construct of a protective hockey helmet, a necessity in a dynamic and often violent game, is disappearing, becoming engulfed and wrapped up in soft and shimmering folds.

The hockey configurations flow loosely and fluidly. In a temporary clearing in the fabric studio and in a brief moment when the fabric hockey adornments are securely fastened, a small group of children cluster together and face Adrienne. Small bodies are poised as they sway back and forth in a hockey-player rhythm

Figure 2.2 The fabricated hockey game.

anticipating the possibility of a game beginning. Long, narrow tubes of rolled paper find their way into this assemblage and become hockey sticks. Ben announces, "We want to play hockey," and he nominates Adrienne as referee. "You be the referee," he insists. Adrienne steps into the game and responds, "Do you want me to drop the puck?" There is another brief pause as we look around in search of the perfect puck-object. Sylvia presses a soft yellow knit and felted heart into the palm of Adrienne's hand as a question and possibility: "Could this be a puck?"

With the arrival of the yellow heart-puck, anticipation intensifies. Adrienne holds out the yellow heart-puck in her hand in a referee-like gesture, the moment feeling sonorous with excitement and possibility, and begins to sing the first line of "Oh Canada," the national anthem. The hockey-clad children begin to sing along, and the emergence of this song permeates throughout the studio and creates a much larger pregnant pause as other children and educators turn toward the emerging hockey game. This pause acts as a collective gathering, and as the song grows in volume, others join in, and in this moment, the room is drawn together. Like fabric, the room is temporarily knotted together, undoing as the national anthem comes to a close. As the singing voices trail off, Adrienne releases the heart-puck and drops it to the ground.

Bodies move, paper sticks swing, the little heart-puck spins across the floor, and there is a vibrant entangling of movements and intentions as bodies, fabric and objects come together. Yet there is a particular impermanence to this game. As the game progresses, the fabric begins to unknot and trail away from the children's bodies. What once loosely resembled a hockey helmet becomes unraveled, and as a child runs, long lines of brilliant, translucent blue trail behind his head in a snake-like configuration. The fabric refuses to remain fixed in place, and as it slips away, it takes with it the notion of hockeyness, leaving behind loose bundles and an invitation to recreate and begin again. Thus, the game undoes as it continues and flows into other fabrications. Amid the fragmented flows of fabric and the discarded and bent paper sticks, Griffin, one of the hockey players, approaches Adrienne and drapes a long swath of green fabric over her hand. As she lifts the fabric up to examine it, she wonders aloud: "Let's see what this fabric can do."

Fabricating choreographies

As we attend to what fabric does and what is produced and activated in the studio, we become attuned to a dynamic choreography among educator, material and child, a dance of attentiveness made evident with the fabric. The experience of the studio becomes a moving, sonorous, gestural, textural, material, improvisational "dance of attention,"[13] a dance of attention that is concerned with the "immediacy of mutual action."[14] It is not a focus on *what* is made or fabricated, or on shape, form or product; rather, it is an emphasis on what is put into play, how the conditions for experimentation and "making" are enacted, and the ways we can move in correspondence with the emerging fabrications and choreographies. Manning and Massumi describe this as "an intertwining of fields of emergent experience not yet defined as this or that."[15] In the intertwining, in the play of making, there is a mutual co-composition and fabrication of studio-gatherings-hockey-enactments so that over time, the studio becomes an experience and an event in the making.

Notes

1 Hans-Ulrich Obrist, *Ways of Curating* (New York: Farrar, Straus, and Giroux, 2014).
2 Ibid., 10.
3 Ibid., 13.
4 Hillevi Lenz Taguchi, *Going beyond the Theory/Practice Divide in Early Childhood Education: Introducing an Intra-active Pedagogy* (New York: Routledge, 2010).

5 Veronica Pacini-Ketchabaw, Sylvia Kind, and Laurie Kocher, *Encounters with Materials in Early Education* (New York: Routledge, 2017).
6 Erin Manning, *Politics of Touch: Sense, Movement, Sovereignty* (Minneapolis: University of Minnesota Press, 2007).
7 Manning, *Politics of Touch*, xiv.
8 As an *atelierista*, Sylvia works with children aged 1 to 5 years, educators from the Children's Centre, and adult early childhood education students facilitating artistic engagements, small-group arts-based projects, and various artistic interventions and events in addition to studio investigations and inventions. It is a role similar to an artist-in-residence.
9 Simon O'Sullivan, *Art Encounters Deleuze and Guattari: Thought beyond Representation* (London: Palgrave Macmillan, 2006), 52.
10 Tim Ingold, *Making: Anthropology, Archeology, Art, and Architecture* (New York: Routledge, 2013).
11 Erin Manning and Brian Massumi, *Thought in the Act: Passages in the Ecology of Experience* (Minneapolis: University of Minnesota Press, 2014).
12 Ingold, *Making*, 31.
13 Manning and Massumi, *Thought in the Act*, 5.
14 Ibid., 6.
15 Ibid., 4.

Bibliography

Ingold, Tim. *Making: Anthropology, Archeology, Art, and Architecture*. New York: Routledge, 2013.
Lenz Taguchi, Hillevi. *Going beyond the Theory/Practice Divide in Early Childhood Education: Introducing an Intra-active Pedagogy*. New York: Routledge, 2010.
Manning, Erin. *Politics of Touch: Sense, Movement, Sovereignty*. Minneapolis: University of Minnesota Press, 2007.
Manning, Erin, and Brian Massumi. *Thought in the Act: Passages in the Ecology of Experience*. Minneapolis: University of Minnesota Press, 2014.
Obrist, Hans-Ulrich. *Ways of Curating*. New York: Farrar, Straus, and Giroux, 2014.
O'Sullivan, Simon. *Art Encounters Deleuze and Guattari: Thought beyond Representation*. London: Palgrave Macmillan, 2006.
Pacini-Ketchabaw, Veronica, Sylvia Kind, and Laurie Kocher. *Encounters with Materials in Early Education*. New York: Routledge, 2017.

3

Sticking: Children and the Lively Matter of Sticks

Tonya Rooney

Some children stumble across an ants' nest lying bare and exposed in the middle of an otherwise grassy and lightly treed hillside. One child walks slowly up to the nest's edge, bending over as far as she can to have a look without letting her feet fall forward. Suddenly she straightens up and looks around. Trampling off through the grass, she soon returns with a large stick. From the nest's edge, she reaches out with the stick, placing it as close to one of the ant holes as she can. Tapping impatiently at times, she entreats the ants to come out and to come closer. Realizing this works better if she keeps the stick still, her patience is eventually rewarded. Some ants emerge. They crawl up the length of the stick toward the child's hand. When the point of contact is almost reached, the child releases the stick in a mix of panic and delight. At the thud of the stick, the flurry of ant activity intensifies below.

The term *sticking* carries many meanings. It can refer to the notion of one thing attaching to another, sometimes with the aid of a third binding substance. It also refers to an action of prodding or piercing one object with another. A sense of persistence or loyalty may also be conveyed through actions of sticking at or sticking with/by something or someone. In this chapter, I explore the way children are inexorably drawn to sticks that they come across in the landscape and reflect on the attachments that might be forged with and in these encounters. In witnessing the children's interactions with stick life, I am (in a playful if somewhat literal sense) reminded of what Sara Ahmed refers to as "sticky" attachments.[1] There seems to be something akin to an affective glue or stickiness in the children's relations with sticks: an emerging sticky bond that goes beyond the immediate surface-level point of contact to a mode of sticking that is somehow shaping the children's connection to the world around them.

Walking with children and their sticky companions

Over several months, I have been taking part in regular walks with a group of preschool children through the lightly treed foreshores of an urban lake in Canberra, Australia. These walks form part of an ethnographic research project titled "Walking with Wildlife and Wild Weather Times." This is a collaborative project being undertaken by Affrica Taylor (University of Canberra) and me through which we aim to explore children's everyday material and multispecies relations. In this chapter, I draw on accounts from these walks as documented more fully in our research blog.[2] On our walks, I continue to be surprised at the unexpected happenings that unfold. I also start to notice that some things become a more regular feature of the way children relate to the place, its inhabitants and each other.

Since our early walks, I have been struck by the way the children often pick up sticks and use them to scratch or poke at the earth. In many ways, this is hardly surprising. I remember as a child, and still as an adult, too, the allure of a stick lying on the ground and the desire to reach out and pick it up—to feel its surface, perhaps to then peel back some of the loose bark to expose the textures beneath. As I look more closely, however, at the many things the children do with the sticks on our walks, I notice an unconscious and almost effortless interchange between child and stick that plays out in a multitude of ways. At times, the children simply pick up sticks to carry or drag them along on our walk. At other times, they more deliberately search out a particular kind of stick, for example, one long enough to reach into the middle of an ants' nest or to point to something high up in a tree, or perhaps one sturdy enough to test the depths of the murky lake. Pauliina Rautio, in her work on the phenomenon of children who pick up stones, encourages us to recognize these encounters as one way we might come to know ourselves as part of the world.[3] Based on my observations, I reflect that children's interactions with sticks may also offer insights into our wider (human) connection with the world. This chapter is therefore an invitation to look more closely at the potential significance in these seemingly trivial, yet nonetheless persistent and diverse child-stick encounters. Over time, on our walks I note that the children's interactions with sticks are a feature on every single walk. One girl in particular rarely walks without a stick or a piece of bark. Whether dragging, sweeping or simply holding on, these sticky companions have become part of how she "sticks" to and with the land.

The stickiness of sticky matter

As educators and researchers working with young children, if we start to think about the sticky connections forged in the relations between children and sticks, we may also come to notice the ways that sticks can act as more than random inert tools.

> Strategically positioned, [the sticks] might entice ants to move in a direct line towards children. ... The sticks materialize seamless interconnections—lining up bodies and providing a tangible conduit between human and nonhuman wildlife. It's clear that sticks allow children to exceed the physical limits of their own bodies—to reach out and touch inaccessible wildlife. ... In this affective sense, the sticks could be functioning as "sticky" lines of attachment, adhering or bonding the children with the hard-to-reach creatures of this place.[4]

The combination of prodding, stirring, responding, touching and linking that children exhibit in their encounters with sticks seems to be in part shaping a lively connection with their more-than-human surrounds. Ahmed's notion of sticky attachments characterizes stickiness as not just a tacky or discomforting property that sits on an object's surface but rather a dynamic, ongoing and cumulative relation that binds objects across time and difference.[5] The surface of a stick object does appear to have a kind of sticky allure. It draws the children into contact, where the children are not just doing things with or to the stick, but the stick itself is also doing something. The stick draws the children in, and at the same time, its stickiness is being drawn out. As Ahmed suggests, stickiness then does not so much reside on an object's surface but rather is an effect of surfacing.[6]

Following Ahmed a little further, we could say that the relation between child and stick involves a transfer of affect such that the child becomes sticky. This is because "to get stuck to something sticky is also to become sticky" and with this comes the capacity to "pick up" other objects.[7] Thus, as the children become "sticky," they are also open to new possibilities for connecting or sticking with other materials, places and beings. One of the children's favorite activities is "fishing," where they seek out a stick and dangle it into the water in the hope that something will stick.

> Today, the children spent much time "fishing" with an assortment of sticks and pieces of reed. Bending over the water's edge, the children called "come on fishy" and "come on, you can make it."[8]

Figure 3.1 Sticking with the lake, Canberra, Australia.

A stick therefore is at once an object but also much more. Veronica Pacini-Ketchabaw, Sylvia Kind and Laurie Kocher describe a material object as also "a continuum, a story, an event, a happening, a doing."[9] We can think of a child's encounter with a stick along these lines, as something "set in motion ... marked by a sense of *not knowing*, of hopeful waiting."[10]

The lively matter of sticks

The lively materiality of a stick is not just evident in what the child and stick are doing to each other. It is also revealed under the surface of the sticks when they are cracked or worn away. The children often find sticks or trees marked with holes and insect trails.

> The children were fascinated with the patterns and textures of these bug habitats. They ran their fingers over the lines and bumps. ... Although mysterious and not always easy to read, the inscriptions they were tracing on the surface of the tree trunks seemed to bear witness to the fact that these trees have had their own lives and stories to tell.[11]

The surface therefore reveals to the children that a stick is not simply a dead static object but a home to various creatures (such as borers and spiders), perhaps a place for plants to cling (such as lichen or moss) or at times highly friable, such as when a decaying stick crumbles at a child's touch. The children in turn find their own ways of relating to the lively impermanence of sticky matter.

> As a couple of the children climbed through the lower branches [of the tree], another heeded "Be careful. You might take all the skin off it." This reference to the shedding bark captured a sense of vulnerability that seemed to surround this otherwise imposing and tall eucalypt.[12]

The children's sticky encounters, with both the sticks and other wildlife, seem to provide a connection to the circulating bonds of life, decay, death and reemergence. On one of our walks, we came across a lone possum tail lying on the ground. In response to this surprising and slightly gruesome sight, the children started searching around for a stick.

> For some time, the children stood around the tail, keeping slightly back as if not sure what to expect; some thinking the tail might still be alive. ... But the tail remained still. Emboldened by its inertness, one child picked up a stick to prod it. ... Eventually, the other children also decided that it might be safe to prod, and one by one they all set off searching for prodding sticks: "I'm going to find a stick." "Me too."[13]

As the children pick up sticks and become more sticky, they thus seem to find new ways to forge connections with a multitude of other creatures, materials, times and places, connections that at times sit at the very nexus of life and death, fear and hope.

It is not just individual sticks that surface stickiness and open up new ways of connecting with the world. On our walks, I often find myself looking down at the mass of sticks strewn all across the ground. This collective mesh of sticky matter is hard to ignore. It is crunchy underfoot and also at times prickly and scratchy. I come to understand this as another form of sticky surface, one that stretches as a mat of matter across the place where we walk. Despite the discomfort, the children do not avoid these areas but rather continue moving through and over the brittle and often uneven surface, pausing at times and reaching down to select a single stick. In these moments, as I watch a child grasp, twist, yank and then pull free a stick from the tangled surface, I witness again the liveliness of matter as the sticky floor first resists, holds back and then relaxes when an object finally breaks away into a child's grasp. The points of connection between child and stick are therefore far from singular and isolated from the world but rather seem to be always entangled in a messy collective of more-than-human worldly relations.

Risking sticky attachments

In acknowledgment of the somewhat notorious status of children's play with sticks, as shown through the frequent remonstrations from adults to children—"put the sticks down" or "don't play with sticks"—it would be remiss not to mention that the attachments children forge with and through sticks inevitably come with some risks. Sticks can be sharp, rough, smooth, fragile, sturdy, splintered or broken. They can scratch or cut us and, in this real physical sense, prompt a painful reminder of the fragility of our own human surface or skin. Yet, despite the occasional scar left by a sticky exchange, the children continue to be drawn to sticks as they shape, test and forge new relations along the course of our walks. Perhaps then, rather than see these risky encounters as moments children should best avoid, we could think of children's interactions with sticks as a reminder of the value of what Lesley Instone refers to as a "reaching out and risking attachment with all manner of unlike others."[14] As Instone and others suggest, the wider human condition of vulnerability requires of us to confront rather than ignore the uncertainty and fragility of the times in which we live.[15] Recall the opening vignette. In this, the children, as they reach into the middle of the ants' nest with their sticks, are not only forging a type of sticky attachment but are also risking attachment. Through their sticks, they are drawing the ants out and bringing closer an understanding of the limits of their own vulnerability, and at the same time, they are surfacing an affective awareness of the mutual vulnerabilities in multispecies relations. In this risky encounter, the children seem to be showing us how vulnerability is something to understand and learn with, not something we need to leave alone.

The risky sticky connections that the children engage with on our walks invoke a strong sense that they are somehow sticking with the place and its inhabitants in a way that they will carry on with them. This can be seen in both the affective traces of a(n) (ac)cumulating history of contact between child, stick and land and more literally in the way children carry sticks or bark with them for the duration of our walk. Strands of stickiness stretch therefore beyond the immediacy of each moment and at times become part of the growing bond among the children themselves.

> The base of a eucalyptus tree was littered with long strips of newly fallen bark. The children were intent on finding the longest possible piece to play with. Once located, this length of bark accompanied the children for quite some time. They took it in turns to carry it along with them. The children seemed to be holding onto the long bark as a thread of connection; one that linked them together as they walked and as well acting as a moveable thread of attachment to the entities and places they were passing by and through.[16]

Conclusion

In observing children's relations with sticky matter, we witness a lively, ongoing interchange that forges relations in and with the environment. In these simple everyday moments, it seems that something important is going on in the way children risk attachment to and stick with their sticky companions. By reaching out to sticks, the children seem to bring to the surface our entanglements with/in long histories of contact that stick with us over time and place. As we take the time to notice what is happening in these child-stick relations, we might also reflect on the figure of the stick as it continues in our adult lives. Perhaps, when we grab a stick to help us as we climb a hill, or simply to feel the stick's texture in our hands, we are seeking out a mode of connection that works by both unsettling and (re)binding the points of connection between human and more-than-human worlds, not to challenge the boundary between these worlds but to remind ourselves that it has never really been there.

Notes

1   Sarah Ahmed, *The Cultural Politics of Emotion* (New York: Routledge, 2004); Affrica Taylor and Tonya Rooney, "Sticks and Stickiness," *Walking with Wildlife in Wild Weather Times* blog, 9 April 2016, https://walkingwildlifewildweather.com/2016/04/09/stickiness-and-sticks/.
2   Taylor and Rooney, "Sticks and Stickiness."

3   Pauliina Rautio, "Children Who Carry Stones in Their Pockets: On Autotelic Material Practices in Everyday Life," *Children's Geographies* 11, no. 4 (2013): 394–408.
4   Taylor and Rooney, "Sticks and Stickiness."
5   Ahmed, *The Cultural Politics*, 91.
6   Ibid., 90.
7   Ibid., 91.
8   Taylor and Rooney, "Sticks and Stickiness."
9   Veronica Pacini-Ketchabaw, Sylvia Kind, and Laurie Kocher, *Encounters with Materials in Early Childhood Education* (New York: Routledge, 2016), 34.
10 Pacini-Ketchabaw et al., *Encounters*, 35.
11 Taylor and Rooney, "Returning to the Fallen Trees," *Walking with Wildlife in Wild Weather Times* blog, 8 August 2016, https://walkingwildlifewildweather.com/2016/08/08/returning-to-the-fallen-trees/.
12 Taylor and Rooney, "Lakeside at Last," *Walking with Wildlife in Wild Weather Times* blog, 19 July 2017, https://walkingwildlifewildweather.com/2017/07/19/lakeside-at-last/.
13 Taylor and Rooney, "Bones, Teeth, Claws, and Tails," *Walking with Wildlife in Wild Weather Times* blog, 19 July 2017, https://walkingwildlifewildweather.com/2017/07/19/bones-teeth-claws-and-tails/.
14 Lesley Instone, "Risking Attachment in the Anthropocene," in *Manifesto for Living in the Anthropocene*, ed. Katherine Gibson, Deborah Bird Rose, and Ruth Fincher (New York: Punctum Books, 2015), 36.
15 Also see, for example, Myra Hird, "Waste, Landfills, and an Environmental Ethic of Vulnerability," *Ethics and the Environment* 18, no. 1 (2013); Affrica Taylor and Veronica Pacini-Ketchabaw, "Learning with Children, Ants, and Worms in the Anthropocene: Towards a Common World Pedagogy of Multispecies Vulnerability," *Pedagogy, Culture, & Society* 23, no. 4 (2015): 507–529.
16 Taylor and Rooney, "Threads of Connection," *Walking with Wildlife in Wild Weather Times* blog, 14 June 2016, https://walkingwildlifewildweather.com/2016/06/14/threads-of-connection/.

Bibliography

Ahmed, Sara. *The Cultural Politics of Emotion*. New York: Routledge, 2004.
Hird, Myra. "Waste, Landfills, and an Environmental Ethic of Vulnerability." *Ethics and the Environment* 18, no. 1 (2013): 105–124.
Instone, Lesley. "Risking Attachment in the Anthropocene." In *Manifesto for Living in the Anthropocene*, edited by Katherine Gibson, Deborah Bird Rose, and Ruth Fincher, 29–36. New York: Punctum Books, 2015.

Pacini-Ketchabaw, Veronica, Sylvia Kind, and Laurie Kocher. *Encounters with Materials in Early Childhood Education*. New York: Routledge, 2016.

Rautio, Pauliina. "Children Who Carry Stones in Their Pockets: On Autotelic Material Practices in Everyday Life." *Children's Geographies* 11, no. 4 (2013): 394–408.

Taylor, Affrica, and Veronica Pacini-Ketchabaw. "Learning with Children, Ants, and Worms in the Anthropocene: Towards a Common World Pedagogy of Multispecies Vulnerability." *Pedagogy, Culture, & Society* 23, no. 4 (2015): 507–529.

Taylor, Affrica, and Tonya Rooney. "Walking with Wildlife in Wild Weather Times" blog, 2016. https://walkingwildlifewildweather.com.

4

Literacying: Literacy Desiring in Writers' Studio

Candace R. Kuby

Two grade 2 (7- to 8-year-old) students, Ashley and Joseph,[1] are working with a game board they created after researching Egyptian pyramids. I sit down and have a conversation with them. Joseph tells me they can develop games by "playing to fix them" (i.e., edit and revise). Ashley articulates that they are creating the game so younger children who don't like to read could play a game and learn. She goes on to explain the board game, how to roll the dice and move through the squares. I asked them to tell me about some of the changes they made as they played the game yesterday.

Joseph explains they made "three starts" as he points to purple, red and yellow squares. Ashley says they are going to make one or two more (orange and brown). She explains that they also accidentally wrote arrows on the game board where they were not supposed to be (which would be confusing to players). They decided to glue paper on top of the arrows to cover them up.

I inquire: "So by playing the game, you developed the game?" They agree. I ask: "So what is your plan after developing it?" Joseph: "Let everybody play." Ashley chimes in that they will share it with a classmate's sister's kindergarten class (5–6 years old) to see if they want to play it. I ask if they think it is important to play a game first in order to develop it. Both say "Yes!"

Ashley explains what might happen if she played the game as the red game piece and went in a direction where there wasn't an arrow to guide her: This is why they needed to develop the game by playing it.

This is a story about literacying: the lively literacy desirings of the Egyptian pyramid game board coming to be. Drawing on a researcher-teacher partnership since 2010 in a grade 2 Writers' Studio, I discuss our (i.e., those of the teacher, students, myself as researcher, the writing materials) entangled becomings as writers: our literacying. Over the years, our[2] research focus has been (re) imagining and (re)defining writing and writing pedagogy through documenting via note-taking, photographs and video recording the unfolding, emerging literacies in Room 203. We refer to this process as pedagogical documenting, inspired by Reggio Emilia early childhood education practices.[3] In this chapter, I consider what was produced when Tara (the teacher) invited children to "go be writers" with a range of materials (e.g., paper, pencils, stencils, yarn, iPads, paint, computers, cotton balls, feathers). We were inspired by and quite familiar with the scholarship on multiliteracies, multimodality and New Literacy Studies.[4] These bodies of literature see literacy as political and never neutral and contend that all texts are multimodal. However, as we invited children to become writers with a range of materials, these theoretical perspectives weren't enough for thinking beyond human- or child-centered pedagogies and methodologies. In other words, they didn't feel adequate to help us attend to the relationship *between* material-discursive bodies (human, nonhuman and more-than-human bodies). We began to read scholarship that attends to human becoming as an inseparable entanglement of/with/in the world, particularly Gilles Deleuze and Félix Guattari's works,[5] Karen Barad,[6] and early childhood teachers/researchers[7] who think with post-theories.

In this chapter, I focus on the unfolding of the Egyptian pyramid game board that came to be at the end of a school year. In doing so, I share some of the intra-active ways we engaged with and produced research with children-materials in an ongoing, rhizomatic way of literacying or, as we conceptualized, based on Deleuzian notions of desire, literacy desiring(s).[8] The aim of this storying is to share how research as an entangled becoming-with children and materials produced newness—new ways of thinking/be(com)ing/doing/knowing literacies. In other words, literacy is not (only) a noun but a verb: a doing, an intra-active[9] becoming, a force. My hope is that this story will entangle with you, the reader, and produce a (new) space to (re)consider literacy(ies), specifically, writing with young children.

Game path becoming game board

The next day, Ashley is working to flatten a cardboard box. To measure the size she'll need to cut out, she places the game board on top of the cardboard box. She uses scissors to cut like a knife around the game board. Tara comes by and wonders if Ashley needs to cut through one piece of cardboard or both. In other words, if the box is torn apart, there will only be one layer to cut through. Tara asks if she can

Literacying 55

help her tear it apart and suggests tracing the game board so Ashley doesn't cut the game board she's worked so hard on. Ashley doesn't take up Tara's offer. Tara leaves.

Ashley takes the game board off, cuts some cardboard, and puts the game back on to trace it with a marker around the edges. Then Ashley pulls off the game board, puts it aside, and begins cutting out the cardboard. A friend comes to help her cut. The scissors are difficult. They struggle to cut the cardboard. Periodically Ashley stops to rest and stretch her hands. After cutting out a rectangle, she lays the game board on top of the cut-out cardboard and gets glue to secure it to the board. The two students work together to rub and smooth the paper on the board. They use their entire bodies, palms, and knuckles to flatten and smooth.

I notice several squares colored "start" on the game board, perhaps inspired by a familiar game called Sorry that they've played before (see Figure 4.1). Squares to place "chance" cards are scattered all over the game board. A "mummy jail" space is in the middle; it says "lose 2 turns and stay there." I see an "explore pyramid section" and the word "finish" at the pyramid.

I wonder what inspired Ashley and Joseph to create the variety of colored spaces and places (e.g., mummy jail, pyramid) on the game board. What from their days of researching about Egyptian pyramids intra-acted with them as they collaboratively drew the game board? We wondered what prior experiences playing other game boards served as mentor texts for them as they imagined the multiple possible experiences others would have playing their game. This is literacy desiring. We conceptualize literacy desiring as

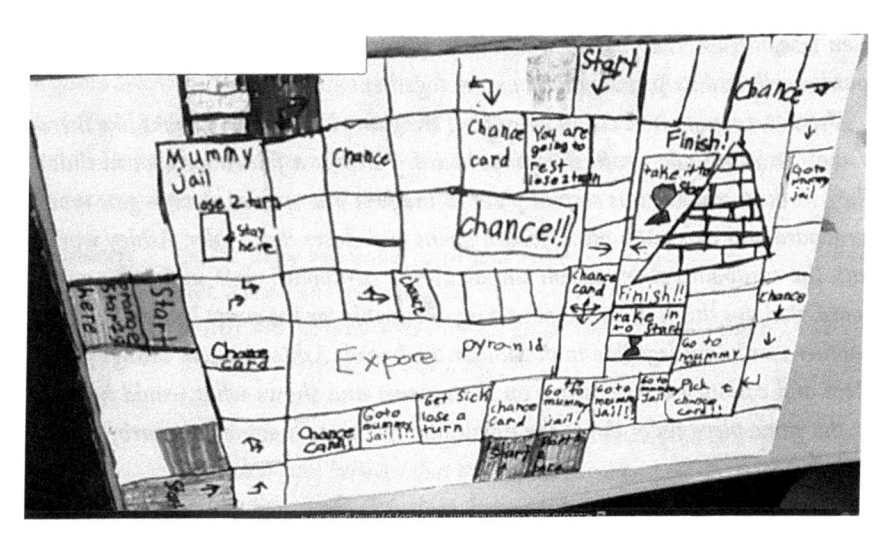

Figure 4.1 Game board.

Ashley:	We're into trouble a little because this [cardboard leg] won't stick up. It keeps falling down.
Joseph:	It's a problem.
Candace:	Any ideas, Joseph?
Joseph:	No. I can't think of it.
Candace:	Hmm. … So what is your plan?
Joseph:	So think.
Candace:	To keep thinking?
Ashley:	Uh-huh (yes).

It was fascinating to me how Ashley and Joseph had researched about Egyptian pyramids in books and online, but in the moment of making a game board, the materiality of possible futures, possible users' experiences with the game board *and* their readings of life under the pyramids intra-acted together to spark newness: an underground jail with a slide to get there. This newness was produced in the (new) relationship of people (Ashley and Joseph) with Egyptians of long ago, with boxes, squares on game boards, tape, staplers and so forth.

Joseph and Ashley seemed fine with a plan of continuing to think (with materials). They weren't frustrated to the point of stopping or giving up. Instead, they worked longer with materials to try and produce what they hoped would become an underground jail.

What was produced as I talked with them about the material troubles they were working with as composers? For myself and Tara, it produced many conversations on what counts as writing. Is composing an Egyptian pyramid game board writing? Is it a way to share research with others or/and for others to experience a pyramid? As we've written about elsewhere,[13] we struggle with the labels of "writing" or "not writing." These categories produce binaries, which posthumanist scholarship works to resist. When we draw lines or circles around what counts as writing, then we limit possibilities of new literacies—new ways of knowing/be(com)ing/doing. For Tara, the politics of schooling played out in how she framed Writers' Studio to administrators, teachers and families. Tara was expected to have a time of the day to teach the district's adopted writing program. However, she worked within the striated space of the program to find and create smooth spaces with children and materials as writers. Deleuze and Guattari[14] write of supple, bending, porous, nomadic spaces as smooth and the rigid, sedentary, inactive spaces as striated. They also state that these spaces only exist in a mixture. So while creating a game board might not look like writing in the traditional sense, we found that the children in the classroom—much like in this example—spent time and worked with materials to revise and edit. We noticed and had conversations with children on *their* writing processes, not the typical linear process of writing often taught in schools (i.e., brainstorm, draft, revise, edit, publish).[15]

Ashley and Joseph continue thinking and working with materials and each other. Underneath the game board are several cardboard slides. As discussed above, it seems they've realized a slide isn't enough: There needs to be supports to hold it up. The supports for the slide are cut out of cardboard, and they are working to secure them all with a stapler.

After working with the slides-supports-stapler for a while, Joseph tears off the slide. Jacob stops and says, "Can I help you?" Ashley says yes. The three continue to work with the cardboard cutouts and the stapler. One of them gets a box in the middle of the table and puts the game board on top of it. The game board comes off. Joseph still works with stapler and cardboard slide in an effort to secure it. Eventually Ashley exclaims, "It worked!"

This literacying story ends here, sort of. We do not have any video or audio footage of what came to be after these clips from Writers' Studio. We do not know what end product was produced from these desirings with materials and each other. We do not know if, when or who played the "final" game. We are okay with that. As we watch these clips again, we hear Deleuze and Guattari's[16] voices describing entering in the middle [of a plateau, there is no beginning or end] and Maggie MacLure's[17] voice describing data that glow [data that call out, that you can't let go of]. We recognize that something in our researching together grabbed us in the becoming literacies, the lively reconfigurings that happened as Joseph–stapler–Ashley–cardboard–research-on-pyramids–Jacob–Candace–scissors–Tara–school-discourses–and … and … and … worked together. Literacy desiring is about the relationships, realities and knowledges produced. Barad[18] and Hillevi Lenz Taguchi[19] conceptualize this entangled production as the ethico-onto-epistemological ways the world comes to be. Literacy desiring is unpredictable, rhizomatic rather than linear, and can feel uncertain, especially to teachers. But we found that literacy desiring was necessary for opening up intra-active pedagogical spaces for literacies to come to be—literacying.

Notes

1 All student names are pseudonyms.
2 Candace authored this chapter and therefore many statements are written with "I." However, "we" is also used in the chapter to signify and acknowledge the

5

Intergenerationaling: Children, Elders and Materials Making Waves

Rachel Heydon and Elisabeth Davies

We are two researchers who are navigating posthumanist waters, being guided by our experiences with intergenerational learning and what happens when young children and elders create art together. For us, elders are persons who, by virtue of age and experience, have reached the status of a senior person in their context.[1] Rachel, an educational researcher, has been researching intergenerational programs, with a concentration on intergenerational art, since 2003, and has recently been collaborating with Elisabeth, an information science researcher, on a study of integrating digital tools into intergenerational curricula. These programs' *classroom curricula,* which the literature defines as what actually happens in teaching and learning situations,[2] draws us in. The data from across these studies are asking new questions of us, especially those data that signal directly or indirectly to issues of death and dying. We are most curious about how to create spaces for working with and through intergenerational curricula that widen our view, allowing curricula to deal with "unforeseen events"[3] so we might more fully consider "the roles of affect, embodiment [and] perception,"[4] as well as other potential constituents of the curricula and what they generate in their dynamic entanglements.

Karen Barad teaches that the "materiality" of bodies "plays an active role in the workings of power,"[5] and when society marks some bodies (e.g., children, senior citizens), this has materializing effects in the world. We conduct our research in an era when human capital theory[6] and the legacies of modernist developmental psychology forward a particular onto-epistemological definition of education and care for young and old. Human capital theory aligns people's worth with their participation in the economy, which can minoritize[7] the knowledge of children and elders.[8] Furthermore, developmentalism upholds an "adult-child dichotomy"[9] whereby adults are said to be able to identify the normal, progressive "domains"[10] through which children are purported to progress, thereby permitting them to determine what is developmentally appropriate (i.e., keeping with the norm).[11] In previous studies, Rachel found that early childhood educators' discomfort with death and dying and their reliance on developmentally appropriate practice, which rendered these topics taboo, led to death and dying becoming a *null curriculum*.[12] In this null curriculum, death and dying were not pedagogically addressed in the explicit curriculum, though the omission had deleterious effects; for instance, some elders withdrew from children when they became ill, and educators underestimated intergenerational relationships.[13]

In this chapter, we use this null curriculum to explore the following questions: What are the constituents, movements and effects of the intra-relations[14] that give rise to and occur within intergenerational art-making events and practices? How might risky texts[15] or difficult knowledge be part of these intra-relations and with what consequences for participants' knowledge, bodies, identities and relationships with each other? Our exploration involves sharing narrative impressions of our postqualitative methodic practice, which includes children, elders, materials, artwork, affects and the other elements of intergenerational curricula created in/through our inquiries. These narrative fragments are offered as provocations for openings to the unpredictable[16] and the "unrequited."[17] We focus on *felt focal moments*[18] from the data that raise the complementarity of life and death and the intervals in between what we can empirically know. We did not initially look for these disturbances, these rogue waves of data, but they arose and demanded our attention. We conclude the chapter with some considerations of what early childhood researchers might attend to when working in inter- or monogenerational contexts.

Let's talk of the end first

A woman who has always enjoyed coming to intergenerational art class stops coming. At a different adults-only art class, the researcher asks her why she has not been at the intergenerational class. The researcher poses the query as she watches the woman paint an angel on top of a roof to announce her death. The woman tells of the shame of her body that is bloated from cancer and the fear of bringing that close to children. "Some children think we're monsters," she explains. Later, she tells of the intergenerational home where she lives: "They never want you to know who's died. … When I die, I want them to send out the trumpets so everyone knows. I want to go out with the trumpets!" Turbulence—she's going to roil the water.

In another country, another woman who is a regular in an intergenerational art class draws an abstract image as she waits for class to start. She always arrives at art class after a daily loop around the grounds. Even in Canadian winters, she wears shorts ("I'm always hot!") and almost sprints, despite her cane and advanced age. When explaining her artwork, the woman points to a series of dots and relates that

> these are the voices from my past and those of the children who call to me from the play area. I am very aware of how limited our time is and how we are connected to the past and to the future. These are the voices that surround me and remind me that we are here for just a brief time.

Wavelength changes—the distance between waves becomes shorter.

An educator in an intergenerational program shared that he's had cancer, and after returning from sick leave, he's noticed that he's been keeping a bit of a buffer between the children and the elders. He's *afraid*, now that he's been sick, that he's *like* an elder, and he wants to keep a distance between the children and death, and himself and death. He's being pulled under the waves and is frightened by the depths.

A child stands at an intergenerational art show, waiting for her elder partner from art class. They've both painted rabbits—companion paintings—and the child waits beneath them to introduce her partner to her family. The child waits beneath two framed rabbits for someone who will never come again. On the other side of the continent, the elder partner's adult daughter writes a thank-you note to the intergenerational researcher who acknowledged her mother's recent death. It is spring—a time of rebirth and a time of rabbits. Refraction—waves are changing direction.

But can we talk of life without death?

An elder, like all the other participants in his intergenerational art class, takes up the invitation to create an electronic art portfolio documenting the processes and products of class. In his portfolio, he includes a color digital photograph entitled "Painting like Georgia O'Keeffe." The photo is of himself and his child partner side by side, each painting his own image of leaves. The photo shows the duo, eyes trained on their paintings, paintbrushes in hand, the child with his tongue out, concentrating, the elder hunched, serious. On the following page of the e-portfolio, the elder has uploaded a photograph of his finished painting, all thick brushstrokes of yellows, oranges, black, contained by a fuzzy circle of calming blues. Above this he included the caption: "I had a bad night last night. I am telling you this because I came in here and painted and forgot all about my pain." Later in the e-portfolio, a black line drawing with wisps of pink, purple and green is present in between and the caption. "It's the body of what will become a butterfly. A larva. It's changing." What he doesn't say: "I am sick. I am dying. I will be dead shortly after I have added the last entry in this e-portfolio." What he makes instead: a video of himself, talking about a collage he's made of a bright sun and a smiling face, inspired by the tattoo on the back of his hand: "People regularly say, 'Oh, I love your tattoo,' and I think they're talking about what they feel and we all feel, beautiful colors, and I am pleased to carry it on my hand." A look at the child's e-portfolio shows images parallel to his elder partner's— paintings done in the same style, similar or exact subject matter, photographs of the child and elder working together. The data implore us not to see them separately; these data overlap and create new data.

The children have been missing their classmate, a nonagenarian with a knack for storytelling. Today the elder is back, finally well enough to venture to intergenerational art class, though the vestiges of her illness are apparent in the oxygen tube she now has in her nose and the difficulty we can hear in her breath. Their collective cloth painting is going well. Two children stand around the elder, each adding their own images to the cloth. A boy holds the delicate chalk and draws an egg. Then, perhaps inspired by the elder's narrative flare, he tells a tale about the snake who will emerge from the egg. During the telling, the elder begins to cough a terrible cough, and the children's eyes become wide, but the calm, resourceful class volunteer rubs the elder's back, explains to the children what is happening and invites them to support the elder in this moment. Guided by the volunteer and their love for the elder, the children relax, speak to the elder in soothing tones, rub her hands and resume drawing and telling stories. The spell passes. The rise, the fall, the ebb, the flow.

"There is an end, but no conclusion"[19]

At the start of this chapter, we wondered at the intra-relations[20] implicated in intergenerational art programs. We let the data push undercurrents to the surface from a variety of studies of intergenerational art programs, undercurrents about who and what were implicated, including difficult knowledge. As a collective, the narratives signal some of what early childhood researchers might attend to when working in inter- or monogenerational contexts. Here is some of what we have noticed.

The narratives underscore the ontological inseparability of agentially intra-acting "components"[21] or, what we name at the start of this chapter, constituents of the classroom curricula. Striking for us was the physicality of the various constituents and how they related to each other: the intermingling of, for example, young and old bodies that engaged with each other and artistic media, like paint and iPads, plus physical properties like colors, shapes, line and dimensionality, to collectively and mutually make a new happening. In the curriculum, this new happening included the physical art work and the uploads to the e-portfolios which transformed the original works. It also included affective relationships between participants and between participants and materials. Witness, for instance, that the relationships between the children and elders were mediated through art making and instantiated in the art itself. Recognizing materials as active participants in people's learning and text making[22] collapses the dichotomy between animate humans and inanimate materials, allowing researchers to see how materials coproduce and intra-actively shape one another.[23] This recognition allows for a more fulsome accounting of intergenerational art making than might be otherwise possible. It also has more far-reaching implications.

The recognition calls for a rethinking of classic curriculum theory. Joseph Schwab taught that all curricula involve five commonplaces: teacher, student, subject matter, milieu and curriculum making.[24] This is a teaching that is often repeated today.[25] The narratives illustrate, however, that at least one other commonplace is missing—the material: paint, cloth, iPads and hands (to name a few). Further extending another bit of classic curriculum theory is how acknowledging the importance of intra-actions of the human and nonhuman in the experience of curriculum can help researchers to rethink the nature and production of lived curriculum. Conventionally, lived curriculum refers to the teacher's or student's experience of curricula.[26] The narratives viewed with a widened lens ask instead for the lived curriculum to be read as an experience created in multiple, in and through a range of human and nonhuman commonplaces.

Complexifying commonplaces and curriculum as a whole repeals the binary between child and adult and reveals the complementarity of intergenerationaling. We are told that the "dwellers of this planet at this point in time are interconnected but also internally fractured by the classical axes of negative differentiation" of which "age and ablebodiedness continue to index access to normal humanity."[27] The narratives convey the *in-it-togetherness* of the curriculum, where child, adult and all other constituents are vital to the intra-relations that have possibilities of producing important effects. Such an onto-epistemology has a crucial ethical component, laboring "to produce a workable frame for the actualization of the many missing people, whose 'minor' or nomadic knowledge is the breeding ground for possible futures."[28] Isolating children is thus impossible and undesirable. Difficult knowledge will become part of any classroom curriculum; relegating death and dying in such a case to the null curriculum is an abdication of pedagogical possibility and responsibility. The narratives surface and (re)value children's capacity to deal with difficult knowledge, make trite a discussion of modernist developmental appropriateness and suggest that how this knowledge is dealt with pedagogically needs to be considered within the intra-relations of the classroom curriculum as a totality.

Thinking this way about intergenerational curricula is an eminently hopeful endeavor. It signals a diffraction of curriculum, children, elders and world bending to each other to intra-act. As Rosi Braidotti says,

> "We" are in *this* together. This is a collective activity, a group project that connects active, conscious and desiring citizens […] As a project, it is historically grounded, socially embedded, and already partly actualized in the joint endeavour, that is, the community of those who are actively working toward it. If this be utopian, it is only in the sense of the positive affects that are mobilized in the process, the necessary dose of imagination, dreamlike vision, and bonding without which no social project can take off.[29]

The diffraction is already there and trying to make itself seen: the ripple of children and elders sharing time, chalk, space and artistic practice; the ripple of the educators who are uncomfortable, pushing them to erase opportunities and create the missing, yet speak about it suggesting a change; the ripple of a young child's witnessing of his elder friend drawing his transition out of this life; the ripple of the researchers who are there. All of us making waves together.

Notes

1   Rachel Heydon and Susan O'Neill, *Why Multimodal Literacy Matters: (Re)Conceptualizing Literacy and Well-being through Singing-infused Multimodal, Intergenerational Curricula* (Rotterdam: Sense, 2016).

2   Walter Doyle, "Curriculum and Pedagogy," in *Handbook of Research on Curriculum*, ed. Phillip W. Jackson (New York: Macmillan, 1992).

3   Martin Müller and Carolin Schurr, "Assemblage Thinking and Actor-network Theory: Conjunctions, Disjunctions, Cross-fertilisations," *Transactions of the Institute of British Geographers* 41 (2016): 217–229.

4   Rachel Heydon and Jennifer Rowsell, "Phenomenology and Literacy Studies," in *Routledge Handbook of Literacy Studies*, ed. Kate Pahl and Jennifer Rowsell (London: Routledge, 2015), 458.

5   Karen Barad, *Meeting the Universe Halfway: Quantum Physics and the Entanglement of Matter and Meaning* (Durham, NC: Duke University Press, 2007), 65.

6   Gary Becker, "Investment in Human Capital: Effects on Earning," in *Human Capital: A Theoretical and Empirical Analysis, with Special Reference to Education*, 2nd ed., ed. Gary Becker (Cambridge, MA: National Bureau of Economic Research, 1975).

7   Russell Bishop, "Effective Teaching for Indigenous and Minoritized Students," *Procedia Social and Behavioral Sciences* 7 (2010): 57–62.

8   Rachel Heydon, *Learning at the Ends of Life: Children, Elders, and Literacies in Intergenerational Curriculum* (Toronto: University of Toronto Press, 2013).

9   Gaile Cannella, "History of Early Childhood Curriculum," in *Encyclopedia of Curriculum Studies*, vol. 1, ed. Craig Kridel (Thousand Oaks, CA: SAGE, 2010), 307.

10 Ibid.

11 Luigi Iannacci and Pam Whitty, eds., *Early Childhood Curricula: Reconceptualist Perspectives* (Calgary: Detselig, 2009).

12 Rachel Heydon, "We Are Here for Just a Brief Time: Death, Dying, and Constructions of Children in Intergenerational Learning Programs," in *Early Childhood Curricula: Reconceptualist Perspectives*, ed. Luigi Iannacci and Pam Whitty (Toronto: Detselig, 2009), 217–241; Elliot W. Eisner, *The Educational Imagination: On the Design and Evaluation of School Programs*, 2nd ed. (New York: Macmillan, 1985).

13 Heydon, "We Are Here for Just a Brief Time."

14 Barad, *Meeting the Universe Halfway*.

15 Roger Simon and Wendy Armitage-Simon, "Teaching Risky Stories: Remembering Mass Destruction through Children's Literature," *English Quarterly* 28, no. 1 (1995): 27–31.

16 Müller and Schurr, "Assemblage Thinking."

17 Nigel Thrift, "Afterwords," *Environment and Planning D: Society and Space* 18 (2000): 214.

18 Ty Hollett and Christian Ehret, "Bean's World: (Mine)Crafting Affective Atmospheres for Game-play, Learning and Care in a Children's Hospital," *New Media & Society* 17, no. 11 (2015): 1849–1866.

19 Michael Oakeshott, "An Essay on the Relations of Philosophy, Poetry, and Reality," in *What Is History? and Other Essays: Selected Writings*, ed. Luke O'Sullivan (Exeter: Imprint Academic, 2004), 182.
20 Barad, *Meeting the Universe Halfway*.
21 Ibid., 33.
22 Veronica Pacini-Ketchabaw, Sylvia Kind, and Laurie Kocher, *Encounters with Materials in Early Childhood Education* (New York: Routledge, 2017).
23 Barad, *Meeting the Universe Halfway*.
24 Joseph Schwab, *The Practical: A Language for Curriculum* (Washington, DC: National Education Association, 1970).
25 Zongyi Deng, "The 'Why' and 'What' of Curriculum Inquiry: Schwab's The Practical Revisited," *Education Journal* 41, nos. 1–2 (2013): 85–105.
26 Ted Aoki, "Legitimating Lived Curriculum: Towards a Curricular Landscape of Multiplicity," *Journal of Curriculum and Supervision* 8, no. 3 (1993): 255–268.
27 Rosi Braidotti, "Critical Posthuman Knowledges," *The South Atlantic Quarterly* 116, no. 1 (2017), 93.
28 Ibid.
29 Rosi Braidotti, *Nomadic Theory: The Portable Rosi Braidotti* (New York: Columbia University Press, 2011), 294–295.

Bibliography

Aoki, Ted. "Legitimating Lived Curriculum: Towards a Curricular Landscape of Multiplicity." *Journal of Curriculum and Supervision* 8, no. 3 (1993): 255–268.

Barad, Karen. *Meeting the Universe Halfway: Quantum Physics and the Entanglement of Matter and Meaning*. Durham, NC: Duke University Press, 2007.

Becker, Gary. "Investment in Human Capital: Effects on Earning." In *Human Capital: A Theoretical and Empirical Analysis, with Special Reference to Education*. 2nd ed., edited by Gary Becker, 13–44. Cambridge, MA: National Bureau of Economic Research, 1975.

Bishop, Russell. "Effective Teaching for Indigenous and Minoritized Students." *Procedia Social and Behavioral Sciences* 7 (2010): 57–62. doi:10.1016/j.sbspro.2010.10.009.

Braidotti, Rosi. "Critical Posthuman Knowledges." *The South Atlantic Quarterly* 116, no. 1 (2017): 83–96.

Braidotti, Rosi. *Nomadic Theory: The Portable Rosi Braidotti*. New York: Columbia University Press, 2011.

Cannella, Gaile. "History of Early Childhood Curriculum." In *Encyclopedia of Curriculum Studies*, vol. 1, edited by Craig Kridel, 306–308. Thousand Oaks, CA: SAGE, 2010.

Deng, Zongyi. "The 'Why' and 'What' of Curriculum Inquiry: Schwab's *The Practical* Revisited." *Education Journal* 41, nos. 1–2 (2013): 85–105.

Doyle, Walter. "Curriculum and Pedagogy." In *Handbook of Research on Curriculum*, edited by Phillip W. Jackson, 486–516. New York: Macmillan, 1992.

Eisner, Elliot. *The Educational Imagination: On the Design and Evaluation of School Programs*. 2nd ed. New York: Macmillan, 1985.

Heydon, Rachel. *Learning at the Ends of Life: Children, Elders, and Literacies in Intergenerational Curriculum*. Toronto: University of Toronto Press, 2013.

Heydon, Rachel. "We Are Here for Just a Brief Time: Death, Dying, and Constructions of Children in Intergenerational Learning Programs." In *Early Childhood Curricula: Reconceptualist Perspectives*, edited by Luigi Iannacci and Pam Whitty, 217–241. Toronto: Detselig, 2009.

Heydon, Rachel, and Susan O'Neill. *Why Multimodal Literacy Matters: (Re)Conceptualizing Literacy and Well-being through Singing-infused Multimodal, Intergenerational Curricula*. Rotterdam: Sense, 2016.

Heydon, Rachel, and Jennifer Rowsell. "Phenomenology and Literacy Studies." In *Routledge Handbook of Literacy Studies*, edited by Kate Pahl and Jennifer Rowsell, 454–471. London: Routledge, 2015.

Hollett, Ty, and Christian Ehret. "Bean's World: (Mine)Crafting Affective Atmospheres for Game-play, Learning, and Care in a Children's Hospital." *New Media & Society* 17, no. 11 (2015): 1849–1866.

Iannacci, Luigi, and Pam Whitty, eds. *Early Childhood Curricula: Reconceptualist Perspectives*. Calgary: Detselig, 2009.

Müller, Martin, and Carolin Schurr. "Assemblage Thinking and Actor-network Theory: Conjunctions, Disjunctions, Cross-fertilisations." *Transactions of the Institute of British Geographers* 41 (2016): 217–229. doi:10.1111/Tran.12117.

Oakeshott, Michael. "An Essay on the Relations of Philosophy, Poetry, and Reality." In *What Is History? and Other Essays: Selected Writings*, edited by Luke O'Sullivan, 170–183. Exeter: Imprint Academic, 2004.

Schwab, Joseph. *The Practical: A Language for Curriculum*. Washington, DC: National Education Association, 1970.

Simon, Roger, and Wendy Armitage-Simon. "Teaching Risky Stories: Remembering Mass Destruction through Children's Literature." *English Quarterly* 28, no. 1 (1995): 27–31.

Thrift, Nigel. "Afterwords." *Environment and Planning D: Society and Space* 18 (2000): 213–255.

6

Muscling: Doing Physiologies with Pedagogies in Education Research

Nicole Land

Belly, fascicle, fiber, fibril, filament. This mantra, an abbreviation of the physiological structure of muscle, echoes through my brain as I crouch onto the forest floor. I remember when these anatomical concepts would escape my brain as I frantically scribbled their order down on the corner of my exams. As I push my right shin flat into fallen cedar branches, I am surprised that this physiological understanding of how muscles are built has returned to my thinking. I can now readily recite how physiology knows muscles:[1] muscle belly, the squishy muscle I can poke; muscle fascicles, the bundled cells that cohere as muscle bellies; muscle fiber, the tiny cells knitted together to compose fascicles; myofibrils, the many contractile threads layered together in any one fiber; and myofilaments, the microscopic proteins that generate muscled force. One of the children that I am with in the forest, Avril, lowers her stomach onto a fallen tree that stretches between two dirt hills. Filament, fibril, fiber, fascicle, belly.

In physiology courses, I was taught that skeletal muscles are designed to be biomechanically efficient and that muscles generate power via contractile proteins that produce purposeful movement.[2] Currently, I think with muscles as I participate in a collaborative pedagogical inquiry project with children and early childhood educators in Canada. This work explores how movement happens in a child care program with toddlers and preschool-aged children by foregrounding questions of how, where and why bodies and motion entangle with children's learning. I often trace how a physiological understanding of muscle locates muscles as a stable, science-described material that produces force from within a human body. Muscle becomes knowable as something we are composed of, that we can describe, and that is valued for the motion it generates.[3] This is a conception of muscle that education researchers know well:

the finger muscles that we use to write field notes with but seldom notice as research participants; the eye muscles that fatigue with a day of writing but that we rarely acknowledge as data; the shoulder muscles that tense with exertion or anxiety or excitement but are hardly cited for their contribution to knowledge production. In this chapter, I argue that this taken-for-granted physiological understanding of muscle relies on assumptions of stability and boundedness and becomes vulnerable when immersed in the complexities of how muscles matter as lively, expansive and demanding activities in early childhood education.

Beginning from where the tree meets the dirt, Avril reaches hand over hand, rapidly tugging her body, winter boots, and rain pants across the knotty bark until she reaches the middle of the tree as it spans the gap. Muscles. Bending under her weight, the tree unsettles tiny avalanches of soil from its anchor points. Avril asks if I am taking photographs. I answer yes. I ask if her body feels strong and safe. Shrugging her deltoid muscles toward her ears, Avril lays her cheek against the bark. Different muscles. My hip flexors are starting to quake, so I lower my other leg into kneeling position. Avril starts to swing her legs, rotating from her hip to build momentum for traveling farther across the branch. Moving muscles? One leg pushes powerfully and springs her abdomen to the border of the branch. Arms, exhilaration, legs, risk, abdominal muscles, the tree, back muscles, and fear move together, and winter boots, then legs, then hips, and then her flowery jacket slip off the branch. Muscles? Avril's arms curl around the tree, with biceps, triceps, digitalis flexor and extensor muscles pulling against the wood until they tumble, landing in a puff of soil.

While Avril dusted her jacket off and hopped back onto the branch, I debated physiological conceptions of muscle alongside the muscled complexities that had just unfolded. "Belly, fiber, filament, fibril" felt inadequate as a mode of engaging the muscled motion I had just witnessed. I felt unsettled by a methodological impulse to engage muscles otherwise, beyond familiar frames of naming muscles or noticing muscles only for the movement they generate. Muscles, in this

Figure 6.1 How do muscles matter with tree trunks and tumbling?

moment, were more than tools that produce motion to carry Avril's body across the tree. Muscles did more than slip, fall or fail with the branch, camera and dirt. If I understand that existing methodological habits for attending to movement fall short in taking seriously the nuances of muscled motion, what happens when I shift from noticing movement to thinking with muscles with/in moving?

What I cannot readily locate in the ways that I have been taught to engage with muscles are methods that follow how muscles weave with everyday inquiry practices: how might we *do muscles methodologically* in education research? I take up this question in this chapter. Asking how we might move beyond describing muscled movements or stretch science-based descriptions of muscle into practices of *doing* muscle,[4] I tug physiological accounts of muscle toward a layered, partial and uncertain understanding of how intentional methodological practices might *do* muscles as/with knotting and activity. I wonder how "muscle" might be an active research process, rather than a stable component or taken-for-granted form of bodied data, and deploy a methodology of muscling as I work to think with muscles as muscles happen—to *do* muscles as they muscle.

Bellies, fascicles and fibers

Sitting at my computer, I slide my left and right index fingers across the trackpad to zoom in on an image of Avril as her hands tug her body along the suspended tree branch. I notice how her fingers dig into the satin bark of the fallen tree and anchor her palms against the few knots the tree offers. I wonder what composes Avril's finger muscles in this moment—what (who?) participates in mooring Avril's body? When I attend to muscles here, what am I tending with?[5] What crafts the muscles I am noticing and mobilizing?

Physiology knows muscles as bundles of muscle fibers, nerves and blood vessels knitted together.[6] Muscle fibers gather in fascicles, fascicles sheathed in connective tissue adhere to other fascicles, and connective tissues extend beyond muscle bellies to grab onto bones. Within any one muscle, physiology makes visible muscle fibers of different length and diameter, gathered into strategically situated fascicles, which tug at different angles on different joints such that muscle bellies can perform different movements. As Avril negotiates the tree branch with physiology, she does so with an array of strategically layered muscle tissues, with flesh that is biomechanically designed to allow her human body to navigate the world and the tree branch with dexterity, expertise and efficiency built literally into her muscle's structure.

This is an organized and highly structured bundling of muscle fibers and fascicles, one concerned with an architectural and structural layering. All skeletal muscles, with this physiological method for making muscles perceptible, are composed of the same basic features and can exact movement in a predictable fashion. Such a method of making these muscle bellies visible is a precise methodological practice. Methodology is embedded within this nicely organized, predictable conception of muscle. For example, when I understand that what Avril lives as muscle is made of fibers aligned into fascicles, arranged into perfectly adept muscle bellies, I can attend to the moment of Avril's body and the branch in specific ways, including as a lack of abdominal and arm strength to anchor her body against gravitational forces. Here, I might read this moment as muscle failure. The muscles that I make possible are muscles that succeed only in their mastery, in their fulfillment of their tightly controlled structural function. This interpretation feels, to me, inadequate—and, more importantly, drawing on conceptions of muscles that allow for my analysis to readily overlay narratives of falling as failure makes clear how muscle, and our practices of doing muscle, are ethical and political concerns.

What else, how else, might the muscles in this moment be crafted? How can crafting muscles become an intentional methodological practice? As an intervention into prestructured hierarchical methods of organizing and mobilizing knowledges and bodies, Donna Haraway lends "knotting" as an ongoing feminist practice of making connections that "make a difference; they weave paths and consequences but not determinisms."[7] What muscles are possible in education research beyond determinate, functionally structured muscles? I borrow inspiration from Haraway's contention that we must work to make Euro-Western hegemonic knowledges "seriously unthinkable: not available to think with"[8] and wonder how I might make understandings of muscles that appreciate only their biomechanical function unthinkable. Layering camera-captured frames of the moment with Avril and the log on and through one another, I literally lose sight of when "falling" happens and any ability to pinpoint distinct muscle bellies or functions becomes vulnerable. This is not to argue that lived muscles stop existing or mattering. Rather, my methodological attention is necessarily shifted. Physiology, belly, fascicle and fiber become unsettled as frames for knowing muscle. This, I argue, is a muscling practice. I am forced to generate unfamiliar, situated methods for inhabiting muscles. I need to ask, each time I encounter these muscles, what I am intentionally attending to. I am implicated in the muscles that I make possible. I actively participate in (a) muscling.

Figure 6.2 How do we notice (with) muscles?

Fibrils and filaments

This moment of Avril negotiating with the tree and dirt and winter boots and camera unfolded rapidly. Palmar foot muscles encased in boots hit soil, finger muscles tugged at bark, neck muscles held eyes and ears from contacting the forest floor. In freeze-frames built from the rapid shutter speed of a camera, this pace and progression stutters. I have toggled, in my brain, between the moment and documentation so many times that the activity of muscles is becoming a question: how are these muscles active? What, and how, are these muscles doing, making, creating? Where does this muscle start or move; where does this muscle pause or finish? How, and why, might I trace these muscles' contours?

For physiology, skeletal muscle activity is easy. It is purposeful human movement generated by the ongoing work of muscle contractile proteins. When activated, contractile proteins (myofilaments) continually slide over one another in a coordinated stream of action to generate a muscular contraction.[9] Muscle action is inaugurated at the microscopic scale with the sliding of one muscle filament over another. This tiny motion builds as myofilaments are knitted together into myofibrils. These microscopic forces propagate, cascading and building into functional muscle action. Muscle action is made knowable as the cumulative product of an incredible mass of myofilament labor.

This conception of muscle activity is a methodological concern because it makes possible specific methods for engaging with muscle. When muscle activity is a cumulative product or an outcome, muscled work has a beginning and a conclusion. Avril's left quadriceps muscle is activated to steady her body—muscle delineated (certain myofilaments are activated). Avril swings her right leg over the branch—movement begins. Avril's left rotator cuff fights to hold her swinging body's weight—muscle delineated (other myofilaments get to work). Avril tumbles—movement over. Purposeful muscle activity stops. Muscles, here, are made perceptible in a very specific methodological frame.

How might I attend to muscle activities otherwise? Anna Tsing argues that "our own human involvement in multispecies worlds is thus a place to begin. Our doings are a way to trace the doings of others."[10] Weaving Tsing's provocation with muscles, winter boots and fallen trees, I wonder how I might burrow into how muscles move human bodies and then work to actively refuse this frame of reference. Picking up the layered image of Avril's muscling, I trace what I have been taught to follow as muscles. Quickly, this becomes impossible. The movement is too fragmented, too fast, too unfamiliarly bounded. I cannot find where only myofilament action translates into only purposeful muscle movements. For Tsing, "if a rush of troubled stories is the best way to tell about

Figure 6.3 How do we make muscles perceptible, differently?

contaminated diversity, then it's time to make that rush part of our knowledge practices."[11] Tree, blur, finger, myofibril, camera shutters: these compose the muscles I can make visible and that I can attend to. Rather than asking "Is that a muscle?" my muscling question becomes "Should I disentangle this from muscle?" Muscling, then, entails a practice of noticing how muscles are expansive and collective, while wondering what borders I draw, and what methodological decisions I make, to parse this or that border in any moment.

Muscling

Muscling foregrounds how and why muscles matter in education research. When muscle is no longer an easily graspable materiality, muscling becomes an ongoing, situated, uncertain and partial practice of making muscles perceptible—and of becoming accountable to the consequences of the muscles we make matter. My muscling refuses physiological determinism but tugs physiology into how muscles come to matter, momentarily, before tossing physiology into the messy complexities of doing muscles. What matters, when muscling extends beyond the margins of this research story, is that *this muscling* is situated; it is partial, momentary, imperfect and crafted with my finger muscles as they trigger a camera shutter and tap against my keyboard, with puffs of dirt, with Avril's bodied motion as her shoulders turn and re-turn through our documentation, with fallen trees, with our pedagogical inquiry with children's movement. We—our methodological attunements, loyalties and intentions—are implicated in how muscles are made visible, and thus we are answerable to how the muscling that we participate in creates different possibilities for doing (with) muscle otherwise in early childhood education. I contend that muscles are neither universal nor stable nor methodologically inert; muscles are lively and localized, complex and consequential participants that cogenerate and are generated with/in research practices in education. How we make muscle visible extends our methods for attending to children's movement in early childhood education, which generates possibilities for considering how muscles might entangle with pedagogies beyond traditional frames of reference, while novel pedagogies with/in muscled movement double back through muscles to complexify how, where and why muscles matter to children's learning, thus demanding that we attune to muscles otherwise—again. Muscling, then, offers a practice of taking seriously *how* muscles participate in research while *doing* muscles as intentional, active methodological undertakings.

Notes

1. William McArdle, Frank Katch, and Victoria Katch, *Essentials of Exercise Physiology* (Baltimore, MD: Lippincott Williams & Wilkins, 2006).
2. Keith Moore, Arthur Dalley, and Anne Agur, *Clinically Oriented Anatomy* (Baltimore, MD: Lippincott Williams & Wilkins, 2010); Dee Unglaub Silverthorn, *Human Physiology: An Integrated Approach* (San Francisco, CA: Pearson Education Inc., 2007).
3. Examples of dominant early childhood education resources that make muscle visible through describing the outcomes of muscled movement include Canadian Society for Exercise Physiology, *Canadian 24-hour Movement Guidelines for the Early Years (0–4 years)*, http://www.csep.ca/view.asp?x=696; Canadian Sport for Life Society, *The ABCs: Useful in All Sports*, 2016, http://canadiansportforlife.ca/physical-literacy/abcs-useful-all-sports.
4. Additional examples of early childhood education resources that value muscle for its instrumental functions as described via scientific conceptions of muscle physiology include Vivienne Temple and Alison Preece, *Healthy Opportunities for Preschoolers* (Vancouver, BC: Legacies Now, 2007); Chronic Disease Prevention Alliance of Canada, *Healthy Beginnings for Preschoolers 2–5* (Ottawa: CDPAC, n.d.).
5. Pauliina Rautio, "Thinking about Life and Species Lines with Pietari and Otto (and Garlic Breath)," *TRACE: Finnish Journal for Human-animal Studies* 3 (2017): 94–102.
6. Moore et al., *Clinically Oriented Anatomy*; McArdle et al., *Essentials of Exercise Physiology*.
7. Donna J. Haraway, *Staying with the Trouble: Making Kin in the Chthulucene* (Durham, NC: Duke University Press, 2016): 31.
8. Ibid., 30.
9. Jacob Krans, "The Sliding Filament Theory of Muscle Contraction," *Nature Education* 3, no. 9 (2010): 66.
10. Anna L. Tsing, "More Than Human Sociality," in *Anthropology and Nature*, ed. Kirsten Hastrup (London: Routledge, 2013), 34.
11. Anna L. Tsing, *The Mushroom at the End of the World: On the Possibility of Life in Capitalist Ruins* (Princeton, NJ: Princeton University Press, 2015), 34.

Bibliography

Canadian Society for Exercise Physiology. *Canadian 24-hour Movement Guidelines for the Early Years (0–4 years)*. http://www.csep.ca/view.asp?x=696.

Canadian Sport for Life Society. *The ABCs: Useful in All Sports*. 2016. http://canadiansportforlife.ca/physical-literacy/abcs-useful-all-sports.

Chronic Disease Prevention Alliance of Canada. *Collaborative Action on Childhood Obesity, Phase 2: Healthy Beginnings for Preschoolers 2–5*. Ottawa: CDPAC, n.d.

Haraway, Donna J. *Staying with the Trouble: Making Kin in the Chthulucene*. Durham, NC: Duke University Press, 2016.

Krans, Jacob. "The Sliding Filament Theory of Muscle Contraction." *Nature Education* 3, no. 9 (2010): 66. https://www.nature.com/scitable/topicpage/the-sliding-filament-theory-of-muscle-contraction-14567666.

McArdle, William, Frank Katch, and Victoria Katch. *Essentials of Exercise Physiology*. 3rd ed. Baltimore, MD: Lippincott Williams & Wilkins, 2006.

Moore, Keith, Arthur Dalley, and Anne Agur. *Clinically Oriented Anatomy*. 6th ed. Baltimore, MD: Lippincott Williams & Wilkins, 2010.

Rautio, Pauliina. "Thinking about Life and Species Lines with Pietari and Otto (and Garlic Breath)." *TRACE: Finnish Journal for Human-animal Studies* 3 (2017): 94–102.

Silverthorn, Dee Unglaub. *Human Physiology: An Integrated Approach*. 4th ed. San Francisco, CA: Pearson Education Inc., 2007.

Temple, Viviene, and Alison Preece. *Healthy Opportunities for Preschoolers*. Vancouver, BC: Legacies Now, 2007. http://www.decoda.ca/wp-content/uploads/Hop_ELPR_Book_English_lr.pdf.

Tsing, Anna L. "More Than Human Sociality." In *Anthropology and Nature*, edited by Kirsten Hastrup, 27–42. London: Routledge, 2013.

Tsing, Anna L. *The Mushroom at the End of the World: On the Possibility of Life in Capitalist Ruins*. Princeton, NJ: Princeton University Press, 2015.

Part Two

Relations with Other Species

7

Crowing: Coevolving Relationships

Kathleen Kummen

This chapter is a collection of lively crow stories that are shared as a provocation to (re)think with crows in early childhood spaces. John Marzluff and Tony Angell describe the long, close relationship between humans and crows as one that has inspired art, tales and myths.[1] The Coast Salish peoples, on whose traditional lands these crow-child events occurred, have for millennia shared tales of the crow's adventures as teachings and legends. The stories I share emerged from a multispecies ethnographic research inquiry in a children's center situated in a small urban teaching university. The research follows a common worlds framework.[2] Bruno Latour's concept of common worlds refers to a broader understanding of the social to include all constituents of our worlds, including nonhuman life forms, forces and entities.[3] Multispecies ethnography from this viewpoint is "characterized by an attempt to move beyond research practices that confine themselves to exclusively human (or social) concerns and interests.[4]" Using an actively inclusive more-than-human framework, this research resists the onto-epistemological division that is often perceived between sociocultural contexts and natural environments. Such resistance is necessary in order to reimagine and engage with/in 21st-century pedagogical practices that acknowledge the complexities of children's real-life worlds.[5] This chapter offers crowing as a researching method that attended to the imperfect and complex relationships in child care, relationships that are haunted by multiple legacies of inequity and social injustices.

Coevolution

John Marzluff, professor in wildlife sciences at the University of Washington, has studied the cultural relationship between humans and crows and argues that both species' cultures have been shaped by the other.[6] Marzluff hypothesizes that contact between the two species at crucial moments provoked cultural coevolution in both species. Cultural evolution is defined as the "change through time in socially transmitted behaviors that results because the behavior either affects the practitioner's survival or reproduction or it is chosen or imposed on others by conscious or unconscious decision making."[7]

Marzluff and Angell describe this nonlinear coevolution in a simple tale that, as they caution the reader, belies the extraordinary complexity and unpredictably of coevolution.[8] The story begins with crows finding a new food source in the fish laid out by humans to dry. Human irritations arising from discovering the crows poaching their fish resulted in the human need to create a culture of crow scaring or scarecrows. In response to this human persecution and bullying, crows developed the ability to work together to respond aggressively to humans and were able to pass this knowledge on to successive generations. The innovation, cunning and brutality of crows both impressed and horrified humans, who then represented these feats in legends, tales and myths. This symbiotic dance between crows and humans continued as each species' behavior produced a change in the other. Today, humans and crows rely on the learnings constructed and reconstructed through and in coevolution to guide their encounters with each other. Coevolution is an ongoing, nonlinear process in which current encounters between crows and humans are not isolated moments but rather part of larger, complex, ongoing crow-human entanglements.

Crow time

With tears streaming down his cheeks after kissing his mother goodbye, Jack runs to the glass door that leads from the room of the early childhood center to the outdoor play deck. He stops short at the door, his crying silenced by the harsh call of a crow from a tree in the forest across the street. "Caw! Caw! Caw!" Jack looks up and points to the trees where Crow is perched. Kathleen opens the door so that she and Jack can meet Crow. "Caw! Caw! Caw!" They scan the trees, searching for Crow. "Caw! Caw! Caw!" Crow is perched in the highest branches. Ornithologists theorize that bursts of one to nine caws followed by silence are companion calls that a crow will use to attract another bird's attention.[9] Jack does not possess this piece of knowledge as he waves his arm (a human companion act) in Crow's direction. "Caw! Caw! Caw!" says Crow.

The next morning as Kathleen walks to the early childhood center, she hears the hoarse call of Crow and stops to see the bird swoop down to pick up something off the road. It is early, and she thinks that perhaps Crow was watching for the food that often falls to the ground as humans move about the university campus.

She enters the infant room to find Jack at the glass door. "Caw! Caw! Caw!" calls Crow. When she opens the door so that she and Jack can go outside to look for Crow, Jack lifts up his arms for her to pick him up so that he can look into the trees to locate Crow. Suddenly, Crow swoops down, lands on a branch and flies from one tree to another. Kathleen and Jack watch in silence, their necks stretched out so that their eyes can scan the world above. "Caw! Caw! Caw!" They see dark clouds moving with the wind that brought last night's rain. The morning sky is filled with shades of grey flowing into the greens and browns of the forest. "Caw! Caw! Caw!" A flash of black appears as another crow flies across the skyline. Crow's companion call invites Kathleen and Jack to notice the sky's west-coast palette of colors.

Thinking with developmental theory, these two stories may provoke conversations around separation anxiety and developmentally appropriate practice.[10] Developmental theory positions Jack and Kathleen as the main protagonists in these stories, and as such they are seen as *the* agentic actors. Solely positioning agency within Jack and Kathleen, as the attention is focused on human emotion and knowledge, silences the agentic force of the more-than-human.

Thinking with crows decenters the humans in the narrative and repositions these stories as crow-human encounters. Lesley Instone suggests that we move in this world alongside "multiple others, human and nonhuman, and how we move is likewise not only a human achievement, but shaped by the more-than-human worlds through which we step."[11] Such encounters, Donna Haraway reminds us, "make us more worldly."[12] Thinking with crows moves children and educators from the center of the pedagogical conversations and calls for researchers and educators to pay attention to the relational and coshaping events taking place in children's common worlds. Many argue that such a move is necessary in order to enact alternative practices in early childhood education that respond to the legacies faced by 21st-century children.[13]

These encounters occurred when the human-made clock moved between 8:00 and 8:30 a.m. Pacific Standard Time. At the university where the early childhood center is located, this time of the day is performed in actions regulated by the movement of time as measured by the clock. For example, human bodies moving between campus buildings signify the start or the end of classes. Yet our classroom encounters were invitations made available only when we acknowledged crow time—not a new time but one we were unaware of before[14]—in which Crow invited us into new ways of being with/in the world.

Crows, along with nutcrackers, jays and ravens, are members of the avian family *Corvidae*, who existed long before humans did. They have their own rhythm and flow to their days. In the evenings, they gather in large flocks to roost for the night; in the mornings, they leave the roost in search of food. Highly attuned to predictable routes and schedules, crows will return to particular locations at the times they know food will be plentiful there, such as lunchtime at the university when humans scurry between buildings, often dropping food scraps as they eat on the go, or in the early morning when maintenance staff collect garbage containers.

In responding to Crow's companion call, Jack entered a relationship that would invite the other children and the educators into a world of crow time. I share the two encounter narratives, not so that we might consider how Crow invited us to appreciate the beauty of nature. Rather, I am interested in how crows and humans share a common world in which crow time creates possibilities for both species through their entangled relationship. This is a reciprocal relationship that honors species diversity rather than one in which the crow is anthropomorphized to serve a human purpose, such as evoking nature's beauty. Michelle Bastian explains that by recognizing nature as agentic, humans cannot "attempt to incorporate nature within the smooth even flow of absolute time as it was conceived by Newton."[15] Bastian asserts that recognizing nature's agency makes space for humans to be alert to the unexpected and unpredictable changes in nature as occurring in nature times, such as crow time.[16]

Droppings

As she walks from her car in the morning, Kathleen notices the crows high in the cedar trees of the forest that houses our campus. Ornithologists posit that crows living in spaces inhabited by humans are keenly attuned to changes in human behavior.[17] This ability to adjust their own behavior in response to the unpredictable nature of humans has evolved over time, allowing crows to exploit humans' habits as a means of survival.

The children are sitting outside and the ground is covered with bits of food, dropped by hands attempting to bring morsels to mouths. A crow is perched in one of the trees, appearing content to watch the feasting and food dropping, occasionally emitting a series of sharp companion caws. "Caw! Caw! Caw!" and a flash of black announces a second crow's arrival who lands on the branches of another tree. Now both crows call out with a series of short caws. "Caw! Caw! Caw!" As the toddlers leave the space, a third crow swoops down, landing on a cedar tree near the place where the feast had been held. Entering the room, we hear the sharp calls, "Caw! Caw! Caw!" and our eyes are drawn to the windows to view the three crows feast on children's food droppings.

Just as Crow's ancestors did to our human ancestors, Crow and her companion crows attracted our attention, creating opportunities for new encounters and relationship. Like our ancestors, we watched in awe as Crow and the companion crows displayed for us their foraging skills developed from their ancestors' relationships with humans.[18] The children and I watched with admiration as the crows swooped in with accuracy to retrieve our food waste left on the ground.

Marzluff and Angell assert that by attending to the more-than-human world, we humans can rethink our image of ourselves in the world.[19] Revisiting this story and our thinking with crows as data, I become curious about how the relationship between crows and humans evolved with and through their mutual relationship with waste. This curiosity led me to enact a different kind of pedagogy, a crowing pedagogy. Crowing pedagogies are situated within a conceptual shift from "matters of fact" to what Latour refers to as "matters of concern."[20] Mindy Blaise, Catherine Hamm and Jeanne Iorio explain that matters of fact in an early childhood setting are traditional early childhood practices of observation that compare children to universal standards and norms. Matters of concern, they explain, "engage with the broader, relational contexts that children inhabit as integral parts of the universe."[21]

Thom van Dooren and Deborah Bird Rose assert that ethnographic storytelling invites us to develop "the openness and the sensitivities necessary to be curious, to understand and respond in ways that are never perfect, never innocent, never final and yet always required."[22] In weaving these crowing stories, I was invited to challenge my thinking and to consider my own implications in the world, the consequences of my practices as a teacher-researcher, and what future possibilities these practices might produce. Thinking and writing the preceding story drew my attention to the waste relationship between crows and humans. I was provoked to consider how the children and I are implicated in the neoliberal project of becoming and being consumers who produce waste and how the crows participate in that project as waste consumers. If we can think of coevolution with crows, then, van Dooren and Rose remind us, we can imagine coextinction.[23] Questions of how our practices work to reinscribe particular values around materials and resources such as food begin to emerge.

I am haunted by concerns of excess as I am drawn to the droppings produced by children and adults in early childhood spaces, droppings that have significant material consequences for our common worlds. How are the children, the crows and I continuing to (co)evolve within this historic dance of dropping and scavenging food? What are the possibilities for new ways of being in the world if we attend to this mutual dance? How might these attentions challenge our pedagogical practices to become practices of responsibility and concern?

I do not end this chapter with neat and tidy answers or matters of fact because I do not conceptualize or live teaching as a technological practice where we can follow what to do by rote. Rather, my common worlds researching framework brings me to conclude this chapter with an invitation to teachers and researchers, including myself, to take up activism in our work so as to reimagine and enact early childhood education as matters of concern. It is an invitation to move beyond localized observations of children and teachers for the purpose of applying generally to teaching practices to attend instead to entanglements that provoke complex and difficult conversations of what it means to live well with others, human and more-than-human, in particular situated contexts. The crow-human narratives shared in this chapter illuminate that pedagogies are always already political and ethical. Crowing pedagogies call us to recognize the diverse entanglements of children's common worlds and to make visible the connections and commitments we choose to support. Crowing pedagogies invite educators, researchers and children to engage as political agents so that classrooms are sites where political and ethical practices for living well with others can flourish.

Notes

1 John Marzluff and Tony Angell, *Gifts of the Crow: How Perception, Emotion, and Thought Allow Smart Birds to Behave Like Humans* (New York: Atria Books, 2013).
2 Common World Childhoods Research Collective, "Children's Relations with Place, with Materials, and with Other Species," 2017, http://commonworlds.net/research/.
3 Bruno Latour, "Why Has Critique Run Out of Steam? From Matters of Fact to Matters of Concern," *Critical Inquiry* 30, no. 2 (2004): 225–248.
4 Veronica Pacini-Ketchabaw, Affrica Taylor, and Mindy Blaise, "De-centring the Human in Multispecies Ethnographies," in *Posthuman Research Practices in Education*, ed. Carol Taylor and Christina Hughes, 149–167 (Basingstoke, UK: Palgrave Macmillan, 2016), 151.

5   Veronica Pacini-Ketchabaw and Kathleen Kummen, "Shifting Temporal Frames in Children's Common Worlds in the Anthropocene," *Contemporary Issues in Early Childhood* 17, no. 4 (2016): 431–441.
6   Marzluff and Angell, *Gifts of the Crow*.
7   John Marzluff and Tony Angell, *In the Company of Crows and Ravens* (New Haven, CT: Yale University Press, 2005), 15.
8   Marzluff and Angell, *Gifts of the Crow*.
9   Marzluff and Tony Angell, *Crows and Ravens*; ibid.
10 Carole Copple and Sue Bredekamp, *Developmentally Appropriate Practice in Early Childhood Programs Serving Children from Birth through Age 8*, 3rd ed. (Washington, DC: National Association for the Education of Young Children, 2008).
11 Lesley Instone, "Walking as Respectful Wayfinding in an Uncertain Age," in *Manifesto for Living in the Anthropocene*, ed. Katherine Gibson, Deborah Bird Rose, and Ruth Fincher (Brooklyn, NY: Punctum Books, 2015), 136.
12 Donna J. Haraway, *Modest_Witness@Second_Millennium.FemaleMan_Meets_OncoMouse: Feminism and Technoscience* (New York: Routledge, 1997).
13 Pacini-Ketchabaw et al., "De-centring the Human."
14 Haraway, *Modest_Witness*.
15 Michelle Bastian, "Inventing Nature: Rewriting Time and Agency in a More-than Human World," *Australian Humanities Review* 47 (2009): 113.
16 Michelle Bastian, "Fatally Confused: Telling the Time in the Midst of Ecological Crises," *Environmental Philosophy* 9, no. 1 (2012): 23–48.
17 Marzluff and Angell, *Crows and Ravens*; Marzluff and Angell, *Gifts of the Crow*.
18 Marzluff and Angell, *Crows and Ravens*.
19 Marzluff and Angell, *Gifts of the Crow*.
20 Latour, "Why Has Critique Run Out of Steam?"
21 Mindy Blaise, Catherine Hamm, and Jeanne Marie Iorio, "Modest Witness(ing) and Lively Stories: Paying Attention to Matters of Concern in Early Childhood," *Pedagogy, Culture, & Society* 25, no. 1 (2017): 32.
22 Thom van Dooren and Deborah Bird Rose, "Lively Ethography: Storying Animist Worlds," *Environmental Humanities* 8, no. 1 (2016): 90.
23 Ibid.

Bibliography

Barad, Karen. *Meeting the Universe Halfway: Quantum Physics and the Entanglement of Matter and Meaning*. Durham, NC: Duke University Press, 2007.

Bastian, Michelle. "Fatally Confused: Telling the Time in the Midst of Ecological Crises." *Environmental Philosophy* 9, no. 1 (2012): 23–48.

Bastian, Michelle. "Inventing Nature: Rewriting Time and Agency in a More-than Human World." *Australian Humanities Review* 47 (2009): 99–116.

Blaise, Mindy, Catherine Hamm, and Jeanne Marie Iorio. "Modest Witness(ing) and Lively Stories: Paying Attention to Matters of Concern in Early Childhood." *Pedagogy, Culture, & Society* 25, no. 1 (2017): 31–42. doi:10.1080/14681366.2016.1208265.

Common World Childhoods Research Collective. "Children's Relations with Place, with Materials, and with Other Species," 2017. http://commonworlds.net/research/.

Copple, Carole, and Sue Bredekamp. *Developmentally Appropriate Practice in Early Childhood Programs Serving Children from Birth through Age 8*. 3rd ed. Washington, DC: National Association for the Education of Young Children, 2008.

Haraway, Donna J. *Modest_Witness@Second_Millennium.FemaleMan_Meets_OncoMouse: Feminism and Technoscience*. New York: Routledge, 1997.

Instone, Lesley. "Walking as Respectful Wayfinding in an Uncertain Age." In *Manifesto for Living in the Anthropocene*, edited by Katherine Gibson, Deborah Bird Rose, and Ruth Fincher, 133–138. Brooklyn, NY: Punctum Books, 2015.

Latour, Bruno. "Why Has Critique Run Out of Steam? From Matters of Fact to Matters of Concern." *Critical Inquiry* 30, no. 2 (2004): 225–248.

Marzluff, John, and Tony Angell. *Gifts of the Crow: How Perception, Emotion, and Thought Allow Smart Birds to Behave Like Humans*. New York: Atria Books, 2013.

Marzluff, John, and Tony Angell. *In the Company of Crows and Ravens*. New Haven, CT: Yale University Press, 2005.

Pacini-Ketchabaw, Veronica, and Kathleen Kummen. "Shifting Temporal Frames in Children's Common Worlds in the Anthropocene." *Contemporary Issues in Early Childhood* 17, no. 4 (2016): 431–441. doi:10.1177/1463949116677930.

Pacini-Ketchabaw, Veronica, Affrica Taylor, and Mindy Blaise. "De-centring the Human in Multispecies Ethnographies." In *Posthuman Research Practices in Education*, edited by Carol Taylor and Christina Hughes, 149–167. Basingstoke, UK: Palgrave Macmillan, 2016.

van Dooren, Thom, and Deborah Bird Rose. "Lively Ethography: Storying Animist Worlds." *Environmental Humanities* 8, no. 1 (2016): 78–94. doi:10.1215/22011919-3527731.

8

Shimmering: Animating Multispecies Relations with Wurundjeri Country

Mindy Blaise and Catherine Hamm

Scholars who align themselves with the emerging field of environmental humanities are experimenting with different ways of knowing the world. Part of this work involves writing practices that make room for new relations to emerge. These practices require an experimental orientation toward the world, including curiosity about knowledge construction. In this chapter, we are curious about the effects of binary logic and linguistic imperialism and how they are invisible tools of colonization that continuously separate humans from nature. We utilize the grammar of animacy to help us tell lively and animate stories about multispecies relations with Wurundjeri Country.

This chapter moves beyond our narrow disciplinary trainings in early childhood education by taking a more open, generous and curious view to knowledges. Initially, this required us to move away from focusing exclusively on the human child or the human child acting on nature, toward thinking with multispecies relations. In our previous work[1] we argued that the field of early childhood seems to have lost its ability to think creatively and experimentally. We originally drew from Bruno Latour,[2] who encouraged us to reconsider how early childhood educators usually pay attention to the world. Latour contends that a more expansive logic is necessary to create opportunities for connectivity and relationality, rather than being constrained by binary reasoning such as nature/culture or reason/emotion. Therefore, shifting attention from focusing on "matters of fact" toward making room for "matters of concern" entails foregrounding relational and connected knowledge processes. It also involves making room for more-than-human relations. These shifts require that we try out some new practices. One of these practices includes experimenting with writing lively animate stories as a way to activate new multispecies relations.

We are inspired by Deborah Bird Rose's lively stories about flowering gum tree and flying fox encounters.[3] In these stories, Rose shows how *shimmer*, the Aboriginal ancestral power of life, arises in relationship and encounter. Shimmer exceeds human action. It captures our attention, like the ways in which leaves, wind and sun bring together a brilliant sparkling effect of leafy light patterns and connections that can literally stop us in our tracks or take our breath away for the slightest moment. It is here, within this moment, when something more is possible: an encounter, a change, a connection, an event. The starting point for Rose is always through her connection to Aboriginal Australia. She shows how her Aboriginal teachers taught her about multispecies kinship, connectivity and care.

These stories are not about describing the gum tree and the flying fox (although careful description is needed). Rather, they are about the pulses that bring together multispecies relationships and encounters. For Rose, these encounters are only possible when she engages in "passionate immersion."[4] She is able to do this because she attends to the ways in which she is connected to, rather than separate from, the multispecies world. She suspends the human desire to always *know* the facts about flowering gum trees and flying foxes and instead learns *with* the entangled world she is part of. Human exceptionalism prevents us from learning with multispecies relations and encounters because it is predicated on the desire to know what the species is and why it is relating this way or that way. We are interested in something different. We are curious about what we might learn by paying attention to the pulses of multispecies relations and encounters and how these moments call us into relation. We already live in a pulsing and shimmering multispecies world, but we are not always open to these encounters. When we recognize that we are always already called into relation with human and more-than-human others, the nature/culture binary is diffused. We offer a lively animate story to show how shimmering makes us curious and draws us to our connections within multispecies worlds and worldings. In doing so, we argue that shimmering makes us accountable and responsible.

The following lively animate story does not aim to tell more truthful accounts by stating the "facts" of what we see and hear on our weekly "out and about" walks with young children and teachers. We are not trying to be clever with our storying and what we know about this place. Instead, our writing and storytelling is a political doing. We are curious to experiment with writing in ways that dissolve the hierarchies that typically situate human and more-than-human entities as separate and unequal. Our storying challenges human exceptionalism by activating multispecies relations that bring nature and culture together. We experiment with animacy,[5] referring to the grammatical effects of lively nouns, pronoun use and sentence structure to move ideas and activate multispecies relations.

The lively narrative shows how we attend to the animacies of the world and how shimmering calls other species to one another and also calls us into connection. When we are called into connection, something new is produced. Rose,[6] drawing from Isabelle Stengers's concept of "reciprocal capture," is instructive for understanding the political potential of shimmer to activate new modes of existence that are not transcendental. According to Rose, shimmering is prone to a "reciprocal capture" with Western thought: "It is a process of encounter and transformation, not absorption, in which different ways of being and doing find interesting things to do together."[7] While reading the following lively animate story, we invite you to pay attention to when it calls you into connection, to see if you are able to engage in "passionate immersion" and to consider how "reciprocal capture" occurs.

Shimmering: Creek-egretta-child-yabbie relations

It is Iuk Eel season in Wurundjeri Country.[8] Hot north winds are beginning to abate, and the high temperatures are slowly dropping. Wind, water, trees and animals pulse and hum with the changing Kulin seasons. Wind moves in gusts back and forth, rustling the bright pink buds of Manna gum that are just starting to flower, luring Lorikeet and Eastern Rosella Parrot to her branches. It is hard to ignore Lorikeet and Parrot as they screech and fight boisterously for nectar. Rainfall is increasing and Frog, Possum, and Parrot begin their breeding rituals. The creek on Wurundjeri Country, now known as Stony Creek, flows strongly with the recent heavy rainfall. Creek moves the water, Eel, and other water-based animals, such as crustaceans and macro-invertebrates, in waves along her stony bottom. These animals were once plentiful in this creek and a food source for both the humans and other animals of this place. Now, they are fewer in number, or perhaps we humans have a difficult time paying attention to their everyday happenings and relations.

Egretta novaehollandiae (White-faced Heron) glides along the waterway. Her wings move slowly, effortlessly as she swoops low over the water. At a small bend, Creek appears still. But suddenly there is movement. Water is rippling. Or did Water make a splash? A single brown leaf floats through the air. Leaf is swirling up, down, and around until Creek catches the stem, taking Leaf down her flowing waters.

Egretta returns again, now standing on top of Rock. Her thin, stick-like legs stand out. There is something disarming about her bright yellow legs. And yet, in the distance they blend in with Grass: yellow, tall, thin and soft. She is standing still on Rock. Waiting. But for what? An insect? A small crustacean moving slowly along the bottom of Creek, trying to hide among the rocks and water weeds? Sun's

Figure 8.1 Creek-egretta-child-yabbie relations. Author's photograph.

rays, shining onto the water, sparkle, and Ripple invites. Egretta moves, so slowly, deliberately, and finally comes to rest on the edge of Creek. Egretta continues to wait.

A group of preschoolers and their teachers encounter Egretta on their regular walk along Creek. This is not the first time she has attracted their interest. They have had regular encounters with her. They are excited to see her today because she has not been around the waterway for several weeks. Her beak is a different color to the last time they saw her. It has changed from dusty yellow to dark gray-black. Iuk Eel season also signifies the breeding season for herons. The change in the color of her beak shows that she is ready to find a mate. The Creek-Egretta-human encounter today is not like others before. Egretta lures their attention and the humans become immersed in her doing something new.

Egretta stands motionless on the grassy edge of Creek, her eyes focused down toward the water. She stretches one foot out, placing it in the shallow water, and quickly scratches. Once, twice, three times. She finds a steady place to wait in the water. Quickly her long gray neck jerks down into the water and then rises up. What has she caught in the water? Does she have Yabbie (a small freshwater crustacean)? Slowly, carefully, and rhythmically she walks from the water with Yabbie dangling from her bill and finds a place on the creek bank to eat.

The children and their teachers stand in silent awe, watching as Egretta devours Yabbie. She crunches the hard carapace shell with her beak to reveal the soft flesh beneath. In a few short moments, the only evidence of her feast are Yabbie's claws that she drops from her mouth onto the creek's bank. As the humans see the claws fall to the ground, connections are made: The humans have seen Yabbie's claws on the bank before and wondered how they got there.

Animating

In our previous experimental writing, we have provided examples of different kinds of narrations to show the shifts that are required to move from factual observations to more lively affect-focused stories.[9] In that work we hoped to draw readers into connection through the lively stories. We realize that this can be problematic because it relies on a linear and progressive logic as we present one story followed by another that moves from the simple to the complex. In the spirit of experimentation, and with the aims of this lively doing book, we have tried something different. Robin Wall Kimmerer[10] alerts us to linguistic imperialism and how it distances us from the world, positions nature as an object and "renders the land lifeless." The effects of linguistic imperialism are great and have meant there is loss, for instance, the loss of original Indigenous plant, animal, place and season names. Linguistic imperialism also keeps humans and nonhumans separate. Kimmerer argues that nonhumans become relegated and assigned a pronoun that reduces them to inanimate objects *in* nature rather than subjects *within* natureculture. The English language groups objects together and names them "it" (e.g., I watch the heron fly away. It quickly moves away). Through linguistic imperialism, this has become a dominant way of thinking and knowing that has erased other worldviews. In contrast, Indigenous worldviews use the language of animacy to recognize living beings as subjects rather than objects. This is important, because the language of animacy recognizes how humans are always already in relation to multispecies worlds. Dissolving the divisions between humans and nonhumans helps make us accountable and responsible for the common world we share.

In our story, we have brought the *language of animacy* into relation with *shimmer*. We used the language of animacy as a way to articulate the shimmer to attend to the pulses and movements in multispecies worlds.

Activating something more

In this chapter we have drawn on Rose's[11] idea of "passionate immersion" as a way to activate you, our reader, to be in relation with our story. Our attempt was to draw you into the multispecies worlds where our story is situated. We intentionally shaped our narrative in a nonlinear way, moving with the ebbs and flows of multispecies relations with Creek, with Yabbie, with seasons and with the world. We used pronouns as a way to engage with the more-than-human protagonists as subjects, rather than objects. We have chosen not to conclude our chapter with a more traditional "summing up" of the main ideas and specific writing strategies we used but rather invite you to animate a story that involves multispecies knowledges and relations. We offer the following questions for activating something more:

How can you animate stories that make the more-than-human relations the most important subject? How do you position the more-than-human and these relations in a sentence? What kind of grammar do you use?
How might you replace verbs with nouns?

How can the beginning of each sentence be reframed or refocused? How do you write-in blurriness, overlappings, pasts and presents?

Instead of only writing about relations between species, how might you rewrite playful relations between species in ways that do not separate out the species and their individual actions?

How might the tone of a sentence or phrase be used in ways that make relations less certain, more partial or noninnocent?

How can your writing work to dissolve the hierarchies that are created by linguistic imperialism?

How might you activate your writing as political and response-able, experimenting with making the more-than-human subjects rather than objects?

As a political and ethical practice, how might you enliven your storying to create different kinds of relations between humans and nonhumans?

Notes

1. Mindy Blaise, Catherine Hamm, and Jeanne M. Iorio, "Modest Witness(ing) and Lively Stories: Paying Attention to Matters of Concern in Early Childhood," *Pedagogy, Culture, & Society* 25, no. 1 (2017): 31–42.
2. Bruno Latour, "Why Has Critique Run Out of Steam? From Matters of Fact to Matters of Concern," *Critical Inquiry* 30, no. 2 (2004): 225–248.
3. Deborah Bird Rose, "Shimmer: When All You Love Is Being Trashed," in *Arts of Living on a Damaged Planet: Ghosts and Monsters of the Anthropocene*, ed. Anna Lowenhaupt Tsing, Heather Anne Swanson, Elaine Gan, and Nils Bubandt (Minneapolis: University of Minnesota Press, 2017), G51–G63.
4. Ibid., 53.
5. Mel Y. Chen, *Animacies: Biopolitics, Racial Mattering, and Queer Affect* (Durham, NC: Duke University Press, 2012).
6. Rose, "Shimmer."
7. Ibid., G51.
8. The Wurundjeri people are one of the traditional landowners of Melbourne, Australia. They are one of the five groups that make up the Kulin nation of southwest Victoria. The people of the Kulin nation describe seven seasons, rather than the imperial four seasons. See https://museumsvictoria.com.au/forest/climate/kulin.html. In Australia, March is Iuk Eel season. The changes in seasons are the pulses of relationality of land, sea, sky and all species.
9. Blaise et al., "Modest Witness(ing)."

10 Robin Wall Kimmerer, *Braiding Sweetgrass: Indigenous Wisdom, Scientific Knowledge, and the Teaching of Plants* (Minneapolis: Milkwood Editions, 2013); Robin Wall Kimmerer, "Speaking of Nature," *Orion Magazine*, 2017.
11 Rose, "Shimmer."

Bibliography

Blaise, Mindy, Catherine Hamm, and Jeanne M. Iorio. "Modest Witness(ing) and Lively Stories: Paying Attention to Matters of Concern in Early Childhood." *Pedagogy, Culture, & Society* 25, no. 1 (2017): 31–42. doi:10.1080/14681366.2016.1208265.

Chen, Mel Y. *Animacies: Biopolitics, Racial Mattering, and Queer Affect*. Durham, NC: Duke University Press, 2012.

Gibson, Katherine, Deborah Bird Rose, and Ruth Fincher, eds. *Manifesto for Living in the Anthropocene*. Brooklyn, NY: Punctum Books, 2015.

Kimmerer, Robin Wall. *Braiding Sweetgrass: Indigenous Wisdom, Scientific Knowledge, and the Teaching of Plants*. Minneapolis: Milkwood Editions, 2013.

Kimmerer, Robin Wall. "Speaking of Nature." *Orion Magazine*, 2017. https://orionmagazine.org/article/speaking-of-nature/.

Latour, Bruno. "Why Has Critique Run Out of Steam? From Matters of Fact to Matters of Concern." *Critical Inquiry* 30, no. 2 (2004): 225–248.

Rose, Deborah Bird. "Shimmer: When All You Love Is Being Trashed." In *Arts of Living on Damaged Planet: Ghosts and Monsters of the Anthropocene*, edited by Anna Lowenhaupt Tsing, Heather Anne Swanson, Elaine Gan, and Nils Bubandt, G51–G63. Minneapolis: University of Minnesota Press, 2017.

Tsing, Anna Lowenhaupt, Heather Anne Swanson, Elaine Gan, and Nils Bubandt, eds. *Arts of Living on a Damaged Planet: Ghosts and Monsters of the Anthropocene*. Minneapolis: University of Minnesota Press, 2017.

9

Tracking: Cultivating the "Arts of Awareness" in Early Childhood

Narda Nelson

In the 21st century, young children's more-than-human relations have become a topic of concern in childhood studies, in conjunction with the naming of a new Anthropocene era to mark the profoundly disruptive influence of human activity on planetary systems.[1] Often romanticized and framed as curative in their essence, child–animal relations tend to be underscored by two powerful narratives in contemporary Euro-Western society. On the one hand, post-Enlightenment stories depict young children as "close to nature," placing emphasis on interspecies relationships as a conduit for children's emotional, moral and cognitive development.[2] On the other, Anthropocene narratives imbue childhoods with an overwhelming sense of anxiety and loss, wherein the "future child" stands poised to inherit an abbreviated life, denied the opportunity to "meet with" a growing list of near-vanishing animals in wake of Anthropocene foreclosures.[3]

Both stories universalize childhood, suspending it in an innocuous state of not-yet-fully-formed existence.[4] Neither place young children "near the action" in these challenging times, nor depict them as capable of creating new possibilities for living together with others. They also fail to account for the active role histories, plants, animals and landscape forms play in co-constituting children's everyday relations and, indeed, the very places we live.[5] It is against this backdrop that tracking animals with educators, researchers and a group of 3- to 5-year-old children emerges as a potential method for taking up feminist anthropologist Anna Tsing's call to cultivate the "arts of awareness"[6] to respond to living and learning in troubling times by opening ourselves up to new understandings of our shared vulnerabilities with others in this place.[7]

And so we track.

Figure 9.1 Something happened here.

Trace encounters

The impetus for tracking began when a group of educators I work with shared their desire to engage in a process of collective inquiry into relationships with the animals they and the children encounter on a day-to-day basis. Because animals are not always on call or visibly present, we walk together every week looking for tracks and traces to help stretch our conceptualizations of this place beyond the human-centric preoccupations that influence understandings about who belongs here. Misha Myers suggests that walking is a method that "brings attention to the landscape ... [allowing for] patterns, paces and paths of walking as experienced in the breath, rhythm, sweat and memory of the walker[s]."[8] Following Miller, Myers describes it as an "ideal strategy for witnessing [and inviting engagement with] embodied, participatory, and spontaneous modes of responsiveness and communicability ... a mode of travel that encourages convivial and social interaction with inhabitants of places."[9]

Tracking with young children follows a similar tack. Doing so requires us to attune our senses to something more than the dominant narratives that tend to order this place. For those of us who are settlers in Lekwungen-speaking peoples' territories, attunement includes the added complexity of learning to see ourselves as embodiments of the dominant narratives that continue to occupy

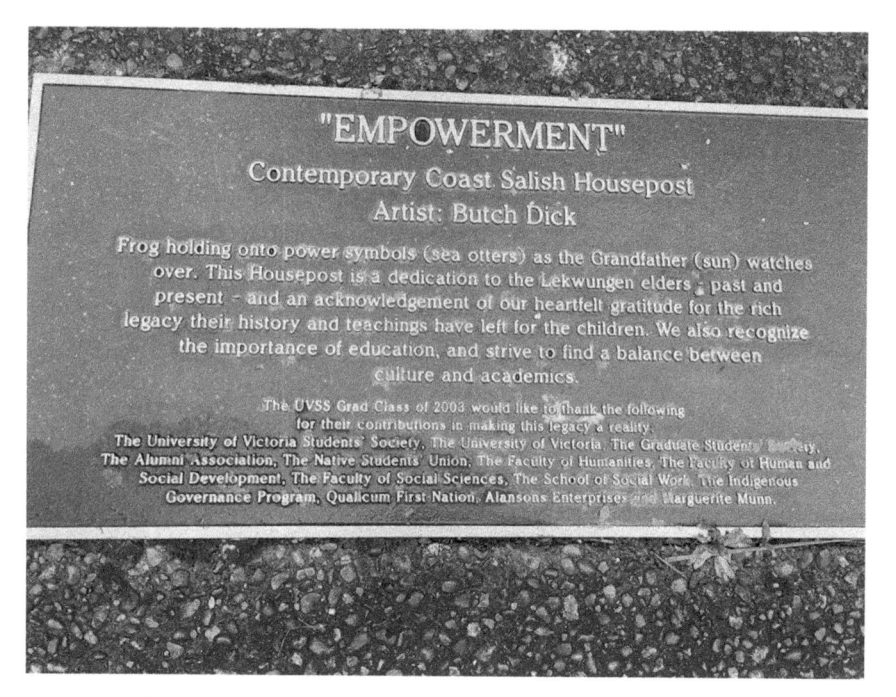

Figure 9.2 Past, present and ongoing connections.

these territories. Learning to walk, scan and "move with" the land's response to another creature's passing through necessitates learning to do so without simultaneously "vanishing" those on whose territories we track.[10] As we move, we stop to notice the weave of past, present and ongoing place connections, while speculating about bent blades of grass, depressions in the ground, a pile of poop and other traces that tell stories about this place too.

For us, tracking with young children also includes walking with questions of what it means to share space in this urban setting[11] while attempting to engage with our more-than-human neighbors who move through it according to their own needs and desires. We began the inquiry by focusing on crows who gather, like us, to scour the grass and cement campus area where a myriad of bodies leave things behind. As often happens with creatures deemed "difficult to live with," these birds seem to have an uncanny knack of showing up when they are not wanted and being absent when we want to engage. But, like us again, they leave behind traces that hint at their having passed through. Sometimes we see garbage strewn around the campus fountain. Other times we follow the scratch mark of a claw or the poke hole of a beak left behind in the mud. Once, a bike mirror revealed itself in the crook of a tree, leading to speculations about it being a special place for crows to stash treasures. As we are learning, this place is much more than a static backdrop for childhood development and human comings and goings! A multitude of connections story this place in ways that both include and exceed our own.

Tracking together with the children has become a means through which we learn to pay close attention to animal others who story this place in their own unique ways. Following Tsing, Donna Haraway and other scholars in the social sciences and humanities, Thom van Dooren, Eben Kirksey and Ursula Münster argue for cultivating the "'arts of attentiveness': modes of both paying attention to others and crafting meaning/ful response[s]"[12] to the challenging times we live in. Tsing highlights "passionate immersion"[13] as part of the symbiotic ways that plants, animals and other creatures story place as part of the process of cultivating such relationships. Cultivating the arts of awareness in this way, that is, by paying close attention to the way that more-than-human stories coshape the places we live and learn, feels vital in a society seemingly bent on perpetuating untenable patterns of living underscored by logics that are buoyed by seeing humans as existing apart.[14] Small ruptures in an otherwise seamless expanse of manicured grass become points of intrigue. We notice a group of ducks working up a low-lying section of the terrain, beaks buried in pursuit of something we cannot see but can hear as they sift the watery mud. Gulls and crows make appearances around the fringe of a newly formed spring wallow, hop-flying away when we get too close. We have plenty of hoof prints, bike treads, *homo sapiens* tracks and other traces to think with too.

Reading for refusal

With a Saskatchewan provincial field guide in hand, we are clearly not reading for accuracy in this west coast terrain.[15] But we find similarities enough amid the animal guidebook discrepancies to keep us scouring the ground for evidence of other stories, and we speculate together about what else might be happening in this place beyond its dominant expression of a place designed with "higher" (human) achievements in mind. The fact that other animals not only pass through but continue to call this place home is part of what van Dooren and Deborah Bird Rose refer to as a complex weave of interspecies, intergenerational achievements.[16] In his book *Flight Ways*, van Dooren talks about the need to come to new ways of understanding what a species is about. "Scientific fact" is one way of getting to know another species, but he suggests that focusing on the "time, energy, and labor required to keep successive generations in the world"[17] might also be an important step in getting to appreciate our coshaping community dwellers. Generations of crows, deer and others thrived here long before the university was built. Certainly, the daily patterns of these now urban critters have shifted significantly. But they are still choosing to make futures here. What does this say?

van Dooren refers to this intergenerational place loyalty as site fidelity. Fidelity can also mean being faithful, which I interpret as a relationship to place that speaks to past, present and future connections: we have been successful in this place and have memories and stories about this place, we live here now in relative safety and abundance, and we believe it will continue to sustain us as a good place to live and raise our families. This reminds me of the places we return to every day and the traces we leave behind. These places are bound tightly into our daily patterns of living through connections of love, friendship, recreation, spirituality, safety, memory, waste, life, death and hope. Paying attention to connections matters. I wonder about the possibility of noticing shared drives through tracking that root us in places and influence decisions to coexist in this urban space.

Sometimes place fidelity is disrupted, as evidenced in the forcible removal of the Lekwungen-speaking children and families from the very places we track. Tracking in what Veronica Pacini-Ketchabaw, Taylor, Blaise and de Finney call our "colonized and ecologically challenged lifeworlds"[18] does not guarantee a change in anyone's perspective. As such, tracking here also requires us to pay close attention to the specific histories of Lekwungen-speaking people's past, present and future relations with this place and its inhabitants that exceed our own settler colonial modes of relating. This includes noticing traces of the ongoing relations that Songhees, Esquimalt and WSÁNEĆ peoples have with their land and the land's more-than-human inhabitants. For example, during our walks, we sometimes stop to notice a Garry oak meadow expanse, totem poles in progress, house posts and medicinal plants that tell stories of more-than-human connections that were never understood as separate from the original peoples of this place to begin with.[19]

Perhaps we are learning to read for refusal or the resolve to persist. Paying close attention to the ability of others to continue and thrive in this heavily governed place with its histories of colonization feels like an achievement worth celebrating in a time of accelerated mass extinctions.[20] This is especially so in the case of creatures like the local black-tailed deer, who tend to be constructed

Figure 9.3 Reading for refusal.

as little more than an urban problem in need of fixing through a process that obscures histories of colonization that created the contemporary urban dynamics with which we must all now contend and attempt to craft more livable ways forward together.[21]

The way we notice together in early childhood contributes to understanding the places we live in as multispecies sites of coexistence versus human-only spaces. It also gives us a chance to learn through encounter and close observation with animals instead of projecting what we know about how, why and where they should live, thereby undermining the hierarchical so-called Great Chain of Being.

Given the challenges of living in these rapidly narrowing times, I have to ask myself what exactly I am advocating for through this method. What exactly are we orienting ourselves to in the process of tracking with young children? It is helpful here to think with Jenny Cameron in her call for researchers to

> [drop] the falsehood of neutral and objective research [in] "taking a stand" for certain worlds and for certain ways of living on the planet, and taking responsibility for helping to make these worlds more likely and these ways of living more widespread. ... An ethics of research in the Anthropocene therefore

means not just foregrounding the realities our research is helping to build, but also attending to how our research methods might help to bring these realities into being.[22]

In light of Cameron's words, it is important to remember that any attempt to measure the so-called success of our ongoing, seriously playful methodological experimentation must be understood as more than training innocent settler children's imaginations to go visiting on these colonized lands. The practice of tracking with young children also requires us to cultivate what Vinciane Despret and Michel Meuret,[23] following Hâche, refer to as the art of consequences. Through tracking engagements, we are committed to trying to orient ourselves and our early childhood practices to undo the myths of superiority and homogeneity so embedded through colonial relations in these Anthropocene times. Among other things, we are learning to read the responses of the land and its inhabitants to a rapidly changing world. Whose lands are we tracking on? We are looking for *otherwise stories*, those stories that draw us in while defying quantification, learning to read temporalities beyond the now of our own being here.[24] We are learning to read for refusal and resolve in the hopes that it will translate into new possibilities for sharing space with others in this place.

Notes

1 Karen Malone, Son Truong, and Tonia Gray, eds., *Reimagining Sustainability in Precarious Times* (Singapore: Springer, 2017); Fikile Nxumalo and Veronica Pacini-Ketchabaw, "'Staying with the Trouble' in Child-insect-educator Common Worlds," *Environmental Education Review* 23, no. 10 (2017): 1414–1426; Affrica Taylor, "Beyond Stewardship: Common World Pedagogies for the Anthropocene," *Environmental Education Review* 3, no. 10 (2017): 1448–1461.
2 Silvia Collado and Henk Staats, "Contact with Nature and Children's Restorative Experiences: An Eye to the Future," *Frontiers in Psychology: Environmental Psychology* 7 (2016): 1–6; Daniel T.C. Cox et al., "Doses of Neighborhood Nature: The Benefits for Mental Health of Living with Nature," *BioScience* 67, no. 2 (2017): 147–155; Richard Louv, *Last Child in the Woods*. New York: Algonquin Books of Chapel Hill, 2008.
3 Ursula K. Heise, *Imagining Extinction: The Cultural Meanings of Endangered Species* (Chicago: University of Chicago Press, 2016); Joshua Russell, "'Everything Has to Die One Day': Children's Explorations of the Meanings of Death in Human-animal-nature Relationships," *Environmental Education Research* 23, no. 10 (2016): 75–90.

4   Affrica Taylor, *Reconfiguring the Natures of Childhood* (New York: Routledge, 2013).
5   Donna J. Haraway, *Staying with the Trouble: Making Kin in the Chthulucene* (Durham, NC: Duke University Press, 2016); Taylor, "Beyond Stewardship," 1448–1461.
6   Anna L. Tsing, *The Mushroom at the End of the World: On the Possibility of Life in the Capitalist Ruins* (Princeton, NJ: Princeton University Press, 2015).
7   Haraway, *Staying with the Trouble*; Deborah Bird Rose, "In the Shadow of All This Death," in *Animal Death*, ed. Jay Johnston and Fiona Probyn-Rapsey (Sydney, Australia: Sydney University Press, 2013), 1–20; Tsing, *The Mushroom at the End of the World*.
8   Misha Myers, "'Walk with Me, Talk with Me': The Art of Conversive Wayfinding," *Visual Studies* 25, no. 1 (2010): 59.
9   Ibid., 67, drawing from Miller.
10 Veronica Pacini-Ketchabaw and Affrica Taylor, "Introduction," in *Unsettling the Colonial Places and Spaces of Early Childhood Education*, ed. Veronica Pacini-Ketchabaw and Affrica Taylor (New York: Routledge Taylor & Francis Group, 2015), 1–17.
11 Thom van Dooren and Deborah Bird Rose, "Storied Places in a Multispecies City," *Humanimalia: A Journal of Human/Animal Interface Studies* 3, no. 2 (2012): 1–27.
12 Tsing, *The Mushroom at the End of the World*; Haraway, *Staying with the Trouble*; Thom van Dooren, Eben Kirksey, and Ursula Münster, "Multispecies Studies: Cultivating the Arts of Attentiveness," *Environmental Humanities* 8, no. 1 (2016): 1.
13 Anna L. Tsing, "Arts of Inclusion, or, How to Love a Mushroom," *Australian Humanities Review* 50 (2011): 19.
14 Natasha Myers, "Ungrid-able Ecologies: Decolonizing the Ecological Sensorium in a 10,000-year-old NaturalCultural Happening," *Catalyst: Feminism, Theory, Technoscience* 3, no. 2 (2017): 1–24.
15 We did acquire a few BC animal tracking guides, Saanich ethnobotany, and west coast fungus guidebook to work with as the project progressed.
16 van Dooren and Rose, "Storied Places."
17 Thom van Dooren, *Flight Ways: Life and Loss at the Edge of Extinction* (New York: Columbia University Press, 2014).
18 Veronica Pacini-Ketchabaw, Affrica Taylor, Mindy Blaise, and Sandrina de Finney, "Learning How to Inherit in Colonized and Ecologically Challenged Lifeworlds: An Introduction," *Canadian Children* 40, no. 2 (2015): 3.
19 Pacini-Ketchabaw and Taylor, "Introduction."
20 Heise, *Imagining Extinction*; van Dooren, *Flight Ways*.
21 Veronica Pacini-Ketchabaw, "Postcolonial Entanglements: Unruling Stories," *Child & Youth Services* 33, nos. 3–4 (2012): 303–316.

22 Jenny Cameron, "On Experimentation," in *Manifesto for Living in the Anthropocene*, ed. Katherine Gibson, Deborah Bird Rose, and Ruth Fincher (Brooklyn, NY: Punctum Books, 2015), 100.
23 Vinciane Despret and Michel Meuret, "Cosmoecological Sheep and the Arts of Living on a Damaged Planet," *Environmental Humanities* 8, no. 1 (2016): 24–36.
24 van Dooren et al., "Multispecies Studies."

Bibliography

Cameron, Jenny. "On Experimentation." In *Manifesto for Living in the Anthropocene*, edited by Katherine Gibson, Deborah Bird Rose, and Ruth Fincher, 99–101. Brooklyn, NY: Punctum Books, 2015.

Collado, Silvia, and Henk Staats. "Contact with Nature and Children's Restorative Experiences: An Eye to the Future." *Frontiers in Psychology: Environmental Psychology* 7 (2016): 1–6.

Cox, Daniel T.C., Danielle F. Shanahan, Hannah L. Hudson, Kate E. Plummer, Gavin M. Siriwardena, Richard A. Fuller, Karen Anderson, Steven Hancock, and Kevin J. Gaston. "Doses of Neighborhood Nature: The Benefits for Mental Health of Living with Nature." *BioScience* 67, no. 2 (2017): 147–155.

Despret, Vinciane, and Michel Meuret. "Cosmoecological Sheep and the Arts of Living on a Damaged Planet." *Environmental Humanities* 8, no. 1 (2016): 24–36.

Haraway, Donna J. *Staying with the Trouble: Making Kin in the Chthulucene*. Durham, NC: Duke University Press, 2016.

Heise, Ursula K. *Imagining Extinction: The Cultural Meanings of Endangered Species*. Chicago: University of Chicago Press, 2016.

Louv, Richard. *Last Child in the Woods*. New York: Algonquin Books of Chapel Hill, 2008.

Malone, Karen, Son Truong, and Tonia Gray, eds. *Reimagining Sustainability in Precarious Times*. Singapore: Springer, 2017.

Myers, Misha. "'Walk with Me, Talk with Me': The Art of Conversive Wayfinding." *Visual Studies* 25, no. 1 (2010): 59–68.

Myers, Natasha. "Ungrid-able Ecologies: Decolonizing the Ecological Sensorium in a 10,000-year-old NaturalCultural Happening." *Catalyst: Feminism, Theory, Technoscience* 3, no. 2 (2017): 1–24.

Nxumalo, Fikile, and Veronica Pacini-Ketchabaw. "'Staying with the Trouble' in Child-insect-educator Common Worlds." *Environmental Education Review* 23, no. 10 (2017): 1414–1426.

Pacini-Ketchabaw, Veronica. "Postcolonial Entanglements: Unruling Stories." *Child & Youth Services* 33, nos. 3–4 (2012): 303–316.

Pacini-Ketchabaw, Veronica, and Affrica Taylor. "Introduction." In *Unsettling the Colonial Places and Spaces of Early Childhood Education*, edited by Veronica Pacini-

Ketchabaw and Affrica Taylor, 1–17. New York: Routledge Taylor & Francis Group, 2015.

Pacini-Ketchabaw, Veronica, Affrica Taylor, and Mindy Blaise. "Decentring the Human in Multispecies Ethnographies." In *Posthuman Research Practices in Education*, edited by Carol A. Taylor and Cristina Hughes, 149–167. London: Palgrave Macmillan, 2016.

Pacini-Ketchabaw, Veronica, Affrica Taylor, Mindy Blaise, and Sandrina de Finney. "Learning How to Inherit in Colonized and Ecologically Challenged Lifeworlds: An Introduction." *Canadian Children* 40, no. 2 (2015): 3–8.

Rose, Deborah Bird. "In the Shadow of All This Death." In *Animal Death*, edited by Jay Johnston and Fiona Probyn-Rapsey, 1–20. Sydney, Australia: Sydney University Press, 2013.

Russell, Joshua. "'Everything Has to Die One Day:' Children's Explorations of the Meanings of Death in Human-animal-nature Relationships." *Environmental Education Research* 23, no. 10 (2016): 75–90.

Taylor, Affrica. "Beyond Stewardship: Common World Pedagogies for the Anthropocene." *Environmental Education Review* 3, no. 10 (2017): 1448–1461.

Taylor, Affrica. *Reconfiguring the Natures of Childhood*. New York: Routledge, 2013.

Tsing, Anna Lowenhaupt. "Arts of Inclusion, or, How to Love a Mushroom." *Australian Humanities Review* 50 (2011): 5–22.

Tsing, Anna Lowenhaupt. *The Mushroom at the End of the World: On the Possibility of Life in the Capitalist Ruins*. Princeton, NJ: Princeton University Press, 2015.

van Dooren, Thom. *Flight Ways: Life and Loss at the Edge of Extinction*. New York: Columbia University Press, 2014.

van Dooren, Thom, and Deborah Bird Rose. "Storied Places in a Multispecies City." *Humanimalia: A Journal of Human/Animal Interface Studies* 3, no. 2 (2012): 1–27.

van Dooren, Thom, Eben Kirksey, and Ursula Münster. "Multispecies Studies: Cultivating the Arts of Attentiveness." *Environmental Humanities* 8, no. 1 (2016): 1–23.

10

Rabbiting: Troubling the Legacies of Invasion

Affrica Taylor

The parklands area of the Australian National University campus where we walk with the children is right on the edge of Canberra's central business district. This is Ngunnawal country.[1] Before colonization, and before the city was built, eastern gray kangaroos grazed on the native grasses and sheltered under the box gum trees. Today, this remnant native grassy woodland urban area is registered as a threatened ecological community and is heritage-listed for conservation.[2] Wild European rabbits have replaced kangaroos as the dominant grazing species. Along with surrounding urban human settlement, it is now rabbits that pose the greatest threat to this native grassy woodlands ecological community.

First tale: Spotting rabbits

"Look! Quick! There's one." "Where?" "It's running away from us." "See that little thing bobbing up and down? Now it's gone." "I can see one over there. It's heading for that tree." "We saw bunnies!" "Hey everyone, we saw two bunnies!"

Rabbit spotting is one of the children's favorite walking activities. These small, shy animals are fast and elusive. When disturbed, they dash off and hide in the long tussock grasses or run down their burrows. So, for the children, it is a compelling challenge to get a good look at the rabbits, and any fleeting sighting is worthy of acclaim. As well as spotting actual rabbits, the children also like to spot rabbit clues. These are abundant. Rabbit scratchings, burrows, and large piles of poo are a ubiquitous feature of the landscape, marking and reshaping it on a seemingly daily basis. The children have become so accustomed to these burgeoning rabbit signs that they've become quite blasé about them. "Another rabbit toilet," they commonly chant, in ho-hum tones, as they walk along.

They were not blasé when they spotted their first dead rabbit, lying next to a burrow. The children solemnly gathered around to inspect it at close quarters. The body was completely intact, so at first they maintained hope: "Maybe it's just asleep?" Despite a gradual realization that the rabbit was indeed dead, the children still seemed moved by its apparent vulnerability. It was inclement weather and the body was exposed to the elements. They were worried about leaving it there all alone. "He might get all wet," one child mused as she and the others looked down at the small, still body.

After this first encounter, stumbling across dead rabbits quickly became a regular occurrence, prompting us to wonder what was going on. The children started speculating: "Maybe a fox grabbed the bunny and pulled out its fur, and then picked it up and ran over here and killed it. But it didn't eat it all, and it ran away down there."

As these grisly dead rabbit spottings became increasingly frequent, a number of children were drawn to closely inspect the decaying bodies or body parts. They seemed to be gaining the kind of confidence that comes from familiar curiosity. "I can see where its eyes were." "I can see its nose. Its nose is peeled." They noted how the fur quickly falls off the rabbits' bodies, exposing the skin and muscles underneath. They set about identifying the different kinds of exposed bones. They used magnifying glasses to closely inspect inside the body cavities and noticed that worms and bugs were often eating the remains. Despite their forensic interest in the decomposition process, the children did not forget that these remains belonged to previously living beings. They punctuated their examinations with spontaneous expressions of sadness and sympathy, such as: "I'm sorry this happen to you, bunny."[3]

Rabbiting

The term *rabbiting* is part of the Australian bush vernacular. It literally means "killing rabbits" and is a state-sanctioned national pastime in rural Australia. The rabbiting saga began in the mid-19th century, when settler gentry imported and released a handful of wild European rabbits to establish the popular British gentlemen's sport of hunting in the Antipodes. The project did not turn out as anticipated. Without predators, wild rabbits quickly multiplied and spread across the continent. They ate every blade of grass in sight, triggering a cascade of native species extinctions. Notwithstanding that Indigenous Australians regard white settlers as invaders and that it was the white settler-invaders who brought the rabbits with them, the indisputable environmental damage caused by the rabbits has since earned them the status of the key invasive species. It has also justified a retaliative settler war against feral rabbits that is ongoing to this day. The invasive rabbit legacy, with all its inherent ironies, is one of the significant settler colonial messes that contemporary Australian children inherit.

Rabbiting can be seen as an exemplar of separation, mastery and control. This is the sequence of delusionary Euro-Western man-over-nature fantasies that environmental philosophers Val Plumwood and Deborah Bird Rose closely associate with white settler colonial beliefs, actions and legacies in the Australian context.[4] Rabbiting requires white settlers (as environmental stewards) to distance themselves from rabbits (as invaders) in order to carry out the violent measures needed to eradicate them. Kate Wright points out that Australian children are a target audience for the eco-nationalist narratives that accompany and rationalize the "redemptive violence" involved in systematically slaughtering rabbits. These narratives seek to convince children that "rabbit love is inappropriate because it conflicts with ecological politics."[5] In other words, Australian children inherit a very troubling settler rabbiting legacy. In direct contrast to the predominantly lovable portrayal of rabbits in European children's popular culture, Australia's settler eco-nationalist popular culture encourages children to dissociate from and ultimately hate invading rabbits in order to prove their love for their country.[6]

Second tale: Becoming rabbits

The children would love to pursue the rabbits when they scurry into the patches of native tussock and lomandra grasses that conceal their warrens. But in summer, the ever-present risk of treading on a snake precludes them from venturing into these thick grasses. So, when the weather cools down and we are sure that the snakes have all hibernated, the children are keen to inspect the rabbits' grassy abodes. They find lots of burrows, scratchings, and droppings secreted throughout, but the rabbits are nowhere to be seen.

Although the children never manage to see live rabbits close up, as soon as they can immerse themselves in the tussock grasses where the rabbits live, they imagine that they are rabbits. This is one of their favorite games. Crouching down in the long grasses, they smell the same grassy smells that the rabbits presumably smell. Pushing their way through the thick tufts, they feel the same friction of spiky grass on their bodies that the rabbits presumably feel. Ensconced in thick, grassy rabbit worlds, they spontaneously become rabbits: hopping around, sitting up on their haunches, twitching their noses and smelling the breeze, simulating nibbling on grass and doing rabbit poos. "Look, I'm a camouflaged rabbit. I'm camouflaged in the grass," *a child calls out, encouraging others to join in. They seem to be trying to get as close as they can to a full sensory embodiment of rabbitness.*

At some point during the year, and in response to the children's growing interest in rabbits, the preschool teacher decided that it was time to introduce the children to a controversial picture book called *The Rabbits*.⁷ This is an allegorical fable about the colonization of Australia. Originally written for older readers, the colonization narrative is categorically structured around the binary of good indigenes and bad foreign invaders. The rabbits are the evil protagonists. They represent the British settler colonizers as invaders and environmental destroyers. The narrator numbats (small marsupials) are meek and innocent. They represent the colonized indigenes who witness from the sidelines with horror as the rabbits destroy their country and steal their children.

We cannot be sure whether or not it was a coincidence, but sometime after reading this book, we noticed a shift in the tone of the children's rabbit play. A group of children transformed into "killer rabbits" that "like eating people." They took to using a weeping acacia tree as their "hideout" from which to plot and execute high-spirited ambushes on adults. Rather than violent, however, the repeated raids of the "carnivore rabbits" were marked by loud and excited laughter.

Grappling

In the Australian settler colonial context, child-rabbit relations are far from straightforward and innocent. This is simply because non-Indigenous Australian children and rabbits are already entangled and co-implicated in messy invasive colonial legacies. Our walks in the grassy woodlands have incrementally uncovered the troubling mess of this inheritance. Once unveiled, the pressing question becomes how best to deal with this trouble. We are cognizant of the increasing pressures on the children to distance themselves from rabbits and thereby disidentify with the invasive and destructive forces of colonization. We realize that expectations are often made that children will align themselves as future environmental stewards and may well be tasked to "save us from the rabbits."⁸

No matter how noble the intentions, heroic white settler stewardship requires us to perform some kind of separation, mastery and control. The children did not do this. We observed how, instead of rehearsing an exonerating and/or vindicating "goodies and baddies" script, the children continued to grapple with the troubling legacies of rabbit invasion, with all their contradictory pushes and pulls. This grappling was expressed through the ways in which they sought connection with the rabbits, even as they were trying to come to terms with the dawning realization that rabbits have a destructive impact on the Australian environment.

The children's grapplings evoke Donna Haraway's urging that we must learn how to inherit by "staying with the trouble" and working in tandem with other species, toward a modest form of recuperation.[9] Staying with the trouble stands in stark contrast to the conceit and folly of seeking ultimate or final "humans-to-the-rescue" solutions. Rather than seeking such heroic solutions, the children's grapplings perform a kind of ongoing relational ethics that includes more-than-human others within the ethical domain. They remind me of the "multispecies ethics of conviviality" that Thom van Dooren and Deborah Bird Rose advocate as they call for more inclusive and respectful ways of living in our increasingly multispecies cities.[10] And finally, the children's ongoing rabbit grapplings exemplify what Rose refers to, in the specifically settler colonial Australian context, as a much-needed "decolonising ethics" for a "wild country."[11]

Third tale: Staying with the rabbits

In light of the children's deepening rabbit relations and grapplings, we decided to take them to the "Rabbits in Australia" exhibition at the National Museum of Australia. It's just down the road from the center. No sooner had we set off, buffeted by strong, cold winds, than we came across a sodden rabbit head in the middle of the footpath. It was an uncanny and foreboding sign. The children broke out in a nervous, rhythmic chant: "Dead bunny head, dead bunny head."

The chilling mood of this unnerving encounter was echoed inside the museum exhibition. Although the museum claims to be representing the diversity of relationships that Australians have had with wild rabbits since European settlement, the children were instantly transfixed by the displays featuring the numerous ways that settler have killed rabbits, for instance, by fumigating, ripping and dynamiting burrows; shooting, poisoning and trapping rabbits; and releasing rabbit calicivirus. From their shocked facial expressions and many incredulous questions, it was clear that they were completely taken aback by all the emphasis on killing, although some also expressed curiosity about how the killing technologies worked. The rabbit traps and poisoned carrots held a particular, grim fascination. The images that revealed the sheer volume of rabbits killed in the ongoing wars waged against them made a huge impression on the children. However, even as the artifactual evidence that millions and millions of rabbits had been killed came across loud and clear, the children struggled to understand why.

Their attention eventually turned to the imposing neon map of Australia up on the wall: the "invasive species" display. They watched it light up in red to show the rapid spread of rabbits across the continent. This seemed to help them register the scale of the rabbit problem. "There's a lot of rabbits in Australia, yeah" and "Whoa! Rabbits all along Australia!" they exclaimed. However, despite our attempts at explaining the ecological rationale behind this "invasive species" display—there were too many rabbits, they were eating all the grass, and this meant that other creatures could not survive and the rabbits needed to be culled—the children's overwhelming sympathy remained with the rabbits.

The final straw came as they clustered around a small screen, watching an early-20th-century documentary ominously entitled Menace of the Rabbit. *The children were aghast at the sight of thousands of frightened and defenseless rabbits being slaughtered and skinned. "Poor bunnies," they kept repeating over and over, and "that's so horrible," "that's not fair for the rabbits." To the children, these horrifying images only served to confirm the impressions they had gained from the entire museum experience. It was the people who were the menacing threat, not the rabbits. They had had enough of it.*

They told us so in no uncertain terms the next time we met. They had been mulling over things they had seen "in the olden days" at the museum. They admitted that they felt scared watching the rabbits being killed. Their own feelings of vulnerability reinforced their empathy for the rabbits, even though they also accepted that too many rabbits cause problems for the environment. They seemed to be able to grasp and hold the deeply ecological understanding that all living beings are both dependent on and vulnerable to each other. In visceral and affective ways, they apprehend that we cannot be separated off—no matter how wild the invasive colonial legacies we are grappling with.

Notes

1 The local Aboriginal people belong to the Ngunnawal language group. Like their ancestors, they are the traditional custodians of this part of the country.
2 Australian National University Services, "Old Canberra House Remnant Grassy Woodlands," https://services.anu.edu.au/planning-governance/project-management/old-canberra-house-remnant-grassy-woodlands.

3   The italicized tales in this chapter are taken from children's encounters with rabbits during the "Walking with Wildlife in Wild Weather Times" project in 2016. This is a common worlds ethnographic research project conducted by Tonya Rooney (Australian Catholic University) and myself with children from the University Preschool and Childcare Centre at the Australian National University. For more information on this project and our multispecies walking method, see the Common Worlds Research Collective, http://commonworlds.net/portfolio_page/walking-with-wildlife-in-wild-weather-times/.
    For more detailed accounts of the tales recounted here, see the project blog *Walking with Wildlife in Wild Weather Times*, https://walkingwildlifewildweather.com/.
4   Val Plumwood, *Feminism and the Mastery of Nature* (London: Routledge, 1993) and Deborah Bird Rose, *Reports from a Wild Country: Ethics for Decolonisation* (Sydney: UNSW Press, 2004).
5   Kate Wright, *Transdisciplinary Journeys in the Anthropocene: More-than-human Encounters* (New York: Routledge, 2017), 126–127.
6   For a detailed analysis of Australian and Canadian eco-nationalist children's literature and popular culture, see Affrica Taylor and Veronica Pacini-Ketchabaw, *Children and Animals: Common World Ethics for Entangled Lives* (London: Routledge, 2018).
7   John Marsden and Shaun Tan (illustrator), *The Rabbits* (Sydney: Lothian, 1998).
8   "Who will save us from the rabbits?" is the concluding question in *The Rabbits*.
9   Donna J. Haraway, *Staying with the Trouble: Making Kin in the Cthulucene* (Durham, NC: Duke University Press, 2016).
10 Thom van Dooren and Deborah Bird Rose, "Storied Places in a Multispecies City," *Humanimalia: A Journal of Human/Animal Interface Studies* 3, no. 2 (2012): 1–27.
11 Rose, *Reports from a Wild Country*.

Bibliography

Australian National University Services. "Old Canberra House Remnant Grassy Woodlands." https://services.anu.edu.au/planning-governance/project-management/old-canberra-house-remnant-grassy-woodlands.

Common Worlds Research Collective. "Walking with Wildlife in Wild Weather Times." http://commonworlds.net/portfolio_page/walking-with-wildlife-in-wild-weather-times/.

Haraway, Donna J. *Staying with the Trouble: Making Kin in the Cthulucene*. Durham, NC: Duke University Press, 2016.

Marsden, John. *The Rabbits*, illustrated by Shaun Tan. Sydney: Lothian, 1998.

Plumwood, Val. *Feminism and the Mastery of Nature*. London: Routledge, 1993.

Rose, Deborah Bird. *Reports from a Wild Country: Ethics for Decolonisation.* Sydney: UNSW Press, 2004.

Taylor, Affrica, and Veronica Pacini-Ketchabaw. *Children and Animals: Common World Ethics for Entangled Lives.* London: Routledge, 2018.

Taylor, Affrica, and Tonya Rooney. "Walking with Wildlife in Wild Weather Times" blog. https://walkingwildlifewildweather.com/.

van Dooren, Thom, and Deborah Bird Rose. "Storied Places in a Multispecies City." *Humanimalia: A Journal of Human/Animal Interface Studies* 3, no. 2 (2012): 1–27.

Wright, Kate. *Transdisciplinary Journeys in the Anthropocene: More-than-human Encounters.* New York: Routledge, 2017.

Part Three

Relations with Place

11

Gathering: An A/r/tographic Practice

Vanessa Clark

Many objects cross my path along my walk and grab my attention. Gathering is a laborious way of connecting to art materials.[1] I stop to pick up small, unwanted objects, objects that have been discarded, lost, stored, hidden, misplaced by people, trees and animals. I am gripped by the unknown worlds of these objects—bits of a pink plastic balloon, a used orange plastic spoon, a half-eaten chestnut. This chapter offers an a/r/tographic practice called *gathering* as a way to practice art, as a way to research and as a way to teach in preservice early childhood care and education. Just as my art practice as research was a gathering where I walked and picked up objects and ideas, this chapter is also an a/r/tographic enactment of gathering: a crafted, nonlinear composition of photographs, stories and ideas that act together and do unpredictable new things together.

I hold a black cloth bag in my hand as I slowly walk around the city where I teach future early childhood educators at a university located in the unceded and ancestral multinational territories of the Coast Salish peoples, including Tsleil-Waututh, Skwxwú7mesh, shíshálh, Lil'Wat, and Musqueam Nations. My a/r/tographic practice grows out of urgent concerns about imperial and settler colonialism in this particular place/space-time. While walking, I see that the ground beneath my feet is constantly changing. The cracked gray cement sidewalk gives way to golden dry grass and flaked red earth. Twigs and dried leaves snap and crunch under my feet as I step onto a brown woodchip path. Soon my path turns to pebbles and stones. These changing grounds tell me of hundreds of years of struggle and conquest, including, for example, the city workers pouring sidewalks to contain nature, the water eroding the cement paths, and the struggles of moss growing in the cracked cement. There is nowhere innocent for me to stand, nowhere for me to hide or escape.[2] These grounds locate me as a white settler—a replacement of the many Indigenous people who had to die for me to be here.[3]

There is an extensive body of writing on imperialism[4] and settler colonialism.[5] In this chapter, I gather inconsumable ideas from this literature, like the objects I gather on my walks, and entangle them through my art and teaching practices to study the mess of imperial and settler colonialism in early childhood inclusive teacher education in Canada. I have endeavored to engage with the rich and sophisticated literature, lectures, talks, and art and museum exhibits of Indigenous peoples and communities. These works, as I explored them with my students in a thirteen-week course on inclusive group settings in early childhood education,[6] raised complex possible/impossible issues, questions and ideas for inclusive practice. The central question and struggle raised in my a/r/tographic practice of gathering during my walks and in my teaching was the very possibility of inclusion and belonging. And, if inclusion is possible, then inclusion for whom, into what and by whom?

(re)Assembling renderings and methods

The days are getting colder, and it is harder to get outside. The ground is frozen and the dirt crunches under my feet as I walk. The ice makes it harder to pick up individual objects. Bending, with my arms stretched out, I tug at a leaf and a whole clump comes together. Precision seems to be impossible when working against the weather.

Within the last two years prior to teaching inclusive practice, I entered into a *living inquiry*. Stephanie Springgay, Rita Irwin and Sylvia Kind articulate six *renderings* for enacting research: contiguity, living inquiry, metaphor and metonym, openings, reverberations and excess.[7] A rendering is an opening, a way of entering into and moving through artistic research. In their words, "renderings are not methods. They are not lists of verbs initiated to create an arts-based or a/r/tographical study. Renderings are theoretical spaces through which to explore artistic ways of knowing and being research."[8] To render allows for an engagement with research in this chapter that is in process—to show the actions, situations and doings of figuring it out (as opposed to showing only the finished product).

While I am interested only in living inquiry for the purposes of this chapter, that rendering is frozen to the other renderings, several ideas and roots. In order to pick up living inquiry, the rendering of metaphor comes with it, and the frozen connections are broken. Although at the time of my gathering I did not realize I gathered reverberations, it was stuck to another rendering and went into my bag, and only later in my research did it appear again. In picking up living inquiry, I tear off the word *living*. Perhaps the idea of living inquiry dishonors those who are not living, in the Western binary sense of living and dead. From this point forward, I refer to living inquiry simply as inquiry.

This inquiry requires that I engage my art and teaching practice as "a philosophical space of inquiry."[9] Linda Tuhiwai Smith asserts that the West compartmentalizes space into "architectural space, physical space, psychological space, theoretical space, and so forth."[10] Here I endeavor to resist compartmentalizing these spaces. Specifically, an art and teaching practice of gathering involves several theoretical actions: Walking. Listening. Stopping. Bending. Stretching. Touching. Holding. Analyzing. Responding. Picking up. Dropping. Assembling. Meeting. Removing. Dislodging. Dislocating. Crunching. Squishing. Cracking. Snapping.

While gathering as an art and teaching practice is more than a method, it requires methods. Over the months, I picked up several materials that allowed for different methods: a black cloth bag that allowed me to carry the objects I picked up; different texts, including Rachelle Clifford and Eve Tuck and Wayne Yang,[11] which gave me terrain to read/walk; a camera to document images; and a journal and pen for writing stories. My teaching intent was not to invite early childhood education students to reproduce my conception of gathering but instead to offer them materials and methods from my conception of gathering to make their own.

According to John Law, one premise of realism in social sciences is that it assumes that the real is tidy and organized. Instead, he suggests that methods might try to be disciplined in their research of mess.[12] If we recognize that imperial and settler colonial worlds are a mess, then gathering might be a way to engage well with the concern. Gathering with a bag might be a way to study the mess. It creates the conditions for meetings among ideas, matters and objects that may be logically divided, and it produces effects from their relationalities that are unpredictable and risky.

My bag as a meeting place / space-time

Gathering is not the same as mixing or combining. Gathering keeps matters separate, whereas mixing makes one substance. Just because matters remain separate, however, does not mean they do not change. The inconsumable objects are taken out of the contexts where they were dropped, and they have been altered in many ways through being picked up and carried in my bag. When I pick up objects and put them in my bag, sometimes they crack, squish, snap or break. My bag is like a meeting place[13]/ space-time where objects rub against one another, and sometimes they grind.

I hear their noises from my bag as I walk. Together, objects communicate something different than they do alone. Gathering requires attention to this change and to the way in which the objects are placed together. Gathering requires ethics to consider with early childhood students what objects we remove (e.g., as a settler, sometimes it is important to leave empty-handed), how objects are held and placed together, and what is produced from their meetings. Importantly, gathering is not in our control, and with gathering comes both possibility and risk of what gathers us and how objects come together.

I was curious how the students would gather and how I would gather with them. What conditions were created that called attention to certain objects and ideas? What ideas and objects would gather students and which would come to matter in their worlds? Where would they walk to gather ideas and objects, and how would they pick them up? What would be dropped and left behind? What and how would students gather together?

Gathering as a place / space-time-specific art practice

Over the semester in the inclusive practice course, the students and I met in various places on and around campus and went on walks together. While walking, I often ask: "Where am I?" In response to Eve Tuck and Marcia McKenzie's important call for social science researchers to engage with place beyond a surface on which research is conducted,[14] here along the way I engage with place/space-time through art. While walking out from Waterfront Station onto West Cordova Street into downtown Vancouver, we are emplaced within a set of historical connections and relations to the city, to the name of the city, to the cement roads and sidewalks beneath our feet. I take up Doreen Massey's, Linda Tuhiwai Smith's and Jodi Byrd's articulations of place and space-time as inextricably linked in that the global scale relates to the local through European planetary conquest, including the complex multi-Nation territories that used to be here and the city that has grown up through the manufacturing of cement and the construction of roads.[15] We often drive these roads to get to school, to the childcare center, to the forest and so forth. The "roads, and their development, through surveying, building, naming, and mapping"[16] have created new insides to the Canadian state in relation to the outsides (e.g., the moss growing through the cracks in the cement) that continue to threaten the state's legitimacy.

But I wonder what other places might be here? What boundaries might shift in the remaking of insides and outsides? Places also stretch beyond fixed histories and identities and are thus porous and unfixed.[17]

We also met at the Museum of Vancouver and went to the exhibit *cəsnaʔəm, the city before the city*, where we explored the Musqueam city and territory, as told by the Musqueam people. Pauline created the portfolio entry in Figure 11.1, and it shows the Musqueam's ancestral and cosmological layer, *cəsnaʔəm*, the ontological roots of the city before the city of Vancouver. It is in this potentiality, perhaps, that this place is unfixed, where there is hope to account for dispossession and for us in early childhood care and education to imagine other forms of belonging in inclusive practice that do not continue Indigenous peoples' disappearance.[18]

Another time we met on campus, and several groups of students decided to go into the forest. The students attended to the trees—in particular, the fallen trees and stumps—as landmarks. They noticed a tree stump rotting that was becoming a nurse tree to another tree. The students opened up possibilities for engaging with trees, their decomposition and their life-giving gestures of nursing. I asked the students to draw a map of their walk, take a picture of their map (e.g., see Figure 11.2) and paste their map's image into their portfolio.

On their walk through the forest, the students made several stops. Their final meeting place was a fallen tree, and students climbed and balanced on it. Morgan wrote,

> As we ventured into the forest, we split up into different groups. Water covered the earth and made the ground slippery. Plants and branches crunch beneath our feet. The canopy provides protection from the rain. Though we took different directions, we ended up in the same place. We help each other balance on the fallen tree.

The students' short walk, what they noticed and the different relationalities with trees offered ideas and possibilities for ways of being together. They found their way with the fallen trees and stumps and supported one another to balance on them. The students explored theories in/through/with their bodies.

Figure 11.1 Portfolio layer.

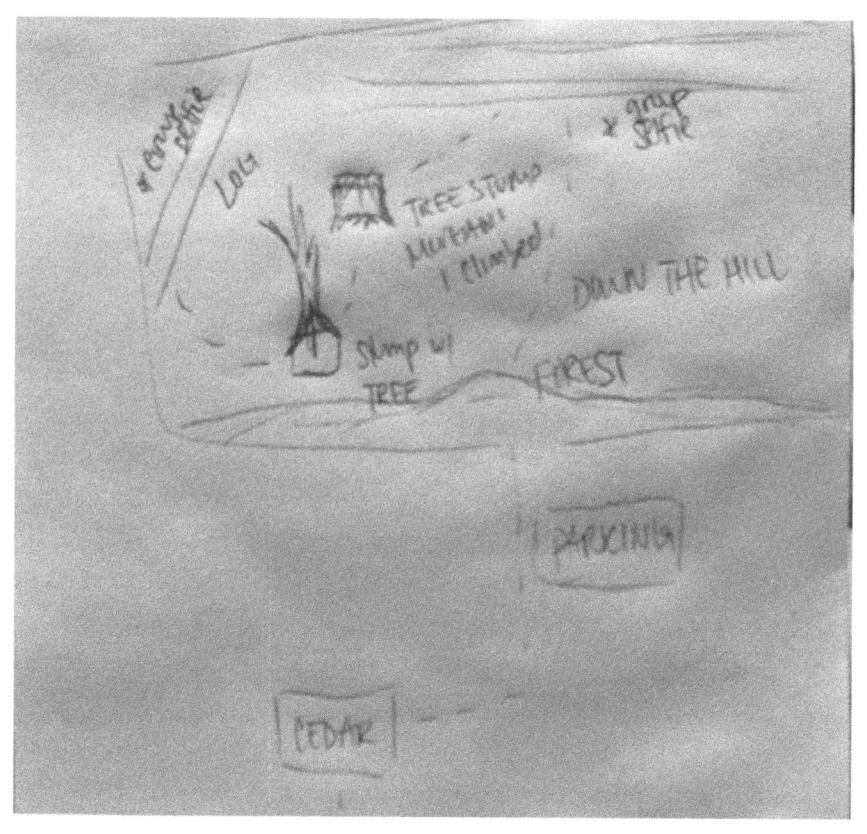

Figure 11.2 Map of walk.

Teaching as gathering

Gathering has allowed me to explore what I call rebodying in teaching. This rebodying includes, for example, the intelligence and logics of walking the earth, the curiosity of hands meeting objects, the knowing of feet on the ground, the questioning of reaching, the bending of arms and legs over tree stumps, the holding of matters of concern in the heart, the guts to walk down certain paths, the ethics it takes to decide when and how to pick up certain ideas and when and how to let others drop, the importance of feeding the spirit. The pedagogical practice of rebodying through gathering allows for attunement to the relational processes and embodied situations of engaging theories. It creates small conditions for moments where communities explore the responsibilities and obligations of walking, balancing and thinking together.

Figure 11.3 Gathering of photographs.

Jungsun, Nina, Maggie, Mingying and Ryan, students in the program, created Figure 11.3 from photographs they took on their walks throughout the course. The gathering in Figure 11.3 speaks to a process of teaching and learning. Together the photos produce a larger, complex, layered picture provoked by an assignment that asked students to create pedagogical responses to a selected concern—in this case, students selected the concern of multiculturalism. After the photograph above was taken, the students disassembled the photos. The "big picture" is a trace of an impermanent assemblage of photos that are contextual and temporal. Perhaps Figure 11.3 speaks to education and learning as collective, situated and temporary. Temporary, but lingering. Perhaps we may together touch on the big picture and hold on to a trace of it before it comes apart. Figure 11.3 might suggest a particular approach to teaching and learning in inclusive practice, both postsecondary and early childhood, inspired by gathering.

Gathering, as an a/r/tographic practice, might offer a way to study and imperfectly respond to ongoing colonial legacies in inclusive practice as it begins to explore the potentials of an ethics of relating differently to things, theories, places and each other in teaching and learning.

Notes

1. Rachelle Clifford, "My Grandfather the Cedar My Grandmother the Wool," MA thesis, Emily Carr University of Art + Design, Vancouver, BC, 2010.
2. Jodi Byrd, *Transits of Empire: Indigenous Critiques of Colonialism* (Minneapolis: University of Minnesota Press, 2011).
3. Scott Morgensen, *Spaces between Us: Queer Settler Colonialism and Indigenous Decolonization* (Minneapolis: University of Minnesota Press, 2011).
4. For example, Linda Tuhiwai Smith, *Decolonizing Methodologies: Research and Indigenous Peoples*, 2nd ed. (London: Zed Books, 2012); Byrd, *Transits of Empire*.
5. For example, Kelly Black, "Localizing Settler Colonialism" (video), 13 March 2016; Byrd, *Transits of Empire*; Sandrina de Finney, "'We Just Don't Know Each Other': Racialised Girls Negotiate Mediated Multiculturalism in a Less Diverse Canadian City," *Journal of Intercultural Studies* 31, no. 5 (2010): 471–487; Eve Tuck and Wayne Yang, "Decolonization Is Not a Metaphor," *Decolonization: Indigeneity, Education, and Society* 1, no. 1 (2012): 1–40.
6. Within the field of early childhood education, "inclusive" has a particular understanding that does not typically reach to the concern of settler colonialism.
7. Stephanie Springgay, Rita Irwin, and Sylvia Kind, "A/r/tography as Living Inquiry through Art and Text," *Qualitative Inquiry* 11, no. 6 (2005): 897–912.
8. Ibid., 899.
9. Stephanie Springgay, "Inside the Visible: Youth Understandings of Body Knowledge through Touch," PhD diss., University of British Columbia, 2004, 43.
10. Smith, *Decolonizing Methodologies*, 53.
11. Clifford, "My Grandfather the Cedar"; Tuck and Yang, "Decolonization Is Not a Metaphor."
12. John Law, *Making a Mess with Method*, http://www.lancaster.ac.uk/fass/resources/sociology-online-papers/papers/law-making-a-mess-with-method.pdf.
13. Doreen Massey, *Space, Place, and Gender* (Minneapolis: University of Minnesota Press, 1994).
14. Eve Tuck and Marcia McKenzie, *Place in Research: Theory, Methodology, and Methods* (New York: Routledge, 2014).
15. Massey, *Space, Place, and Gender*; Smith, *Decolonizing Methodologies*; Byrd, *Transits of Empire*.
16. Black, "Localizing Settler Colonialism."
17. Massey, *Space, Place, and Gender*; Smith, *Decolonizing Methodologies*; Byrd, *Transits of Empire*.
18. Black, "Localizing Settler Colonialism."

Bibliography

Black, Kelly. "Localizing Settler Colonialism." Video. 13 March 2016. https://www.youtube.com/watch?v=xFbJb8FvyU8.

Byrd, Jodi. *Transits of Empire: Indigenous Critiques of Colonialism*. Minneapolis: University of Minnesota Press, 2011.

Clifford, Rachelle. "My Grandfather the Cedar My Grandmother the Wool." MA thesis, Emily Carr University of Art + Design, Vancouver, BC, 2010. http://content.lib.sfu.ca/cdm/ref/collection/ecuths/id/2908.

de Finney, Sandrina. "'We Just Don't Know Each Other': Racialised Girls Negotiate Mediated Multiculturalism in a Less Diverse Canadian City." *Journal of Intercultural Studies* 31, no. 5 (2010): 471–487. doi:10.1080/07256868.2010.513082.

Law, John. *Making a Mess with Method*. Last modified 20 December 2003. http://www.lancaster.ac.uk/fass/resources/sociology-online-papers/papers/law-making-a-mess-with-method.pdf.

Massey, Doreen. *Space, Place, and Gender*. Minneapolis: University of Minnesota Press, 1994.

Morgensen, Scott. *Spaces between Us: Queer Settler Colonialism and Indigenous Decolonization*. Minneapolis: University of Minnesota Press, 2011.

Smith, Linda Tuhiwai. *Decolonizing Methodologies: Research and Indigenous Peoples*. 2nd ed. London: Zed Books, 2012.

Springgay, Stephanie. "Inside the Visible: Youth Understandings of Body Knowledge through Touch." PhD diss., University of British Columbia, 2004. http://m2.edcp.educ.ubc.ca/artog/data/phd/SPRINGGAY.pdf.

Springgay, Stephanie, Rita Irwin, and Sylvia Kind. "A/r/tography as Living Inquiry through Art and Text." *Qualitative Inquiry* 11, no. 6 (2005): 897–912.

Tuck, Eve, and Marcia McKenzie. *Place in Research: Theory, Methodology, and Methods*. New York: Routledge, 2014.

Tuck, Eve, and Wayne Yang. "Decolonization Is Not a Metaphor." *Decolonization: Indigeneity, Education, and Society* 1, no. 1 (2012): 1–40.

12

Mashing: A Practice That Makes Vision Felt

Nikki Rotas

Within this chapter[1] I explore the use of wearable cameras in educational research and offer a proposition that reenvisions the mobile camera, body and image as an entanglement of more-than-representational thought. I borrow María Puig de la Bellacasa's concept of *touching visions*[2] to attend to the affective dimensions of imaging (and/or data making), subjectivity making and movement in feminist postqualitative educational research. I ask if and how moving images alter the child's perceptions in ways that disrupt marginalizing discourses of disengaged children in urban schools. Questions I pose include these: What does the camera-body-image entanglement make possible? In what ways does embodied perception affect thinking and what is in turn thought? Attending to these questions, I introduce *mashing* as a pedagogical practice that grapples with perception. I discuss how the practice of mashing activates new movements of thought that are possible among subjects, objects and environments.

Feminist concerns with affect and the intimacies of subjectivity making, as well as the classic feminist practice of *reclaiming*, have tirelessly worked to open up visions to possibilities that are not out there to be found.[3] Instead visions of a future that have not yet become require the simultaneous movement of making and unmaking. This future time must bear the labor of past and present visions that have historically excluded raced, classed, sexed and more-than-human bodies. Getting messy, mashing things up and *staying with the hot compost*[4] pile of waste that humans have had a heavy hand in making—whether acknowledged or not—is the massive task of worlds, communities, schools and families. The hot compost pile that feminist thinker Donna Haraway describes is not to be understood as a metaphor, but rather as a proposition for collective thought and multiple visions of what living in more-than-human worlds might become. Staying with the hot compost pile is also about staying with the mess of environmental destruction and exclusionary practices that violently persist—such violence cannot be wished away.

Whether or not humans are up for the task of desiring their own hot mess is a speculative thought and provocation that requires difference in education, research, teaching and learning. What is necessary in these intersecting and messy worlds of climate, environment and curriculum expectations are new relations that are open to situated and multiple visions that do not exclude the nonhuman, and rather attend to the materiality of visions that cannot be grasped in the form of "brute data."[5] The compost pile's heat is felt, and as I argue below, one of many ways to stay with the hot compost that children have inherited is to approach teaching and learning through embodied visions of affect and movement. I conclude this chapter making note of Spinozist ethics and how it resonates with Haraway's call for collective thought and action in times of hot mess.

Embodied visions (of curriculum)

Integrating environmental science, technology and arts-based curriculum, the year-long research project that I draw on in this chapter was enacted with grade 2 and grade 3 students in an urban elementary school in Toronto, Canada. Twenty-two students aged 7 and 8 wore small, durable action cameras during research events and/or practices throughout the school day. Wearing the cameras on their back, chest, head and wrist, students, teachers and researcher created embodied visions of curriculum content.[6] The Ontario provincial curriculum, in particular, the grade 2 and 3 *science and technology* curriculum[7] was used in relation to student-initiated practices that included running, gardening, bird watching and composting. Science and technology curriculum expectations related to *soil science* and *big ideas* in elementary science that included understanding that (1) humans are animals and (2) forces exist that cause movement.[8] Both are science and technology curriculum expectations of 7- and 8-year-old children in Ontario public schools.

Wearing the cameras at all times enabled experimentation with curriculum content in ways that touched on yet another curriculum expectation in grade 2 science and technology that requires an understanding of the relation between science, technology and environment. This relation was enacted through the embodied practices mentioned above (i.e., gardening, running, bird watching and composting). Importantly what makes technologies like the wearable camera different from a video camera that, for example, is used on a tripod is its capacity to foreground embodied visions and thus the process of perception as it is forming. Wearable cameras have the capacity to sense what is seen with the body and in relation with environments, creating embodied visions in the very act of doing curriculum. The cameras sense speed, slowness and touch through a wide-angled lens.

My research intent was not to measure movement, nor to capture visions of thought. My intent in using the camera as a relational object was to challenge understandings of perception and to provoke new directions in qualitative research that disrupt data-driven methods of truth about children and their experiences in urban environments. The research project served to affirm the capacity of students to relationally see/live/feel environments and, in this particular project, creatively respond to experiences of urban life that were recorded from an embodied view. The use of wearable cameras, which lack a viewfinder and view screen (used to view and edit video while recording), was significant in staying with the movement of multiple visions that relationally sustain urban environments. Another intention within the research project was to negotiate an understanding of the wearable cameras as co-composing objects of inquiry that *touch visions* in ways that affect and inform perceptions of life.

Touching visions

María Puig de la Bellacasa's notion of touching visions shifts from privileging sight to recognizing sight as a dominant mode of human communication that is leaky with possibilities of seeing through sensorial modes of knowing. Vision, in other words, is felt through the body's sensorial capacity, which informs relations to environment and thus the production of subjectivity. Puig de la Bellacasa questions her invocation of touch and why it is so compelling. She lists many reasons for the use of touch in feminist discourse, noting the potential of touch to (1) generate awareness of embodied perception as it relates to affect and thinking; (2) disrupt boundaries between self, other and object; and (3) attend to the materiality and corporeality of subject–object relations.[9] She sees the potential of touch "to inspire a sense of connectedness that can further problematize abstractions and disengagements of (epistemological) distances—between subjects and objects, knowledge and the world, affects and facts, politics and science."[10] Puig de Bellacasa sees touch as a haptic capacity and strategy for perceiving a micro-politics that is more-than-representational because it operates on an everyday level of interaction that is not visible to the human eye or to the camera's mobile eye..

This level of micro-political engagement engenders an understanding of technologies and modes of epistemological measurement as nonneutral forces that shape what becomes visible. Such thought also engenders an understanding of politics as that which seeks alternative ways of seeing through the affective dimensions of touch. I must, however, note that the wearable cameras do not have the capacity to register or capture touch. The cameras have an extraordinary capacity to record an immersive perspective of pedagogical events as they unfold. The cameras offer unique angles and insights into the everydayness of schools and communities. The immersive and mobile vision that the camera shapes affirms the capacity of students, schools and communities to determine their own touching visions, their own multiple meanings of lived experience. The project was concerned with how technologies, bodies and images moved and merged with multiple experiences, not as a result of a particular experience. Through the practice of mashing, I was, in particular, curious how a video image's reimaging (that was recorded with the wearable cameras) might be approached in excess of facts and instrumental research findings.

Mashing

The practice of mashing involves editing two or more songs together to create a new song. This idea was student generated and proposed as a result of a popular television show titled *Glee*.[11] The show followed the lives of a group of students in an American high school who participated in a glee club. During glee practice, students selected two or more popular songs and mashed them together to form a new song. The students in this research project hacked the practice by mashing the video images that were generated with the wearable cameras' use. They used editing software that the teacher taught the students how to use. Students created digital short videos that enabled them to view, mash up and reclaim their experiences on a computer screen. Throughout the weeks, students recreated their digital short videos by mashing different images.

Upon viewing the raw video footage it became evident that the wearable cameras captured motion. For instance students witnessed phenomena that escaped talk and text methods.[12] Students did not realize that they had done something and did not recall saying something in particular. The children also noted that they and their friends sounded and looked different. Other students felt queasy viewing multiple images, noting the rapid movement of bodies and unfocused shots displayed across the computer screen. The practice of mashing worked to reclaim experience and account for, and thus become *response-able*[13] for, the discursive forms of knowledge that were produced. The practice worked to encounter images in ways that created knowledge. The practice sought to share understandings of material content with other users and in relation to one's own experience and knowledge system. Importantly, mashing added relations to worlds by observing, thinking and reclaiming, which are actions that involved "touching and being touched by what we 'observe.'"[14]

The haptic quality of the images displayed on the computer screen, for example, worked to defamiliarize the self and in turn opened up vision to the durational force of movement, not human-centered motion. In other words the practice of mashing also considered the affective dimensions of vision that are often not intelligible or articulable in language. In this sense mashing and the touching visions that such a practice activated were not merely evocative of the human; they were composed of a multiplicity of more-than-human durations.[15] The mash-ups, therefore, became images that the wearable cameras did not record.

The significance of this material and spatial composition then renders subjectivity making as a collective process and active engagement with worlds. The practice of mashing furthermore puts into question what researchers do with data and/or images that are produced in empirical research studies. Students' active engagement with images further enables a rethinking of agency as an entanglement of multiple visions that are informed by more-than-human bodies across time and space. The question of how to see and/or touch the hot compost pile that humans live and breathe is one that requires collective efforts of thought and action, not limited to the representational eye. An equally important question that Puig de Bellacasa wonders about is the kind of touching that is produced. She asks: "What kind of touching is produced when we are unaware of the needs and desires of that what/whom we are reaching for?"[16]

Desiring compost

Reaching for something in particular and/or wanting something for someone or a group of people is always problematic. To want and/or to desire for others is a circular practice that always returns to the self. Critical and creative practices such as *mashing* potentialize the desire for that which cannot be known in advance. The unknowability of the not-yet is risky terrain to endure, and yet within experiences of endurance, the possibility of thinking, feeling and seeing otherwise exists. The possibility of healing from cruel realities that destroy land and bound Othered bodies to borders is present. Critical and creative practices ask questions that concern the *what if* of engagement. What if student- and community-initiated forms of tangible engagement become committed knowledge practices of worldly transformation?[17] From this perspective, engagement transforms into an ethics of encounter in which value is not committed to knowing, but rather a revaluation of knowing is at stake. The challenge, as Puig de Bellacasa reminds us, is how to encounter knowledge in difference and within epistemological constraints that seek comfort in what is known.

To activate the desire to deal with the hot mess of inheritance is a reality that requires endurance. Within endurance there must be response-ability[18] and attentiveness to the multiple visions and layers of life and death that become the stuff of hot compost. As Haraway writes, communities of compost work to understand "how to inherit the layers upon layers of living and dying that infuse every place and every corridor."[19] The "Children of Compost"[20] desire emergent processes of valuation that multiply and are ongoing. Haraway's call to desire the mess of hot compost echoes Baruch Spinoza's ethics in which he states that many kinds of desires and pleasures hate, love, and hope, and by which bodies are affected and endure.[21] Within endurance a process exists that multiplies visions and that might in turn have a future hand in making hot compost that desires to heal and create worlds worth living.

Notes

1 Fragments of this chapter have been adapted from the author's doctoral dissertation *Three Ecologies of Practice: An Intra-active Account of Learning by Doing*, Ontario Institute for Studies in Education, University of Toronto, 2016.
2 María Puig de la Bellacasa, "Touching Technologies, Touching Visions: The Reclaiming of Sensorial Experience and the Politics of Speculative Thinking," *Subjectivity* 28 (2009): 297.
3 Ibid., 299.
4 Donna J. Haraway, *Staying with the Trouble: Making Kin in the Chthulucene* (Durham, NC: Duke University Press, 2016), 31.
5 Elizabeth Adams St. Pierre, "The Appearance of Data," *Cultural Studies? Critical Methodologies* 13 (2013): 224.

6   Nikki Rotas, "Moving toward Practices That Matter," in *Pedagogical Matters: New Materialisms and Curriculum Studies*, ed. Nathan Snaza, Debbie Sonu, Sarah Truman, and Zofia Zaliwska (New York: Peter Lang, 2016), 183.
7   Ontario Ministry of Education, "The Ontario Curriculum: Grades 1–8 Science and Technology," 2007.
8   Ibid.
9   Puig de la Bellacasa, "Touching Technologies," 298.
10 Ibid.
11 Ryan Murphy, Brad Falchuk, and Ian Brennan, creators, *Glee*, television series, 2009–2015 (Los Angeles, CA: 20th century Fox Television).
12 Jamie Lorimer, "Moving Image Methodologies for More-Than-Human Geographies," *Cultural Geographies* 17, no. 2 (2010): 242.
13 Haraway, *Staying with the Trouble*, 105.
14 Puig de la Bellacasa, "Touching Technologies," 310.
15 Claire Colebrook, "Modernism without Women: The Refusal of Becoming-Woman (and Post-Feminism)," *Deleuze Studies* 7, no. 4 (2013): 437.
16 Puig de la Bellacasa, "Touching Technologies," 300.
17 Ibid., 230.
18 Haraway, *Staying with the Trouble*, 105.
19 Ibid., 138.
20 Ibid., 139.
21 Baruch Spinoza, *Ethics: Treatise on the Emendation of the Intellect and Selected Letters*, trans. Samuel Shirley (Indianapolis, IN: Hackett, 1992), 137.

Bibliography

Adams St. Pierre, Elizabeth. "The Appearance of Data." *Cultural Studies? Critical Methodologies* 13 (2013): 223–227.

Colebrook, Claire. "Modernism without Women: The Refusal of Becoming-Woman (and Post-Feminism)." *Deleuze Studies* 7, no. 4 (2013): 427–455.

Haraway, Donna J. *Staying with the Trouble: Making Kin in the Chthulucene*. Durham, NC: Duke University Press, 2016.

Lorimer, Jamie. "Moving Image Methodologies for More-Than-Human Geographies." *Cultural Geographies* 17, no. 2 (2010): 237–258.

Murphy, Ryan, Brad Falchuk, and Ian Brennan, creators. *Glee*. Television series. 2009–2015. Los Angeles, CA: 20th century Fox Television.

Ontario Ministry of Education. "The Ontario Curriculum: Grades 1–8 Science and Technology, 2007." Last modified 29 September 2017. http://www.edu.gov.on.ca/eng/curriculum/elementary/scientec18currb.pdf.

Puig de la Bellacasa, María. "Touching Technologies, Touching Visions: The Reclaiming of Sensorial Experience and the Politics of Speculative Thinking." *Subjectivity* 28 (2009): 297–315.

Rotas, Nikki. "Moving toward Practices That Matter." In *Pedagogical Matters: New Materialisms and Curriculum Studies*, edited by Nathan Snaza, Debbie Sonu, Sarah Truman, and Zofia Zaliwska, 179–196. New York: Peter Lang, 2016.

Rotas, Nikki. *Three Ecologies of Practice: An Intra-active Account of Learning by Doing.* PhD diss., Ontario Institute for Studies in Education, University of Toronto, 2016.

Spinoza, Baruch. *Ethics: Treatise on the Emendation of the Intellect and Selected Letters.* Translated by Samuel Shirley. Indianapolis, IN: Hackett, 1992.

13

Playing: Inefficiently Mapping Human and Inhuman Play in Urban Commonplaces

Linda M. Knight

I am interested in play, and specifically, play in urban spaces. My use of the term *urban* refers to the world's cities, towns and neighborhoods, across climates, demographies, geographies and affluences. My use of the term *play* is also diverse: I think about play as an enactment/response/communication/exchange/performance by humans, nonhuman animals and inhuman matter. My work is concerned with theorizing play to form new conceptualizations about urban citizenships: Who/what/how is an urban citizen? I also use feminist, posthuman theorizations to consider play and the ethics of urban demarcations and planning. My lively story focuses on drawn mappings of play that I create in my investigations. The maps are purposefully inefficient, enacting a postqualitative methodologic practice that plays with what counts as a researching method as I take notice of play in urban spaces in Australia.

Concepts of play

The literature on the benefits of play to children is significant,[1] especially in early childhood. Early childhood play literature can focus on particular issues, including the benefits of play to aid social development and physical and mental well-being,[2] the problematics of gendered play,[3] and how play helps build relationships with place and nature.[4] Advocacy for urban play provision can hinge on futures discourses about urban population statistics[5] and pathologizing discourses of children disconnected from physical activity and face-to-face social interaction.[6] Humanist play research may have differing contexts and be interpreted through different paradigms, but the consensus is that play is innate and vital for us.

Play is not only a human capacity: ethological studies help extend humanist notions of play to examine how nonhuman animal play in its various forms offers a distraction for pets in the domestic sphere as well as animals living in capture.[7] Animals living in the wild are also seen to possess the capacities for generating and experiencing play, creativity and pleasure.[8] Ethological research is presented as providing a window into the play capacities and habits of nonhuman animals, although the preference for behaviorist/positivist readings tends toward notions that animal play is akin to, or a version of, the acts and motivations for human play.

Existing literature recognizes the need to advance and extend our limited understandings of how and why play occurs.[9] Paying attention to play helps enrich conceptions about relationalities and expressions in humans and animals[10] that extend beyond a hierarchical reading of human/animal binaries. Critical thinking about play beyond a humanist focus helps to expand concepts and ideas about nonhuman animal play as "much more complex"[11] than it being a mirror or facsimile of, or for the same purposes as, human play.

How is play described? Humanist, ethological, posthuman and multispecies contextual analyses offer different articulations that emerge from a range of paradigms. Ethological behaviorist studies see animal play as purposefully intentioned, "not fully functional as it is incomplete, exaggerated or somehow modified."[12] Animals are seen to make cognizant decisions to play and differentiate it from other behaviors. By contrast, Donna Haraway's speculative multispecies encounters are a playing full of "unexpected conjunctions and coordinations of creatively moving partners"[13] that "[break] rules to make something happen."[14] Play occurs spontaneously and contingently in a tangle of energies and movements within the milieu. Humanist readings of play often attend to the affective, honing in on its "opposition to seriousness, morality, and productive work"[15] that "escapes focused attention, reasoned argument, and political debate."[16] Although play is generally understood as being essential to human thriving,[17] human play is often negatively implied: a break from the regular way of being in the world, a temporary escape/return to immaturity and silliness.

Karen Barad's posthuman readings of quantum physics[18] reconceptualize inhuman matter. Barad views "things" less as discrete bodies than as clusters of forces, what she calls "transmaterialities":[19] energy fields of particles moving in times and patterns with lively edges that bounce back and forth. Barad's research into theoretical physics and lightning strikes exposed how even seemingly familiar matter (the electrical charge) is not mechanistic but consists of particles busily playing with possibilities and futures.[20] The highly advanced research equipment she used recorded how lightning bolts send out tracers that play with different route options before selecting the preferred route to the earth. Similarly, Julia Yeomans suggests that "advances in nanotechnology and imaging techniques"[21] have led to "surprises that are challenging theories of non-equilibrium statistical physics."[22] Yeomans notes the unexpected behaviors of "inanimate systems ... [that] operate out of equilibrium and may be considered active"[23] when stimulated by external energy pulses. The energy source should make the fluids active in particular ways, and yet unexpected activations are observed. Technological advancements allow physicists to see how matter also can behave unexpectedly and "[break] rules to make something happen."[24] Matter's vibrancy[25] and vitality are a form of inhuman play.

In my research I consider the behaviors and interactions that are interpreted as play in human and nonhuman contexts to speculate on inhuman play. Specifically I wonder how the idea of play in urban commonplaces might shift from thinking about play in nonhuman and/or human terms and expand to include the inhuman as independently play-full. In thinking about the inhuman, how might the lively doing of playing in urban places acknowledge the agentic play of the inhuman? My big research question, then, is not "Does play matter?" but "Does matter play?"

Urban play spaces

Contemporary playgrounds are a familiar sight, appearing in urban spaces and parks in cities across the globe. Playground equipment often has a design conventionality that is easily recognizable[26] through the inclusion of modules such as climbing frames, swings and slides. Playgrounds are understood as obvious play spaces, a particular type of pedagogic site for children to build social relationships, play and undertake physical activity. Dislocating from a humanist vision of play, a posthuman reading of play in urban commonplaces takes notice of the energies and activities occurring in all manner of spaces beyond a simple interaction between child and play equipment. Factors such as surfaces, light, time, animals, birds, sounds, gestures, shade and rain are seen to possess playful agency. Playing becomes clusters of choreographic, pedagogic intra-actions, bringing about a rethinking and rearticulation of "lively playing" as a complex series of entangled movements, affects and sensations across vast scale and durational differences.[27] Feminist theoretical reconceptualizations around matter[28] help to critique taken-for-granted notions of how space, structures and forms can be allocated particular purposes and how play can be privy to regulating expectations. In thinking critically about play, the playground dissipates and becomes a series of moving, traveling, multibodied events, shifting locations in unpredictable ways through urban commonplaces across the urban location, contesting the humanist approach to urban residential planning that demarcate sites of play via strictly regulated play structures. It is important to critically theorize urban play because even urban green spaces are curated and regulated. The popular "natural" wooden play equipment in early childhood play areas, as well as green spaces such as small woodlands, canals and river ways, and flood plains, are seen as beneficial sites for urban human and domestic nonhuman animal citizens to experience a taste of nature.[29] The socioeconomic and political agendas of local councils that direct government investment toward maintaining select green spaces highlight the ethics of allocating urban spaces for particular purposes and for specific users: humans and permissible nonhuman animals. Other types of animals and inhuman players cannot be kept out, but are not always welcomed in.

Inefficient mapping

In my research-creation work I make "inefficient" drawn mappings of lively playing.[30] Trying to capture lively playings in their entirety is impossible and futile, but partial recordings, or what Dennis Wood terms the "inefficient map"[31]—maps that do not attempt to include everything on a single sheet but focus on aspects—can record playing through such things as affects and the diverse pedagogical happenings that take place through the interactions and interactivities of matter. Mapping, rather than other forms of recording (such as a running record or a video-recording), can be a way to enter into the milieu, to notice some of what goes on without claiming to represent some kind of truthful or whole account of the time-place. The inefficient mappings' graphic orientation allows for visual notation of schizo[32] play activity: overlapping, simultaneous, multiple movements, forms, light and time.

Figure 13.1 is a mapping of a popular reserve. It encompasses a reservoir, running tracks, small woody hills and bush vegetation. The area is really busy with activity at all times of the day and night, variously by humans, domestic dogs and wildlife. It is also popular with air currents, sunlight, moistures, light flashes, pollens and other small particles. During this mapping I made sporadic and partial recordings of light and shade and how they play with topologies

Figure 13.1 Mapping. Pencil on tracing film. 2016. Artist: Linda Knight.

and surfaces, depths and planes, especially during movements through the structures and in negotiation with other human, nonhuman animal and inhuman visitors. The flickerings and pulses generated by the playing, and the resulting disorientation, made the mapping difficult and frenzied.

Figure 13.2 inefficiently maps the bruising and blustering force of air currents when it shifts from being air and becomes wind. Gusts pushed through an urban creek and altered what was before. Not everything moved at the same scale and pace. I recorded snatches of tiny whorlings and huge blasts, exhales and pauses. These forces' imprints showed in arranged flattenings and jagged tearings and in minute vibrations of grasses, trees, webs, grass seeds, pollen motes and insects. Movements were everywhere, overlapping and intercepting the space, pushing the mapping materials in all directions.

As a postqualitative methodologic practice, the mappings closely examine and comment on the ethics of urban planning. They visually mark/mark playful "multisensory encounters that entangle residents of diverse cultural backgrounds, nonhumans, and material things."[33] The mappings might be partial, but they home in on what conventionally can be regarded as unimportant, unsightly, or a problem: things about a place that "spoil" the neighborhood. The mappings linger in urban spaces demarcated for particular activities or ignored as a space with no development/financial potential. My mappings are driven by affect and

Figure 13.2 Mapping. Pencil on tracing film. 2016. Artist: Linda Knight.

are "attentive to the experience of place"[34] but within the faulty capacities of my ability to turn, to look, to see, to mark, and to accurately record. I am aware that I do hardly any justice to capturing all the play that occurs around me, but that is the ethics of it. I am only a tiny part of the "playful events that entangle humans, more-than-human forms of life, and material things."[35] My presence is not crucial or even remotely relevant. I am just one small being in a vast crowd of urban citizens ethically moving and playing together.

My insignificance is, conversely, important to declare. My presence in a space, and my holey mapping, is not intended to authorize a place: it is a modest witnessing[36] of community participation. Although inefficient, the mappings provide a gestural articulation on the importance of having posthuman commonplaces for all citizens to play.

Notes

1 Alaina Roach O'Keefe, Joanne Lehrer, and Debra Harwood, "Introduction: Play in the 21st century," *Canadian Journal of Education* 39, no. 3 (2016): 1–5.
2 Kirti D. Bhonsle and Vinayak S. Adane, "Assessing the Play Provisions for Children in Urban Neighborhoods of India: Case Study Nagpur, Maharashtra," *Buildings*

6, no. 3 (2016): 31–58; John Horton, "Disabilities, Urban Natures, and Children's Outdoor Play," *Social & Cultural Geography* 18, no. 8 (2017): 1152–1174; Susan G. Zieff, Anoshua Chaudhuri, and Elaine Musselman, "Creating Neighborhood Recreational Space for Youth and Children in the Urban Environment: Play(ing in the) Streets in San Francisco," *Children and Youth Services Review* 70 (2016): 95–101.

3   Mindy Blaise, "Interfering with Gendered Development: A Timely Intervention," *International Journal of Early Childhood* 46, no. 3 (2014): 317–326; Rachel Chapman, "A Case Study of Gendered Play in Preschools: How Early Childhood Educators' Perceptions of Gender Influence Children's Play," *Early Child Development and Care* 186, no. 8 (2016): 1271–1284.

4   Kellie Dowdell, Tonia Gray, and Karen Malone, "Nature and Its Influence on Children's Outdoor Play," *Australian Journal of Outdoor Education* 15, no. 2 (2011): 24–35; Horton, "Disabilities, Urban Natures, and Children's Outdoor Play"; Lasse Juel Larsen, "Play and Space: Towards a Formal Definition of Play," *International Journal of Play* 4, no. 2 (2015): 175–189; Affrica Taylor, *Reconfiguring the Natures of Childhood* (New York: Routledge, 2013).

5   Bhonsle and Adane, "Assessing the Play Provisions for Children"; Sri A. Ekawati, "Children-Friendly Streets as Urban Playgrounds," *Procedia—Social and Behavioral Sciences* 179 (2015): 94–108.

6   Magdalena Czalcynska-Podolska, "The Impact of Playground Spatial Features on Children's Play and Activity Forms: An Evaluation of Contemporary Playgrounds' Play and Social Value," *Journal of Environmental Psychology* 38 (2014): 132–142; Sharareh Ghanbari-Azarneir, Sara Anbari, Seyed-Bagher Hosseini, and Seyed-Abbas Yazdanfar, "Identification of Child-Friendly Environments in Poor Neighborhoods," *Procedia—Social and Behavioral Sciences* 201 (2015): 19–29; Horton, "Disabilities, Urban Natures, and Children's Outdoor Play"; Karen Malone, "Street Life: Youth, Culture, and Competing Uses of Public Space," *Environment and Urbanization* 14, no. 2 (2002): 157–168.

7   Ida K. H. Jørgensen and Hanna Wirman, "Multispecies Methods, Technologies for Play," *Digital Creativity* 27, no. 1 (2016): 37–51.

8   Gordon M. Burghardt, "Creativity, Play, and the Pace of Evolution," in *Animal Creativity and Innovation*, eds. Allison B. Kaufman and James C. Kaufman (London: Elsevier Academic Press, 2015), 129–161; Jørgensen and Wirman, "Multispecies Methods."

9   Roach O'Keefe et al., "Introduction."

10 Donna J. Haraway, *When Species Meet* (Minneapolis: University of Minnesota Press, 2008); Jørgensen and Wirman, "Multispecies Methods."

11 Jørgensen and Wirman, "Multispecies Methods," 42.

12 Ibid.

13 Haraway, *When Species Meet*, 241.

14 Ibid., 238.
15 Michele Lobo, "Co-inhabiting Public Spaces: Diversity and Playful Encounters in Darwin, Australia," *Geographical Review* 106, no. 2 (2016): 166.
16 Ibid., 167.
17 Peter Gray, "What Exactly Is Play, and Why Is It Such a Powerful Vehicle for Learning?" *Topics in Language Disorders* 37, no. 3 (2017): 217–228.
18 Karen Barad, *Meeting the Universe Halfway: Quantum Physics and the Entanglement of Matter and Meaning* (Durham, NC: Duke University Press, 2007); Karen Barad, "TransMaterialities: Trans*/Matter/Realities and Queer Political Imaginings," *GLQ: A Journal of Lesbian and Gay Studies* 21, nos. 2–3 (2015): 387–422.
19 Barad, "TransMaterialities."
20 Ibid.
21 Julia M. Yeomans, "Active Matter: Playful Topology," *Nature Materials* 13, no. 11 (2014): 1004.
22 Ibid.
23 Ibid.
24 Haraway, *When Species Meet*, 238.
25 Jane Bennett, *Vibrant Matter: A Political Ecology of Things* (Durham, NC: Duke University Press, 2009).
26 Susan G. Solomon, *American Playgrounds: Revitalizing Community Space* (Lebanon: UPNE, 2005).
27 Linda M. Knight, "Playgrounds as Sites of Radical Encounters: Mapping Material, Affective, Spatial, and Pedagogical Collisions," in *Pedagogical Matters: New Materialisms and Curriculum Studies*, vol. 501, ed. Debbie Sonu, Nathan Snaza, Sarah E. Truman, and Zofia Zaliwska (New York: Peter Lang, 2016), 13–28.
28 Barad, *Meeting the Universe Halfway*; Barad, "TransMaterialities."
29 Bhonsle and Adane, "Assessing the Play Provisions for Children"; Lobo, "Co-inhabiting Public Spaces."
30 Knight, "Playgrounds as Sites of Radical Encounters."
31 Dennis Wood, *Everything Sings: Maps for a Narrative Atlas*, 2nd ed. (New York: Siglio, 2013), 19.
32 Gilles Deleuze and Félix Guattari, *Anti-Oedipus: Capitalism and Schizophrenia*, trans. Robert Hurley, Mark Seem, and Helen R. Lane (Minneapolis: University of Minnesota Press, 1983).
33 Lobo, "Co-inhabiting Public Spaces," 164.
34 Wood, *Everything Sings*, 19.
35 Lobo, "Co-inhabiting Public Spaces," 172.
36 Donna J. Haraway, *Modest_Witness@Second_Millennium.FemaleMan_Meets_OncoMouse: Feminism and Technoscience* (New York: Routledge, 1997).

Bibliography

Barad, Karen. *Meeting the Universe Halfway: Quantum Physics and the Entanglement of Matter and Meaning.* Durham, NC: Duke University Press, 2007.

Barad, Karen. "TransMaterialities: Trans*/Matter/Realities and Queer Political Imaginings." *GLQ: A Journal of Lesbian and Gay Studies* 21, nos. 2-3 (2015): 387-422.

Bennett, Jane. *Vibrant Matter: A Political Ecology of Things.* Durham, NC: Duke University Press, 2009.

Bhonsle, Kirti D., and Vinayak S. Adane. "Assessing the Play Provisions for Children in Urban Neighborhoods of India: Case Study Nagpur, Maharashtra." *Buildings* 6, no. 3 (2016): 31-58.

Blaise, Mindy. "Interfering with Gendered Development: A Timely Intervention." *International Journal of Early Childhood* 46, no. 3 (2014): 317-326.

Burghardt, Gordon M. "Creativity, Play, and the Pace of Evolution." In *Animal Creativity and Innovation*, edited by Allison B. Kaufman and James C. Kaufman, 129-161. London: Elsevier Academic Press, 2015.

Chapman, Rachel. "A Case Study of Gendered Play in Preschools: How Early Childhood Educators' Perceptions of Gender Influence Children's Play." *Early Child Development and Care* 186, no. 8 (2016): 1271-1284. doi:10.1080/03004430.2015.1089435.

Czalczynska-Podolska, Magdalena. "The Impact of Playground Spatial Features on Children's Play and Activity Forms: An Evaluation of Contemporary Playgrounds' Play and Social Value." *Journal of Environmental Psychology* 38 (2014): 132-142. doi:10.1016/j.envp.2014.01.006.

Deleuze, Gilles and Félix Guattari. *Anti-Oedipus: Capitalism and Schizophrenia*, translated by Robert Hurley, Mark Seem, and Helen R. Lane. Minneapolis: University of Minnesota Press, 1983.

Dowdell, Kellie, Tonia Gray, and Karen Malone. "Nature and Its Influence on Children's Outdoor Play." *Australian Journal of Outdoor Education* 15, no. 2 (2011): 24-35.

Ekawati, Sri Aliah. "Children-Friendly Streets as Urban Playgrounds." *Procedia—Social and Behavioral Sciences* 179 (2015): 94-108.

Ghanbari-Azarneir, Sharareh, Sara Anbari, Seyed-Bagher Hosseini, and Seyed-Abbas Yazdanfar. "Identification of Child-Friendly Environments in Poor Neighborhoods." *Procedia—Social and Behavioral Sciences* 201 (2015): 19-29.

Gray, Peter. "What Exactly Is Play, and Why Is It Such a Powerful Vehicle for Learning?" *Topics in Language Disorders* 37, no. 3 (2017): 217-228.

Haraway, Donna J. *Modest_Witness@Second_Millennium.FemaleMan_Meets_OncoMouse: Feminism and Technoscience.* New York: Routledge, 1997.

Haraway, Donna J. *When Species Meet.* Minneapolis: University of Minnesota Press, 2008.

Horton, John. "Disabilities, Urban Natures, and Children's Outdoor Play." *Social & Cultural Geography* 18, no. 8 (2017): 1152-1174.

Jørgensen, Ida Kathrine Hammeleff and Hanna Wirman. "Multispecies Methods, Technologies for Play." *Digital Creativity* 27, no. 1 (2016): 37–51.

Knight, Linda M. "Playgrounds as Sites of Radical Encounters: Mapping Material, Affective, Spatial, and Pedagogical Collisions." In *Pedagogical Matters: New Materialisms and Curriculum Studies*, vol. 501, edited by Debbie Sonu, Nathan Snaza, Sarah E. Truman, and Zofia Zaliwska, 13–28. New York: Peter Lang, 2016.

Larsen, Lasse Juel. "Play and Space: Towards a Formal Definition of Play." *International Journal of Play* 4, no. 2 (2015): 175–189.

Lobo, Michele. "Co-inhabiting Public Spaces: Diversity and Playful Encounters in Darwin, Australia." *Geographical Review* 106, no. 2 (2016): 163–173.

Malone, Karen. "Street Life: Youth, Culture, and Competing Uses of Public Space." *Environment and Urbanization* 14, no. 2 (2002): 157–168.

Roach O'Keefe, Alaina, Joanne Lehrer, and Debra Harwood. "Introduction: Play in the 21st century." *Canadian Journal of Education* 39, no. 3 (2016): 1–5.

Solomon, Susan G. *American Playgrounds: Revitalizing Community Space*. Lebanon: UPNE, 2005.

Taylor, Affrica. *Reconfiguring the Natures of Childhood*. New York: Routledge, 2013.

Wood, Dennis. *Everything Sings: Maps for a Narrative Atlas*. 2nd ed. New York: Siglio, 2013.

Yeomans, Julia M. "Active Matter: Playful Topology." *Nature Materials* 13, no. 11 (2014): 1004–1005.

Zieff, Susan G., Anoshua Chaudhuri, and Elaine Musselman. "Creating Neighborhood Recreational Space for Youth and Children in the Urban Environment: Play(ing in the) Streets in San Francisco." *Children and Youth Services Review* 70 (2016): 95–101.

14

GoProing: Becoming Participant-Researcher

Susannah Clement

Gareth: But whhhhyyyyy does it have to be walking?
Billie: Because that's what the study is about.
Gareth: But why walking?
Billie: So, the lady that came to visit us, when you weren't here, is doing a study about families walking together. And if you ride your bike with the GoPro, she won't be able to use it. ... That's the way it's got to be.

...

Gareth: But what's the difference between walking and riding?
Billie: Nothing in your world, mate, but in Susannah's world, it's her study.

...

Gareth: But ... [starts to sob]
Billie: Okay, I'm not making you walk, you don't have to come with us, okay? You can stay with Daddy. It's okay.
Gareth: It's just that all I want to do is have a go with it. It's not fair! It's not fairrrrr! [crying]

This conversation between Gareth (age nine) and his mother, Billie (late forties), took place while getting ready to go out for a walk from the family's house to a nearby beachside playground. The conversation was recorded by Gareth's sister Ellie (age eleven) on a GoPro Hero3,[1] a small, lightweight video camera lent to the family the week before. Gareth, Billie and Ellie were participants in a research project that explored the everyday walking practices and experiences of families who live in Wollongong, a regional city situated on the east coast of New South Wales, Australia. As Billie tried to explain to her son, the point of using the GoPro was to record the times they walked together, so that I, *"the lady"* from the university, could gain a sense of how it feels for parents and children to walk together in a city which is largely car dependent. Yet for Gareth, the trip's purpose to the playground was less about walking with his mother and sister than about getting to *"have a go"* with the GoPro.

GoPros are small but relatively high-powered, versatile and durable action cameras. The camera weighs only between 80 and 100 grams (depending on the version), is waterproof, and can be mounted using various attachments to bodies, vehicles, or sporting equipment.[2] GoPro is brand name which has become synonymous with wearable camera technologies predominantly marketed targeting amateur filmmakers and participants of adventure sports. They are also increasingly becoming popular tools in ethnographic research. For instance, GoPros and other portable camcorders have been utilized in mobilities research where in situ data collection is important for capturing the intricate movements of daily life.[3] In these studies cameras are mounted to objects such as bicycles,[4] car dashboards,[5] and even surfboards,[6] reducing the inconvenience that comes with having to hold the camera.[7] The GoPro's versatility in being able to attach to equipment and bodies via different accessories made it a useful tool in my research with parents and young children, where carrying things, holding hands and pushing prams made participant-led video-recording particularly difficult. Furthermore, in this project the GoPro reduced the pressure to find suitable times for go-along walks with families (another method used in the study)[8] and allowed them to share their experiences of walking without me being physically present.

Yet, as the opening narrative alludes, the GoPro as a research tool was not an invisible observer of families' walks. The GoPro was often an important topic of conversation during walks. In some instances, its presence was the reason for the walks in the first place, such as Gareth's desire to *"have a go"* with the GoPro that made an outing to the playground appealing. Hence the GoPro was not just a recording device that nonintrusively "captured" everyday life, but rather it was central to the unfolding research encounters. Therefore while I was interested in recording families' everyday walks, what was achieved was more than this. In addition to walking, what was also being recorded was GoProing: a less mundane way of journeying on foot.

GoProing assemblages

From a feminist postqualitative perspective research is always mediated through the means in which it is gathered.[9] Hence video methods are not an objective mode of documenting events which have unfolded, but a subjective way of communicating, describing and making sense of the world.[10] In addition to this feminist postqualitative scholarship highlights the nonhuman's agency in research encounters.[11] For instance Nick Fox and Pam Alldred argue that all research is mediated through a *research-assemblage* that is comprised of the "bodies, things and abstractions that get caught up in social inquiry, including the events that are studied, the tools, models and precepts of research, and the researchers."[12] An assemblage approach, underpinned by the work of Gilles Deleuze and Félix Guattari,[13] moves away from the traditional positivist dichotomy of the *passive* participant "being studied" and the *active* researcher "finding things out." Instead an assemblage approach highlights the multiple human and nonhuman actors which are enrolled in research as a messy, nonlinear and provisional working arrangement. For instance in my research the GoPro's agency (in particular, its affective capacity to shift relations between bodies and places) is important to consider when thinking about the constitution of research encounters and subjects. As the remainder of this chapter explores, the "categories" of participant and researcher are never stable, but become known through affective interactions with technologies, bodies, mobilities and places in order for the working arrangement that is the research-assemblage to be maintained. What this GoProing-research-assemblage achieves is not simply the recording of families' walks but a performative way of moving in which multiple participant and researcher subjectivities emerge.

The "good" participant-researcher

The GoPro is being worn by Gareth via a head strap over his bike helmet.

Gareth: *It's [the GoPro] heavy. Oh god.*
Billie: *You've got to walk your bike, mate. I'll carry your shoes, but you have to walk your bike.*
Gareth: *Can you undo my stand, because I can't do it? Billie kicks the bike stand. Gareth takes the bike, turns, and begins to wheel it, walking barefoot away from the playground. They must be on their way home. Gareth follows behind Billie and Ellie for a few moments before Billie turns around, pointing at Gareth.*
Billie: *No hopping on your bike.*
Gareth: *Hmmmph, fine.*

Despite their initial argument Gareth decided to go with Billie and Ellie to the playground, agreeing to the condition that he walk his bike when wearing the

GoPro. As Billie explained in the follow-up interview, "the rule was that he had to walk his bike, that was the deal we made." In policing what activities could or couldn't be recorded Billie adhered to and reinforced the recording instructions I had given her a week earlier. This example shows that no simple boundary between participant and researcher exists as traditional positivist research methods might leave us to believe. Billie's subjectivity as participant does not preexist; it was not innate within her. Rather Billie was active in constituting herself as the "good" participant through instructing her son how and when to use the GoPro. Furthermore, in doing so, Billie made a judgment about what "going for a walk" was—something that was left open for participants to define for themselves. Billie actively decided what research-worthy material was and, as a result, became embedded in the process of data collection, reduction and analysis. Rethinking recorded walking as GoProing foregrounds how parents, children and wearable cameras are all coproducers of research.[14]

Emotional and coercive entanglements

GoProing was not a neutral, unemotional activity. The GoPro's presence on families' walks caused fascination, excitement, confusion, discomfort and argument.

Gareth is trailing behind Billie and Ellie, walking his bike along a shared footpath. Billie stops for a moment for him to catch up.

Gareth: Hmm, I'm sick of walking.
Billie: Well, if you are sick of walking. ... There are a whole bunch of people behind you! A group of cyclists ride past.
Gareth: I'm walking. [whiny voice]

...

Billie: Are you okay? You're determined to have it [the GoPro]. [chuckles]

Gareth's frustration over the rules and his determination to retain GoPro's use highlight Clifton Evers's argument that the GoPro "not only witnesses and records but also produces affects and emotion."[15] Evers points to how the emotional and affective resonances that emerge between researching bodies and video technologies enable new openings and actions. For Gareth who chooses to walk his bike in order to get the camera's use, the GoPro was seen as an exciting new toy to play with, a desired object that shaped his choices, actions and behavior. As Eva Änggård found when doing research with children and digital cameras, the GoPro proved to be an attractive object for children.[16] This attractiveness was not innate to the GoPro, but became felt through a combination of its well-known brand name and popularity among peers to render the gadget as "cool." Gareth can be heard later in the recording talking about his friend who has a GoPro: "Well, Cameron has his own GoPro."

GoProing as cool opens up ethical questions about informed consent and participant coercion.[17] While Gareth had been explained the project's purpose and design and formally given his consent to participate,[18] his sole motivation for going for a walk was centered on getting to use the GoPro. While the GoPro as a desired object had the benefit of engaging children in the research project, researchers working with children and parents should be aware of the coercive potential of using "fad" recording technologies and the ethical issues that might arise when participants don't fully understand the purpose of their involvement.

Uncomfortable encounters

As well as shifting the routes, routines and motivations for going for a walk, the GoPro's presence in being affixed to bodies made it felt, often in uncomfortable ways.

> Rachel: Yeah it was a nightmare, people were looking and stuff and ummm but it was a bit awkward. And then he [Mike, age five] was complaining and wanted to take it off, and then I thought, well what can I do with it, it's not, I'm not going to wear it. I just felt very uncomfortable, because people were looking, especially in the chemist, and then I think we went to a few shops after that on the recording.

For Rachel (early forties) the GoPro's visible presence and the looks from strangers worked to unsettle the usual flows and atmospheres of shopping with her children. Rachel's discomfort exemplifies the concerns that others have raised regarding the use of recording devices. While the GoPro allows researchers "backstage" views of moments otherwise not accessible,[19] it is important to note, as Evers does, that the "camera as a research method will be more possible at some locations than others" as a result of "cultural codes" that shape the appropriateness of what should or shouldn't be recorded.[20] The GoPro as a wearable technology exacerbates this. The mounts and straps that affix the GoPro to bodies were not particularly discreet. For Rachel the GoPro's presence strapped to her son's head worked to mark her and her children as those breaking the cultural codes of privacy at their local pharmacy.

This example raises questions about types of appropriate times and places for GoProing. In this study the instructions provided to participants were fairly open ended. Participants were instructed to use their discretion to decide what, where and when was appropriate to record. If possible, they were also instructed to record the duration of their walk. Hence in this case, in order to become the good participant by documenting walking with her children around the shops, Rachel persisted with the GoPro despite feeling embarrassed and anxious. This example highlights the importance of explaining to and reminding participants how their research involvement should always be conditional and not filled with undue burden.

Considering GoProing

This chapter has sought to open up discussions about the micropolitics of research with families and GoPros. As examples from my research into families' walking experiences highlight, the GoPro never simply captured everyday mobility or research encounters; instead it played a part in cocreating them. Within this research-assemblage (a working arrangement of bodies, technologies, research discourses, instructions, emotions and affects)[21] recording walking with a GoPro was always more than *just* walking. It became GoProing: a performative way of moving in which multiple subjectivities emerge to blur the lines between traditional research categories. Exploring the moments where these hybrid research-participant subjects are made opens up a number of questions around the practicalities and ethics of doing research with GoPros and families. Despite being instructed to go about their everyday walking routines, parents and children tried helpfully to capture the most interesting, most normal, or right types of data for the research, shifting when they walked and engaged with the spaces around them. GoPros complicated the negotiation of informed consent, research expectations and participant burden, highlighting the need to better recognize and communicate the conditional nature of research relationships. Those toying with the idea of using GoPros in research with children and families should be aware of how this technology intersects with the ongoing maintenance, emergence and embodied performance of research encounters and subjectivities.

Notes

1   GoPro, "How to Update Your HERO3," https://gopro.com/update/hero3.
2   GoPro, "Mounts and Accessories," https://shop.gopro.com/APAC/mounts-accessories/.

3   This chapter specifically refers to GoPro because this was the type of camera used in the research.
4   Justin Spinney, "A Chance to Catch a Breath: Using Mobile Video Ethnography in Cycling Research," *Mobilities* 6, no. 2 (2011): 161–182.
5   Eric Laurier, "Being There/Seeing There: Recording and Analysing Life in the Car," in *Mobile Methodologies*, ed. Ben Fincham, Mark McGuinness, and Lesley Murray (Basingstoke: Palgrave Macmillan, 2010), 103–117.
6   Clifton Evers, "Researching Action Sport with a GoPro™ Camera: An Embodied and Emotional Mobile Video Tale of the Sea, Masculinity, and Men-Who-Surf," in *Researching Embodied Sport: Exploring Movement Cultures*, ed. Ian Wellard (Oxon: Routledge, 2016), 145–162.
7   James Evans and Phil Jones, "The Walking Interview: Methodology, Mobility, and Place," *Applied Geography* 31, no. 2 (2011): 849–858.
8   Susannah Clement and Gordon Waitt, "Walking, Mothering, and Care: A Sensory Ethnography of Journeying On-Foot with Children in Wollongong, Australia," *Gender, Place, and Culture* 24, no. 4 (2017): 1185–1203.
9   Patti Lather and Elizabeth A. St. Pierre, "Postqualitative Research," *International Journal of Qualitative Studies in Education* 26, no. 6 (2013): 629–633; Maggie MacLure, "Researching without Representation? Language and Materiality in Postqualitative Methodology," *International Journal of Qualitative Studies in Education* 26, no. 6 (2013): 658–667.
10 Bradley Garrett, "Videographic Geographies: Using Digital Video for Geographic Research," *Progress in Human Geography* 35, no. 4 (2010): 527.
11 Eva Änggård, "Digital Cameras: Agents in Research with Children," *Children's Geographies* 13, no. 1 (2015): 1–13.
12 Nick J. Fox and Pam Alldred, "New Materialist Social Inquiry: Designs, Methods, and the Research-Assemblage," *International Journal of Social Research Methodology* 18, no. 4 (2015): 400.
13 Gilles Deleuze and Félix Guattari, *A Thousand Plateaus: Capitalism and Schizophrenia*, trans. Brian Massumi (Minneapolis: University of Minnesota Press, 1987).
14 Änggård, "Digital Cameras."
15 Evers, "Researching Action Sport with a GoPro™ Camera," 150.
16 Änggård, "Digital Cameras."
17 Jamie Patrice Joanou, "The Bad and the Ugly: Ethical Concerns in Participatory Photographic Methods with Children Living and Working on the Streets of Lima, Peru," *Visual Studies* 24, no. 3 (2009): 214–223.
18 Following university ethics requirements, consent for children's participation was first gained from their parents/guardians via participant information sheet and signed consent form. Children were then provided with or read an age-appropriate participant information sheet. Following a conversation about this, verbal or written assent was attained.

19 Joanou, "The Bad and the Ugly," 214.
20 Evers, "Researching Action Sport with a GoPro™ Camera," 153.
21 Fox and Alldred, "New Materialist Social Inquiry."

Bibliography

Änggård, Eva. "Digital Cameras: Agents in Research with Children." *Children's Geographies* 13, no. 1 (2015): 1–13. doi:10.1080/14733285.2013.827871.

Clement, Susannah and Gordon Waitt. "Walking, Mothering, and Care: A Sensory Ethnography of Journeying On-Foot with Children in Wollongong, Australia." *Gender, Place, and Culture* 24, no. 24 (2017): 1185–1203. doi:10.1080/0966369X.2017.1372376.

Deleuze, Gilles, and Félix Guattari. *A Thousand Plateaus: Capitalism and Schizophrenia.* Translated by Brian Massumi. Minneapolis: University of Minnesota Press, 1987.

Evans, James, and Phil Jones. "The Walking Interview: Methodology, Mobility, and Place." *Applied Geography* 31, no. 2 (2011): 849–858. doi:10.1016/j.apgeog.2010.09.005.

Evers, Clifton. "Researching Action Sport with a GoPro™ Camera: An Embodied and Emotional Mobile Video Tale of the Sea, Masculinity, and Men-Who-Surf." In *Researching Embodied Sport: Exploring Movement Cultures*, edited by Ian Wellard, 145–162. Oxon: Routledge, 2016.

Fox, Nick J., and Pam Alldred. "New Materialist Social Inquiry: Designs, Methods, and the Research-Assemblage." *International Journal of Social Research Methodology* 18, no. 4 (2015): 399–414. doi:10.1080/13645579.2014.921458.

Garrett, Bradley. "Videographic Geographies: Using Digital Video for Geographic Research." *Progress in Human Geography* 35, no. 4 (2010): 521–541. doi:10.1177/0309132510388337.

GoPro. "How to Update Your HERO3." https://gopro.com/update/hero3.

GoPro. "Mounts and Accessories." https://shop.gopro.com/APAC/mounts-accessories/.

Joanou, Jamie Patrice. "The Bad and the Ugly: Ethical Concerns in Participatory Photographic Methods with Children Living and Working on the Streets of Lima, Peru." *Visual Studies* 24, no. 3 (2009): 214–223. doi:10.1080/14725860903309120.

Lather, Patti, and Elizabeth A. St. Pierre. "Postqualitative Research." *International Journal of Qualitative Studies in Education* 26, no. 6 (2013): 629–633. doi:10.1080/09518398.2013.788752.

Laurier, Eric. "Being There/Seeing There: Recording and Analysing Life in the Car." In *Mobile Methodologies*, edited by Ben Fincham, Mark McGuinness, and Lesley Murray, 103–117. Basingstoke: Palgrave Macmillan, 2010.

MacLure, Maggie. "Researching without Representation? Language and Materiality in Postqualitative Methodology." *International Journal of Qualitative Studies in Education* 26, no. 6 (2013): 658–667. doi:10.1080/09518398.2013.788755.

Pink, Sarah. *Doing Sensory Ethnography*. Thousand Oaks, CA: SAGE, 2009.

Rose, Gillian. "On the Relation between 'Visual Research Methods' and Contemporary Visual Culture." *The Sociological Review* 62 (2014): 24–46. doi:10.1111/1467954X.12109.

Spinney, Justin. "A Chance to Catch a Breath: Using Mobile Video Ethnography in Cycling Research." *Mobilities* 6, no. 2 (2011): 161–182. doi:10.1080/17450101.2011.552771.

15

Presencing: Decolonial Attunements to Children's Place Relations

Fikile Nxumalo

Resist that which makes me a ghost and you a monster. Resist that which makes us living dead. … I love that part of us that is always already before our dispossession—there is nothing that is ruined, that can't be given up or taken back.

Angie Morrill, Eve Tuck and the Super Futures Haunt Qollective, "Before Dispossession, or Surviving It"

Telling **situated stories**, *stories that also think about the means and consequences of their own telling, is vitally important … stories that take the complexity of change, and draw in some of the myriad beings—human and not—for whom this change is all too often experienced as suffering and loss. And so these must also be stories that ask their audiences to be curious and to care.*

Thom van Dooren, "Vulture Stories: Narrative and Conservation"

Indigenous thought [meaning] … is created and communicated through the movement of body and sound, testimony and witnessing, remembering, protest and insurrection, by creating a space of **storied presencing**, *alternative imaginings, transformation, reclamation-resurgence.*

Leanne Simpson, *Dancing on Our Turtle's Back: Stories of Nishnaabeg Re-creation, Resurgence and a New Emergence*

Situating knowledges

This is a partial and situated[1] (re)telling of encounters with natural places with young children in three childcare centers on Coast Salish territories in what is now British Columbia, Canada. These encounters are performatively (re)storied as an intentional unsettling of settler colonial erasures in everyday mountain forest encounters on unceded Indigenous land. Interferences in the absenting of pastpresent settler colonialisms are enacted through research and pedagogical practices of *refiguring presences*.[2] These practices are inspired by Michi Saagiig Nishnaabeg scholar Leanne Betasamosake Simpson's *presencing*[3] as ways of knowing, doing and becoming that create ruptures in the multiple ways that settler colonialism continues to dispossess and erase Indigenous peoples and Indigenous relationalities from their lands. As Eve Tuck and Wayne Yang note, under settler colonialism "land is recast as property and as a resource. Indigenous peoples must be erased, must be made into ghosts."[4] *Refiguring* denotes an orientation to practices that question and complicate the notion of absence, where instead Indigenous relationalities are rethought as absented presences that have never gone away, though normalized colonial worldings would have us think and act otherwise.[5] Importantly, then, refiguring is necessarily an attunement to and resistance to taken-for-granted understandings and relations, entangling matter, meaning and geopolitics in everyday materializations of settler colonialism in early childhood places and spaces.

Refiguring presences is an imperfect, fraught and always incomplete response; much more is needed to decolonize nature-based early childhood education. Restorying places and place encounters is not enough, and it always brings with it risks of appropriation. For instance I acknowledge that I am an uninvited (immigrant) guest to this particular Indigenous territory, doing this work in early childhood contexts with predominantly immigrant and white settler children, but without Indigenous collaborators. Nonetheless refiguring presences aims to create interruptive movements away from colonizing relations to place and its more-than-human inhabitants as mute sites of children's learning and discovery. Refiguring presences aims to create openings toward engaging in unsettling dialogues with places.

Put to work as a research methodology and pedagogical orientation, refiguring presences uses stories and narratives as modes of interfering in all-too-easy colonial worldings that erase Indigenous presences by encountering the forest as simply a romantic site of children's developmentally focused learning and discovery. For the remainder of this chapter I put refiguring presences to work through interruptive stories that both describe and haunt everyday pedagogical encounters with a mountain forest on unceded Musqueam, Stó:lō, Squamish and Tsleil-Waututh territories. These stories are intentionally multiple and contradictory: they emerge from actual everyday encounters, as well as from otherwise place stories that were brought to both research and practice to complicate the narratives of children's encounters as the main or only story to be told of learning and becoming with this place. Rather than explain and interpret these "small stories," I intentionally place them alongside each other and alongside performative questions, such that interferences might also be enacted in their reading.

Forest discovery

The three childcare centers, where I worked as a pedagogical facilitator supporting educators in their pedagogical practices, are built atop a mountain and are one part of several building developments surrounded by second-growth forest that is inhabited by black bears, cougars, deer, coyotes and many other animal and plant species. The mountain is named for a prominent settler who surveyed the area on behalf of the British Empire for colonial settlement and economic pursuits. The "untouched," "wild" and "pristine" nature of this mountain forest is a common narrative used in its description. Much of the mountain forest has been demarcated as a protected conservation park area which is administered by the local municipality.

While encounters with the forest have become an intrinsic part of the children's curriculum making, each walk along the forest trail seems to invite new curiosities, even as we revisit the same places again and again. The hollowed-out ancient western red cedar tree stumps that are remnants of colonial logging; the green, slippery moss that clings to trees and rocks; the multitude of mushrooms encountered in the early fall; the twisted carpet of English ivy that entangles some of the trees; the garbage left behind by the forest trail's other users and many other more-than-human participants all gather to invite questions and embodied encounters as children are encouraged to use all of their senses to "discover" the forest, in accordance with child-centered nature education.[6]

In a local tourism publication that encourages visitors to discover this mountain and its forests and trails, one reference to Indigenous peoples is given, referring to past villages along one of the rivers in the area. On the city's heritage site, the city's history is divided into "early," "pioneer," "boom" and "modern" periods. Indigenous peoples are mentioned only in the early period, in a reference to the significant reduction in their population due to smallpox and other diseases brought by European settlers.

Unsettling discovery

Traditional use of cedar has changed over roughly the past hundred years. Its prominence in Northwest Coast culture is still very high, but many of its uses have notably diminished. Coupled with an escalating demand for western red cedar as a timber species, the quantity of cedar available to First Peoples is only a fraction of its former amount. Alienation from their former land base because of factors such as tree farm licenses and the creation of parks and protected areas has further reduced the availability and accessibility of cedar. In an ongoing treaty and land rights negotiations between First Nations and federal and provincial governments, the availability of cedar features prominently.[7]

What might pausing at the western red cedar tree stumps to honor this land as unceded Coast Salish territories and to tell Coast Salish stories of this place as witnesses to Indigenous active presences refigure and unsettle? Red cedar tree stumps might teach us different stories as witnesses to colonial histories and Indigenous relationalities with the land. What does it mean to tell and listen to these stories amid ongoing Indigenous dispossession and rampant capitalist colonial extraction? What might it mean for us to pause at the tree stumps, not to "discover" nature, but to refigure what is already there? What might this do toward creating openings for different and unexpected affectivities, connections, relations and pedagogical responses that disrupt the "erasing of Indigenous presence"?[8]

There was a real good man who was always helping others. Whatever they needed, he had; when they wanted, he gave them food and clothing. When the Great Spirit [Xá:ls] saw this, he said, "That man has done his work; when he dies and where he is buried, a cedar tree will grow and be useful to the people—the roots for baskets, the bark for clothing, the wood for shelter."[9]

Extraction and assimilation

Extraction and assimilation go together. Colonialism and capitalism are based on extracting and assimilating. My land is seen as a resource. My relatives in the plant and animal worlds are seen as resources. My culture and knowledge are a resource. The act of extraction removes all of the relationships that give whatever is being extracted meaning. Colonialism has always extracted the Indigenous—extraction of Indigenous knowledge, Indigenous women, Indigenous peoples.[10]

Walking the forest trail

Our walks with the children into the forest are along part of an extensive hiking trail system that has been constructed through the mountain forest. Encountering this partly paved trail is to walk literally and figuratively amid tensions. This forest trail is materially and discursively connected to colonial past and present histories. Many of the hiking trails on the mountain incorporate earlier logging roads that were cut into the forest as part of the extensive commercial logging that began in 1903 and accompanied colonial settlement in the area. With the opening of a lumber mill close to the mountain's foot the mountain was quickly cleared of its trees. The lumber processed at the sawmill (at the time one of the largest in the British Empire until it ceased operation thirty years later) was exported to destinations in the British colonies, such as Australia, as well as to other export markets, such as South America. This lumber was used for many purposes, including shingles, railway ties and spars for sailing ships.[11]

Unsettling the forest trail

How might walking this partially man-made trail be enacted as pedagogical practices of unsettling the separation of past/present, constructed/natural, human/nonhuman, nature/culture? What histories, demarcations and boundaries are either enacted, obscured, or perhaps both, by the forest trail and the forest's apparent timelessness when we walk with children? What might educators learn by following extractive settler colonial logging histories in this forest as a past that is not closed but remains as an active *presence* in the forest's fabric, the forest trail, and the *Shxweli*, "the life force that exists in all things"?[12]

Touching tree hollows

The tree cavities carved into the trees invite the children's curiosities. Some tree hollows are close enough to the ground that the children can peer closely and reach in, touching the holes' depths and edges. Another hollowed out tree trunk is large enough for the children to step inside its depths. Encounters with these tree hollows enact many "real" and "imaginary" inhabitants for the children: "acorns"; "a bath for dinosaurs and bears"; "a rabbit hole"; "bear prints"; "a bear hole"; "a giant's prints"; "a special bird" and so on.

On relational life amid the rotting hollows

As Indigenous knowledges teach us, relationality encompasses complex relations to the earth, cosmologies, living and nonliving beings, and all other matter.[13] The life's complex ecologies inhabited in rotting tree hollows might have much to teach early childhood educators about the interdependencies, contradictions and relations of life and death as co-inhabitants of tree hollows. The more-than-human inhabitants of this forest reciprocally change each other as active participants in the situated storying of this place.[14] What histories of the tree hollow as an active participant in this encounter might be told? What might it mean for educators to look out for the entanglements and vibrancies suggested by tree hollows? What might this enact and bring into view in terms of new possibilities for nature pedagogies? It typically takes over a century for decay holes to begin to form in dying trees and often several centuries for a large tree hollow to form.[15] Touching the ancient cedar tree hollow, then, is also touching deep time and wondering about the human and more-than-human pastpresent histories of this place that have been captured through the shaping of the tree hollows.

The tree hollows' materiality that the children touch cannot be thought apart from their signification or narration and the tensions and connections thereof. What might it mean and do for educators to inhabit tree hollows figuratively through ongoing worldings of colonialism? How might seeing tree hollows as figurative for the rot and devastation created by settler colonialism unsettle our (myself and educators') pedagogical practices? As Anishinaabe scholar Damien Lee describes, "Over 500 years of colonial attacks have ripped holes in the fabric of our relationships within our places."[16] Thinking with the tree hollow as a figure for the effects of colonialism might also be helpful to consider the complexities of colonialism: that the Indigenous cannot be relegated to an absence. Complex relationships and relationalities abound, persist and continually shift *amid the holes left by the rot.*

Decolonial futures

I keep a list of theories of change in my pocket so I can remember something more meaningful than raising awareness. Something more material than raising consciousness. Something more to the touch than visibility. My list of theories of change includes **haunting**, *visitations, Maroon societies,* **decolonization**, *revenge,* **mattering**.[17]

Toward refiguring presences

Refiguring presences as a theory of change in early childhood research and practice foregrounds the interruptive potential of stories that attend to settler colonial tensions and Indigenous relationalities in particular places. I have intentionally brought forward stories that create possibilities for ways of relating that unsettle anthropocentric and colonial enactments of nature education and the erasures therein. My intent, then, has been to experiment with possibilities that unsettle innocent and romantic visions of children's relations with nature and take seriously the implications of inheriting settler colonial histories in the particular situated localities of unceded Coast Salish territories. I have attempted to resist a singular master narrative by posing questions rather than definitive answers alongside the stories.

While restorying places might create possibilities toward more equitable orientations and ethical relationalities, it is important to note that this does not present a resolution to the messiness of ongoing colonialisms or to Indigenous peoples' displacements from the places I describe in this paper. Here I have just begun to suggest possibilities for early childhood educators and researchers to pay critical attention to the seeming banalities of everyday encounters with "natural" places in settler colonial contexts. As a theory of change of decolonial potential, I suggest that relating to the mountain forest trail and to tree hollows and stumps in this particular place through multiple material-discursive stories and histories might trouble views of this particular mountain forest as an uninscribed place—and might create openings toward difficult conversations, disruptive understandings and different unsettled place relations.

Notes

1 Donna Haraway, "Situated Knowledges: The Science Question in Feminism and the Privilege of Partial Perspective," *Feminist Studies* 14, no. 3 (1988): 575–599.
2 Fikile Nxumalo, "Forest Stories: Restorying Encounters with 'Natural' Places in Early Childhood Education," in *Unsettling the Colonial Places and Spaces of Early Childhood Education*, ed. Veronica Pacini-Ketchabaw and Affrica Taylor (New York: Routledge, 2015), 21–42.
3 Leanne Betasamosake Simpson, *Dancing on Our Turtle's Back: Stories of Nishnaabeg Re-creation, Resurgence, and a New Emergence* (Winnipeg, MB: Arbeiter Ring, 2011).

4   Eve Tuck and K. Wayne Yang, "Decolonization Is Not a Metaphor," *Decolonization: Indigeneity, Education, and Society* 1, no. 1 (2012): 6.
5   Gayatri Spivak, *The Post-Colonial Critic: Interviews, Strategies, Dialogues*, ed. Sarah Harasym (New York: Routledge, 1990).
6   See Deborah Tippins, Stacey Neuharth-Pritchett, and Debra Mitchell, "Connecting Young Children with the Natural World: Past, Present, and Future Landscapes," in *Research in Early Childhood Science Education*, ed. Kathy Cabe Trundle and Mesut Saçkes (New York: Springer, 2014), 279–297; Ann Pelo, *The Goodness of Rain: Developing an Ecological Identity in Young Children* (Redmond, WA: Exchange Press, 2013).
7   Ann Garibaldi and Nancy Turner, "Cultural Keystone Species: Implications for Ecological Conservation and Restoration," *Ecology and Society* 9, no. 3 (2004): 1–18.
8   Simpson, *Dancing on Our Turtle's Back*, 96.
9   As told by Stó:lō Elder Bertha Peters, cited in Hillary Stewart, *Cedar: Tree of Life to the Northwest Coast Indians* (Vancouver: Douglas and McIntyre, 1995), 22.
10 Leanne Simpson, "Dancing the World into Being: A Conversation with Idle No More's Leanne Simpson" (by Naomi Klein), *Yes Magazine*, 5 March 2013, 11.
11 Fred Braches, "Chile, Peru, and the Early Lumber Exports of BC," *BC History* 42, no. 2 (Summer 2009): 2–7.
12 Stó:lō Nation Lalems ye Stó:lō Si:ya:m, *Stó:lō Heritage Policy Manual*, 5 May 2003.
13 Gregory Cajete, *Native Science: Natural Laws of Interdependence* (Santa Fe, NM: Clear Light, 2000).
14 Thom van Dooren, "Vulture Stories: Narrative and Conservation," in *A Manifesto for Living in the Anthropocene*, eds. Katherine Gibson, Ruth Fincher, and Deborah Bird Rose (New York: Punctum Books, 2015), 51–56.
15 Kristina L. Cockle, Kathy Martin, and Tomasz Wesołowski, "Woodpeckers, Decay, and the Future of Cavity-Nesting Vertebrate Communities Worldwide," *Frontiers in Ecology and the Environment* 9, no. 7 (2011): 377–382.
16 Damien Lee, "Coming Home through Active Presence," *Dibaajimowinan: Four Stories of Resurgence in Michi Saagiig Nishnaabeg Territory* blog, last modified 30 August 2011.
17 Angie Morrill, Eve Tuck, and the Super Futures Haunt Qollective, "Before Dispossession, or Surviving It," *Liminalities: A Journal of Performance Studies* 12, no. 1 (2016): 1–20.

Bibliography

Braches, Fred. "Chile, Peru, and the Early Lumber Exports of BC." *BC History* 42, no. 2 (Summer 2009): 2–7.
Cajete, Gregory. *Native Science: Natural Laws of Interdependence*. Santa Fe, NM: Clear Light, 2000.

Cockle, Kristina L., Kathy Martin, and Tomasz Wesołowski. "Woodpeckers, Decay, and the Future of Cavity-Nesting Vertebrate Communities Worldwide." *Frontiers in Ecology and the Environment* 9, no. 7 (2011): 377–382.

Garibaldi, Ann, and Nancy Turner. "Cultural Keystone Species: Implications for Ecological Conservation and Restoration." *Ecology and Society* 9, no. 3 (2004): 1–18.

Haraway, Donna. "Situated Knowledges: The Science Question in Feminism and the Privilege of Partial Perspective." *Feminist Studies* 14, no. 3 (1988): 575–599.

Lee, Damien. "Coming Home through Active Presence." *Dibaajimowinan: Four Stories of Resurgence in Michi Saagiig Nishnaabeg Territory* blog. Last modified 30 August 2011. http://dibaajimowin.wordpress.com.

Morrill, Angie, Eve Tuck, and the Super Futures Haunt Qollective. "Before Dispossession, or Surviving It." *Liminalities: A Journal of Performance Studies* 12, no. 1 (2016): 1–20.

Nxumalo, Fikile. "Forest Stories: Restorying Encounters with 'Natural' Places in Early Childhood Education." In *Unsettling the Colonial Places and Spaces of Early Childhood Education*, edited by Veronica Pacini-Ketchabaw and Affrica Taylor, 21–42. New York: Routledge, 2015.

Pelo, Ann. *The Goodness of Rain: Developing an Ecological Identity in Young Children*. Redmond, WA: Exchange Press, 2013.

Simpson, Leanne Betasamosake. *Dancing on Our Turtle's Back: Stories of Nishnaabeg Re-creation, Resurgence, and a New Emergence*. Winnipeg, MB: Arbeiter Ring, 2011.

Simpson, Leanne Betasamosake. "Dancing the World into Being: A Conversation with Idle No More's Leanne Simpson" (by Naomi Klein). *Yes Magazine*, 5 March 2013. http://www.yesmagazine.org/peace-justice/dancing-the-world-into-being-a-conversation-with-idle-no-more-leanne-simpson.

Spivak, Gayatri. *The Post-Colonial Critic: Interviews, Strategies, Dialogues*, edited by Sarah Harasym. New York: Routledge, 1990.

Stewart, Hillary. *Cedar: Tree of Life to the Northwest Coast Indians*. Vancouver: Douglas and McIntyre, 1995.

Stó:lōNation Lalems ye Stó: lōSi: ya:m.*Stó: lōHeritage Policy Manual*, 2003. http://www.srrmcentre.com/files/File/Stolo Heritage Policy Manual, May 2003, v1.2.pdf.

Tippins, Deborah, Stacey Neuharth-Pritchett, and Debra Mitchell. "Connecting Young Children with the Natural World: Past, Present, and Future Landscapes." In *Research in Early Childhood Science Education*, edited by Kathy Cabe Trundle and Mesut Saçkes, 279–297. New York: Springer, 2014.

Tuck, Eve, and K. Wayne Yang. "Decolonization Is Not a Metaphor." *Decolonization: Indigeneity, Education, and Society* 1, no. 1 (2012): 1–40.

van Dooren, Thom. "Vulture Stories: Narrative and Conservation." In *A Manifesto for Living in the Anthropocene*, edited by Katherine Gibson, Ruth Fincher, and Deborah Bird Rose, 51–56. New York: Punctum Books, 2015.

Part Four

Relations with Retheorizings

16

Caring: Method as Affect, Obligation and Action

B. Denise Hodgins

Caring means becoming subject to the unsettling obligation of curiosity, which requires knowing more at the end of the day than at the beginning.

Donna Haraway, *When Species Meet*

In a collaborative inquiry with young children in a toddler classroom, four early childhood educators and I thought with several doll-child encounters to explore how children, educators and things become implicated in gendered caring practices. Guided by our overarching curiosity for how conceptualizations (assumptions) and practices of gender and care are intra-actively related,[1] we came to recognize that emerging gender and caring subjectivities touch many material-discursive practices (technologies) in, near and far from the classroom.[2] While care was a subject of/in our research, it was also a doing. As I review our inquiry together, I am struck with the potentiality of *putting care to work* as a method in postqualitative research intended to, as Donna Haraway says, "get at how worlds are made and unmade, in order to participate in the processes, in order to foster some forms of life and not others."[3]

The conceptualization of care that I engage with in this chapter is indebted to feminist science studies, in particular María Puig de la Bellacasa's careful (re)reading of critical feminism and an early feminist ethics of care that illuminated the undervaluation of care as both a value and a practice.[4] This early work challenged care as understood through a public-private binary and thus opened up envisioning care (a) outside of only personal (individual) abilities and affects, (b) beyond the reaches of home life and (c) as an ethic of interdependence that is always already politicized. As Haraway notes, "Feminists have also argued early, often and well, for caring in all its senses as a core needed practice."[5] With a material feminist, more-than-human relational ontology, this conceptualization of care is thickened to include both human and nonhuman relationality and interdependence, where care operates with/in natureculture assemblages.[6] Leaning on Puig de la Bellacasa's view of care as "an affective state, a material vital doing, and an ethico-political obligation,"[7] I consider caring, in all its senses, as a core needed practice for postqualitative research.

I draw on excerpts from our research, which appear as italicized narratives layered through the chapter, to explore caring as method through three key ideas: being called into response, the concept of dis/connection and taking up a transformative ethos.

Being called into response

Angus is by himself at the water table playing with small buckets, pouring water over a peach-colored plastic girl baby doll who is sitting up in the bubbly, soapy water. He has been "bathing" this baby doll for several minutes when he shifts from pouring water on the baby to pouring some water onto the floor. He looks at me, smiles, waits. He pours some more. "I'm making a puddle right there," he announces. Angus pours some more water into his puddle. He returns to the water table and picks up the peach-colored doll he had been bathing, turns and puts the doll face-first in the puddle, and slides her across the floor with his hand, smiling. He jumps over the baby, then steps on the doll, now laughing. Angus kicks the baby doll across the floor. More laughter as Angus runs toward me. Angus quickly returns to the water table and grabs up one of the other dolls there—a dark brown boy baby doll. He brings him to the puddle, placing him down face-first, and kicks him across the floor. He follows the doll, laughing, picks him up again and drops him with the first doll still lying face down on the watery floor.[8]

Documentation of plastic baby dolls that went from being washed in bubbly water to being kicked across the room called to us educator-researchers and "glowed"[9] in a way that drew us in to want to know more. We became deeply curious, which, as Haraway describes, is "the beginning of fulfillment of the obligation to know more as a consequence of being called into response."[10] Thinking with Haraway, caring requires that we take up this obligation of curiosity that has arisen from being called into response. Noticing that we were affected by this moment was instrumental to our efforts to slow down, pay close attention and attend to far more than what was said (what we thought we heard) and what was done (what we thought we saw). While the educators and I were initially called into response through Angus's engagement with the baby dolls in the water table, the Angus–water-table–baby-doll event's traces provoked us to explore, discuss and remember dolls in all their lively more-than-human pastpresent entanglements. Our *putting care to work* included tracing these entanglements and trying to acknowledge and nurture (in other words, be in response with) the multiple, diverse human and more-than-human relationalities.[11] We considered the dolls' color (brown and white), shape (infant/baby) and material (plastic), as well as the developmental logics for having baby dolls in the classroom. We traced their production, marketing and curricular histories and presents and our own personal experiences (memories) with/of dolls. We were troubled by dolls' plasticity (are they safe?), their production (are they ethically made?), their genderedness (who are they really for?) and their pedagogical assumptions (do they really teach nurturance, acceptance, self-worth, innocence?) yet also drawn to the care these dolls could evoke. Through being in response with the doll-child moments from both inside and outside the classroom we came to recognize that it is not only that these dolls matter to some children (and adults): the mattering of these dolls matters.

Dis/connection

I am sitting at my desk writing, trying to write, about dolls. My deep challenge with the histories and present-day socio-political production stories engulfs me, moves me, as I click away on my laptop. I have placed myself beside the family desktop computer whose screensaver is set up to scatter photos randomly across the monitor. It generally catches my eye when I seek a distraction from writing. I notice that an almost nine-year-old picture has turned up of my son, at about a year and a half, feeding one of his dolls with a toy baby bottle. Like the image of Ruby [from our research study] lovingly looking at the baby doll she has wrapped beside her, this photo of my son punctures my moral outrage about plastics and messages of obligatory maternity and domesticity with feelings of pleasure that my son (and I) took in his dolls. I am reminded again of the delight and fun—dare I say care—that can emerge from engaging with dolls. I shift my eyes from the screensaver and return to my writing, but I am different than I was a minute before. As my fingers tap on the keyboard, feelings of conflict, tension and fondness resonate through my body.[12]

Caring, as an adjective, is typically understood as displaying concern for others through kindness, warmth and compassion, and the word *care* in our society tends to conjure images of hand-to-hand or arm-around-another touch (as the word's Google image search indicates). However dictionary definitions of care exceed these understandings and include such words as anxiety, apprehension and uncertainty, with the etymological root of care tracing to the old English and old Germanic words for grief/grieve and lament.[13] In my reviewing of our research study this encompassing view of care is evident. Being called into response with our "obligations of care"[14] (i.e., the dolls, children, educators and situated histories in our inquiry) was not a smooth nor harmonious engagement. As the narratives I revisit in this chapter indicate, the affects evoked were challenging and contentious, as well as pleasurable and joyful. So too was our work to attend, explore, respond and know more at the day's end. Caring as method called forth concern for others that could be warm *and* anxiety provoking. At varying times those others were the children, each other, the dolls, the workers who produced the dolls, the environment in which they were produced and transported and particular histories that are rendered invisible. Puig de la Bellacasa points out that the numerous theoretical and empirical engagements with care reveal how "caring implicates different relationalities, issues, and practices in different settings."[15]

For us as educators and researchers, one of the anxieties that emerged in our research together was in facing the realization that we cannot care for everything or everyone all of the time and that caring for one could be (often is) at the expense of another. Our actions of, with, and for care generated *both* connection and disconnection. Borrowing from Karen Barad's conceptualization of dis/continuity, I put forward that caring is an act of dis/connection. In her agential realist thinking with Bohr's quantum physics Barad troubles causality and the unfolding of time as linear, progressive and tidy[16] and brings this troubling to the modernist binary of continuity versus discontinuity. In her slash's use with dis/continuity as active and reiterative she challenges the presumption that a break or separation exists between the two and offers instead that the act is a "cutting together-apart (one move)."[17] My suggestion is that caring as method not only acknowledges, makes space for and responds to both connections and disconnections, but that our researching materializes these connections and disconnections as well. And with Barad's quantum dis/continuity, these dis/connections are not either/or, separate and isolated events; they are inseparable (and inevitable), produced together-apart. Barad refers to such moves as agential cuts.

A transformative ethos

When I recorded Angus at the water table with baby dolls, my histories and assumptions, the camera's capabilities and my computer, I, Angus, the water and bubbles [and] the dolls, all intra-acted in that moment. When we discussed this and other [doll] moments, the histories and assumptions of my co-researchers, which images and videos I chose, how I cut them together, the computer's volume, the room's size,, the chairs' comfort and so on intra-acted to produce a new moment. When we returned to the classroom, we were different than we were before—differently curious, but differently accountable as well. As I continued my exploration and analyses, layering stories, tracing threads and knots, my curiosity and accountability continued to grow/change. The hi/stories, productions, developmental rationales of/for dolls in the classroom, the children's love and conflict (with each other at times) for them, my love and conflict over them, which stories do I tell? In the middle of gathering and compiling many, many doll hi/stories, including pages of plastic perils and problems, I shared these with one of the co-researchers in this study. She responded by asking me why/how she should/could care about these dolls amid all these problems. Indeed. Then images of Mateo and Ruby, my own son and daughter, holding, snuggling, smiling at baby dolls interfered with any possibility of a straightforward, tidy declarative statement about dolls in ECE.[18]

Puig de la Bellacasa asserts that "adequate care requires knowledge and curiosity regarding the needs of an 'other'—human or not—and these become possible through relating, through refusing objectification. Such a process inevitably transforms the entangled beings."[19] There are two points that I want to bring to this assertion. The first is that, as previously described, this care through relating is an act of dis/connection that evokes, provokes and requires a variety of responses. I suggest that putting care to work as a research method is to consider *how* "our cuts foster relationship"[20] and to take seriously the question "to what and whom is a response required?".[21] Researching from this perspective then is about attending to the mattering of our onto-ethico-epistemological practices. It requires that we stay with the complexities and grapple with the tensions and contradictions doing so brings. Which cares we care, which questions we ask, which stories we tell, which details we attend to, matter. As Haraway writes, "The details link actual beings to actual response-abilities."[22]

The second point I want to bring to Puig de la Bellacasa's assertion is in regard to inevitably transforming these entangled beings. As the narratives suggest, caring changed us (as educators and researchers) and the ways that we met the children, the materials, and each other in the classroom. Transformation through our relating occurred throughout the process together (as opposed to a "so what? now what?" end-point analysis), which shaped our ongoing pedagogy and research choices as we worked to make space for acknowledging and being accountable to our dis/connections. Our "new" researching selves were continuously new and always connected to our histories and hopes. If the researcher is always new, always transforming in relation with others and cannot know beforehand, a different kind of "paying attention" as a researcher is required. Puig de la Bellacasa proposes that "caring is more about a transformative ethos than an ethical application. We need to ask 'how to care' in each situation."[23] This is not only an epistemological project, as Puig de la Bellacasa makes clear, and certainly not one for constructing epistemological (moral) standards. As she points out:

> Formulating the necessity of care as an open question still adds a requirement to constructivism: cultivating a speculative commitment to contribute to livable worlds. As a transformative ethos, caring is a living technology with vital material implications for human and non-human worlds.[24]

My suggestion is that this onto-ethico-epistemological conceptualization of care may well serve commitments from both researchers and educators to fostering equitable, livable worlds. In this chapter I have revisited moments from our collective inquiry regarding gender and care to consider how caring as method in postqualitative research might be an avenue for researchers to engage in the present, while being response-able to/for that which we have inherited and committed to flourishing yet-to-come. As a postqualitative method, caring—understood through Puig de la Bellacasa's "triptych notion of care"[25]—is not about finding the (final) answer, but rather about opening up speculative possibilities. Caring again and again and again. Such caring involves "maintenance doings, affective relations, and ethicality as well as political commitment."[26] At a time when we live with—and will be bequeathing to future generations—the legacies of colonization, rapid technological advancements, human-caused climate change, mass species extinctions and mass migration and displacement, this call for caring as method feels both urgent and necessary.

Notes

1 Karen Barad, *Meeting the Universe Halfway: Quantum Physics and the Entanglement of Matter and Meaning* (Durham, NC: Duke University Press, 2007).

2 B. Denise Hodgins, *(Re)Storying Cars and Dolls: Gender and Care with Young Children* (PhD diss., University of Victoria, 2014).

3 Donna Haraway, "A Game of Cat's Cradle: Science Studies, Feminist Theory, Cultural Studies," *Configurations* 2, no. 1 (1994): 65.

4   María Puig de la Bellacasa, *Matters of Care in Technoscience: Speculative Ethics in More Than Human Worlds* (Minneapolis: University of Minnesota Press, 2017).
5   Donna Haraway, *When Species Meet* (Minneapolis: University of Minnesota Press, 2008), 332, note 8.
6   Puig de la Bellacasa, *Matters of Care: Speculative Ethics*.
7   María Puig de la Bellacasa, "Matters of Care in Technoscience: Assembling Neglected Things," *Social Studies of Science* 41, no. 1 (2011): 90.
8   Hodgins, *(Re)Storying Cars and Dolls*, 120.
9   Maggie MacLure, "The Offence of Theory," *Journal of Education Policy* 25, no. 2 (2010): 277–286.
10 Nicholas Gane and Donna Haraway, "When We Have Never Been Human, What Is to Be Done?: Interview with Donna Haraway," *Theory, Culture, Society* 23 (2006): 143.
11 Donna Haraway, *Modest_Witness@Second_Millennium_Femaleman_Meets_Oncomouse* (New York: Routledge, 1997), 268.
12 Hodgins, *(Re)Storying Cars and Dolls*, 151–152.
13 Oxford English Dictionary, "Care," *Oxford English Dictionary* (Oxford University Press, 2017), https://en.oxforddictionaries.com/definition/care.
14 Haraway, *When Species Meet*, 70.
15 Puig de la Bellacasa, *Matters of Care: Speculative Ethics*, 3.
16 Barad, *Meeting the Universe Halfway*.
17 Malou Juelskær and Nete Schwennesen, "Intra-active Entanglements: An Interview with Karen Barad," *Kvinder, Køn & Forskning* 1–2 (2012): 16.
18 Hodgins, *(Re)Storying Cars and Dolls*, 223–224.
19 Puig de la Bellacasa, "Matters of Care: Assembling," 98.
20 Maria Puig de la Bellacasa, "'Nothing Comes without Its World': Thinking with Care," *The Sociological Review* 60, no. 2 (2012): 204.
21 Gane and Haraway, "When We Have Never Been Human," 145.
22 Donna Haraway, "Awash in Urine: DES and Premarin® in Multispecies Response-ability," *Women's Studies Quarterly* 40 (1&2): 312.
23 Puig de la Bellacasa, "Matters of Care: Assembling," 100.
24 Ibid.
25 Puig de la Bellacasa, *Matters of Care: Speculative Ethics*, 218.
26 Ibid.

Bibliography

Barad, Karen. *Meeting the Universe Halfway: Quantum Physics and the Entanglement of Matter and Meaning*. Durham, NC: Duke University Press, 2007.

Gane, Nicholas, and Donna Haraway. "When We Have Never Been Human, What Is to Be Done?: Interview with Donna Haraway." *Theory, Culture, Society* 23 (2006): 135–158.

Haraway, Donna. "A Game of Cat's Cradle: Science Studies, Feminist Theory, Cultural Studies." *Configurations* 2, no. 1 (1994): 59–71.

Haraway, Donna. "Awash in Urine: DES and Premarin® in Multispecies Response-ability." *Women's Studies Quarterly* 40 (1&2): 301–316.

Haraway, Donna. *Modest_Witness@Second_Millennium_Femaleman_Meets_Oncomouse*. New York: Routledge, 1997.

Haraway, Donna. *When Species Meet*. Minneapolis: University of Minnesota Press, 2008.

Hodgins, B. Denise. *(Re)Storying Cars and Dolls: Gender and Care with Young Children* (PhD diss., University of Victoria, 2014). https://dspace.library.uvic.ca/handle/1828/5740.

Juelskær, Malou, and Nete Schwennesen. "Intra-active Entanglements: An Interview with Karen Barad." *Kvinder, Køn & Forskning* 1–2 (2012): 10–23.

MacLure, Maggie. "The Offence of Theory." *Journal of Education Policy* 25, no. 2 (2010): 277–286. doi:10.1080/02680930903462316.

Puig de la Bellacasa, María. "Matters of Care in Technoscience: Assembling Neglected Things." *Social Studies of Science* 41, no. 1 (2011): 85–106.

Puig de la Bellacasa, María. *Matters of Care in Technoscience: Speculative Ethics in More than Human Worlds*. Minneapolis: University of Minnesota Press, 2017.

Puigde la Bellacasa, María. "'Nothing Comes without Its World': Thinking with Care." *The Sociological Review* 60, no. 2 (2012): 197–216. doi:10.1111/j.1467-954X.2012.02070.x.

17

Learningliving: Aesthetics of Meaning Making

Randa Khattar and Karyn Callaghan

Randa's story

At a conference we attended some years ago atelierista Jason Avery told a story of an encounter with a young child who had made repeated stereotypical paintings of flowers. Jason had asked the child where she sees flowers, and the child replied, "There are roses in my nonna's garden." Jason asked her what a rose looks like in her nonna's garden. She paused, with her gaze fixed on a point somewhere in her mind. Jason projected for us the drawing that she produced after her internal gaze. It is stunning. He pauses while showing this documentation. Each participant at the conference is making meaning of this now-shared experience. After a variety of hushed reactions, audience participants express awe that such a young child could produce something so sophisticated, so beautiful. I wrote in my notebook, "Is the image of the flower beautiful because it has beauty? Is it beautiful because it is an act of meaning making? Is it in the recognition of meaning making at work that there is an aesthetic quality?"

Karyn's story

In July 1985 I set out on an odyssey, driving by myself from Ontario to Santa Fe, New Mexico. Before I left, I was advised to try to track down a fellow named Ifan, who had lived in Ontario but had moved to Santa Fe many years earlier and could perhaps point me toward some interesting people and places. I fell deeply in love with New Mexico—the land, the sky, the smell of the air after rain, the color of the rocks and soil, the stars, the mingling of Indigenous, Mexican, and Anglo food, art, and music in this high desert oasis. This place felt more "home" to me than anywhere I had ever been. I finally located Ifan a few days before I had to return, and he did connect me with bookstores I hadn't yet discovered and with folks who were very generous with their time. When I got home I wrote a letter to thank him, telling the story as best I could of the depth to which Santa Fe had impacted my heart and soul. Fall came and went and winter settled in on southern Ontario, with gray skies and damp cold air. One February day, a letter arrived in my mailbox with a Santa Fe return address. I opened it to find a handwritten note that said, "It's February in Ontario. You should read the words you wrote while under the spell of adobe streets." The note was tucked around the letter I had sent the previous summer that Ifan had read and put back into its envelope. I read my own letter and cried, deeply moved, not only by being transported back to that aesthetic haven, but also that this near-stranger had recognized the emotion in that letter, kept it, and thought to send it back to me at a time when revisiting those stunning days in Santa Fe would lift me out of the gray. Years later when I first heard about the practice in the preschools in Reggio Emilia, Italy, of revisiting the children's words with them through pedagogical documentation, I knew immediately how impactful it was to know your words have been held and cared for, and how this act reveals a deep kind of listening and empathy.

Neoliberal currents

In neoliberal approaches to early childhood education storying as a practice of appreciation for underlying patterns of connection struggles to be taken seriously. Neoliberal educational approaches "cut up thought into disciplines [that] make us unable to grasp 'that which is woven together' or, in the original meaning of the term, the complex."[1] Bill Readings argues that universities and other institutions for learning have the potential to be sites of "doing justice to thought ... trying to hear that which cannot be said but that which tries to make itself heard."[2] But yet the dominant discourse of neoliberal approaches to education fails to hear other voices.[3] Moreover objectivity and quantifiability are granted the full weight of legitimacy for showing evidence of learning. Discrete and easily digestible, neoliberal knowledge can be absorbed, disseminated and transplanted without a sense of place—or story. An undertow is present: the closer we are to the orbit of neoliberal discourses, the further away we are from states of perturbation capable of deepening the senses toward connection making. In an effort to sustain epistemological and ontological scalability characteristic of the neoliberal project, silenced are situated stories of meaning making that enunciate what is local, unassimilable and wild.

In our pedagogical practices we encounter this tension arising every day when two forces are at play: one driving us to analyze and categorize, and the other compelling us to synthesize, to focus on relationships, to realize that context is what connects us. Modern science, like neoliberalism, is one way of thinking, governed by dispassionate logic, and it has dominated Western thinking since the 17th century. It aims to transcend the particular.

Struggling to be heard, embodied moments of attuned listening,[4] as were described in our opening stories, produce ruptures in the neoliberal impulse[5] to reduce the alterity of otherness.[6] They present as disruptors to dominant developmentalist early childhood discourses that, in the name of developmentally appropriate practice, reduce the recalcitrant alterity of children and childhood to a series of predictable, universal, controllable steps toward adulthood.[7] They cultivate an appetite for embracing each moment of encounter. In such attentive moments we are poised to create and exchange stories radically other to dominant narratives of the prophetic pedagogies[8] of neoliberal markets or quality in early childhood education.

In this chapter we offer *learningliving* as a lively aesthetic movement capable of the reconnaissance[9] of *making meaning of meaning making*. We recognize learningliving in the interaction between the child and Jason, made visible through pedagogical documentation. We see child and educator moving relationally in a deeply reciprocal world. We also recognize learningliving in the connection Karyn and Ifan shared across geo-temporal space, made evident through the profoundly powerful act of revisiting experience. How might meaning making through an orientation of learningliving reconfigure our capacity to learn and live with young children?

In every context, in every life, opportunities are present for deep attentiveness—those moments when—and where—we are moved into another kind of awareness and feel a sense of profound connection. The world's official wonders inspire awe in many people. But following the path of an ant that is carrying several times its own body weight, or peering at the luminescent wing of a dragonfly, or seeing the upside-down reflection in a drop of dew are seemingly mundane moments that can be felt as aesthetic experiences. These are moments when we can become present to a relationship with an aesthetic part of ourselves, moments of deep affinity that are suspended, appearing timeless, often wordless. If we are paying attention, we can witness young children and educators engaged in these relationships every day: present, wondering. We have the opportunity to be connected through aesthetic experiences when our senses are ignited (and connected) and when we are listening deeply. Although what is considered beautiful varies over time and place and between individuals, we suggest that the aesthetic experience is desirable and often emotional. We need it. We recognize it in others in real life, in photos, in stories. It matters. These moments connect us to the pulse of breathing, to conscious living, to each other, to our entanglements within the world.

Is beauty a way of knowing?[10]

Vea Vecchi, atelierista in the Diana School in Reggio Emilia, Italy, quotes philosopher Mauro Ceruti as stating "epistemology and aesthetics are synonymous" and further that "aesthetics means caring for our sensibility toward relations."[11] This deep knowing rejects the thought that aesthetics can be considered an add-on, asserting that "aesthetics is the way of knowing"[12] attuned in recognition, affinity and kinship.[13] Gregory Bateson referred to an aesthetic pattern of relations[14] connecting not only how humans come to know, but also how the "starfish and the redwood forest … [learn] to grow into five-way symmetry … [or] to survive a forest fire."[15] This aesthetic sensibility is ontologically and epistemologically *learningliving* the relational.

Thinking through an aesthetic of relationships appears to change the way the educators in Reggio Emilia move through the world. The documentation they create—also often described as beautiful—is not intended to be an objective rendering or representation of "what happened" or storied evidence of desired academic outcomes, but rather is a trace of moments of learningliving. We are made of the stuff of these stories that are infused with spirit and relationality. These stories are always being written; they arise from the stories that came before, stories of children's encounters with their context, with materials, with each other and with the educators. All of this happens within a city where citizens encounter the children's intelligence and competence on a daily basis. Stories are a kind of moving context, not merely a recitation of facts or occurrences. A good story invites us in, knowing that we will see it differently and that the protagonists will also see it differently each time they revisit it, such as we hope for the reader encountering this story/chapter. We come to know ourselves in new ways with each reconnaissance. We bring ourselves into being every time we tell a story to "engage in further entanglements with and become different in ourselves as teachers."[16] Story is built on concern for the human condition: the situation *is* felt. The aesthetic's spirited danceexists with reason. Story proves nothing, attempts to prove nothing. Its uncertainty, as well as its multiplicity, is what gives it power. It requires interpretation and opens up possibilities. Learningliving brings the educator as close to the child as possible, with empathy and respect for their ways of navigating the world's complexity and strategies for bringing their own sense of order *through* relationship. The act of *recording* in this context—recording so as to revisit and consider multiple possible meanings—is the heart's act. The English word *record* is derived from the Latin word *recordari* (to remember), which is rooted in the Latin word for heart (*cor*).This meaning is apparent in the description offered by Simona Bonilauri and Tiziana Filippini of context that is shaped by documentation: "The stories told here belong to the world of relationships and friendships, spoken words and written words. Though simple and direct in appearance, these stories actually conceal a long and delicate experiment in learning to live together."[17]

What we see in documentation are educators who are present, listening, recognizing the impossibility of knowing what is in front of them. They are curious, aware that children have infinite ways of knowing and allowing themselves to be known. They understand that wonder and marvel are key to creating knowledge, both for children and adults. Their documentation is not *actually* about documenting others. Gunilla Dahlberg explains that it is "an attitude about life,"[18] a form of relationship that puts educators in touch with our own assumptions about what we hold most dear, our own certainties and truths. Mere evidence of competence, of children demonstrating skills that are expected, lacks the potential of eliciting emotional responses. Perhaps it is the *making meaning of meaning making* that is beautiful—the relationships that are made visible in documentation and our willingness to give ourselves over to a story. Perhaps when people see the work from Reggio Emilia, they are reminded of the best of themselves, of how things could be.

This sensibility counters neoliberal-inspired approaches that continue to dominate education discourse in our context,[19] where children and educators spend years of their lives, and where the experience of beauty is probably rare. In such environments we are deprived of moments of transcendence. Our lives are diminished, our spirits impoverished when the aesthetic dimension is ignored. Bateson remarks, "I hold to the presupposition that our loss of the sense of aesthetic unity was, quite simply, an epistemological mistake."[20] We are taught at an early age that the way to define something is by "what it supposedly is in itself, not by its relation to other things."[21] What if "relationship could be used as a basis for definition"?[22] What if the meaning making taking place in ordinary encounters and which is made visible in the ongoing process of pedagogical documentation became the basis of what it means to know in schools and in our other learning institutions?

Like nesting dolls, learningliving grows out of stories within stories—a making meaning of meaning making—in a space that has not set up boundaries. This entangled orientation begins the process of articulating a methodology for challenging the dominant neoliberal discourse's pedagogies. Its grammar is an aesthetic of connection that transforms us. Its vocabulary illuminates the ethics and politics of listening to that which appears invisible—the personhood and cultures of children—within the neoliberal stories of markets, quality and high returns that currently dominate approaches to education.[23]

What we suggest is needed in early childhood education is a taste for aesthetic patterns that connect. Such an appetite might draw us to experiment with pedagogies that unfold a radically different way of learningliving. Perhaps such an approach might open up a crack that invites children more consistently into the dialogue.

Notes

1   Edgar Morin, *Seven Complex Lessons in Education for the Future* (Paris: UNESCO, 1999), 16.
2   Bill Readings, *The University in Ruins* (Cambridge, MA: Harvard University Press, 1996), 161–165.
3   Peter Moss, "Power and Resistance in Early Childhood Education," *Journal of Pedagogy* 8, no. 1 (2017): 12.
4   Gemma Corradi Fiumara, *The Other Side of Language: A Philosophy of Listening* (Abingdon: Routledge, 1990); Carla Rinaldi, "The Pedagogy of Listening: The Listening Perspective from Reggio Emilia," *Innovations in Early Childhood: The International Reggio Exchange* 8, no. 4 (2001): 1–4; Carla Rinaldi, *In Dialogue with Reggio Emilia: Listening, Research, and Learning* (New York: Routledge, 2002).
5   Henry Giroux, The Terror of Neoliberalism: Authoritarianism and the Eclipse of Democracy (Boulder, CO: Paradigm, 2004).
6   Paul Bourdieu, "Utopia of Endless Exploiting: The Essence of Neoliberalism," *Le Monde Diplomatique* (December 1998): 1–5.
7   Gaile Sloan Cannella, *Deconstructing Early Childhood Education: Social Justice and Revolution* (New York: Peter Lang, 2008).
8   Paola Cagliari et al., *Loris Malaguzzi and the Schools of Reggio Emilia: A Selection of His Writings and Speeches 1945–1993* (New York: Routledge, 2016), 421.

9   Lella Gandini, "History, Ideas, and Basic Principles: An Interview with Loris Malaguzzi," in *The Hundred Languages of Children: The Reggio Emilia Experience in Transformation*, ed. Carolyn Edwards, Lella Gandini, and George Forman (Santa Barbara, CA: Praeger, 2012), 63.
10 Margie Cooper, "Is Beauty a Way of Knowing?" *Innovations in Early Education: The International Reggio Exchange* 16, no. 3 (2009): 1.
11 Vea Vecchi, *Art and Creativity in Reggio Emilia: Exploring the Role and Potential of Ateliers in Early Childhood Education* (New York: Routledge, 2010), 14.
12 Cooper, "Is Beauty a Way of Knowing?", 1.
13 Gregory Bateson, *A Sacred Unity: Further Steps to an Ecology of Mind* (New York: Cornelia and Michael Bessie Books, 1991), 8.
14 Gregory Bateson, *Mind and Nature: A Necessary Unity* (Toronto: Bantam Books, 1979), 33.
15 Ibid., 4.
16 Hillevi Lenz Taguchi, *Going beyond the Theory/Practice Divide in Early Childhood Education: Introducing an Intra-active Pedagogy* (New York: Routledge, 2010), 88.
17 Simona Bonilauri and Tiziana Filippini, "Messages: Back and Forth," in *The Hundred Languages of Children: Catalogue of the Exhibit* (Reggio Emilia: Reggio Children, 1996), 173.
18 Gunilla Dahlberg, "Pedagogical Documentation: A Practice for Negotiation and Democracy," in The Hundred Languages of Children: The Reggio Emilia Experience in Transformation, 3rd ed., ed. Carolyn Edwards, Lella Gandini, and George Forman (Santa Barbara, CA: Praeger, 2012), 226.
19 Phillip Schlechty, *Schools for the 21st century* (San Francisco, CA: Jossey-Bass, 1990).
20 Bateson, *Mind and Nature*, 19.
21 Ibid., 17.
22 Ibid., 19.
23 Moss, "Power and Resistance," 16.

Bibliography

Bateson, Gregory. *A Sacred Unity: Further Steps to an Ecology of Mind*. New York: Cornelia and Michael Bessie Books, 1991.
Bateson, Gregory. *Mind and Nature: A Necessary Unity*. Toronto: Bantam Books, 1979.
Bonilauri, Simona, and Tiziana Filippini. "Messages: Back and Forth." In *The Hundred Languages of Children: Catalogue of the Exhibit*, 173–179. Reggio Emilia: Reggio Children, 1996.

Bourdieu, Paul. "Utopia of Endless Exploiting: The Essence of Neoliberalism." *Le Monde Diplomatique* (December 1998): 1–5.

Cagliari, Paola, Marina Castagnetti, Claudia Giudici, Carlina Rinaldi, Vea Vecchi, and Peter Moss. *Loris Malaguzzi and the Schools of Reggio Emilia: A Selection of His Writings and Speeches 1945–1993*. New York: Routledge, 2016.

Cannella, Gaile Sloan. *Deconstructing Early Childhood Education: Social Justice and Revolution*. New York: Peter Lang, 2008.

Cooper, Margie. "Is Beauty a Way of Knowing?" *Innovations in Early Education: The International Reggio Exchange* 16, no. 3 (2009): 1–9.

Dahlberg, Gunilla. "Pedagogical Documentation: A Practice for Negotiation and Democracy." In *The Hundred Languages of Children: The Reggio Emilia Experience in Transformation*. 3rd ed., edited by Carolyn Edwards, Lella Gandini, and George Forman, 225–231. Santa Barbara, CA: Praeger, 2012.

Fiumara, Gemma Corradi. *The Other Side of Language: A Philosophy of Listening*. Abingdon: Routledge, 1990.

Gandini, Lella. "History, Ideas, and Basic Principles: An Interview with Loris Malaguzzi." In *The Hundred Languages of Children: The Reggio Emilia Experience in Transformation*. 3rd ed., edited by Carolyn Edwards, Lella Gandini, and George Forman, 27–71. Santa Barbara, CA: Praeger, 2012.

Giroux, Henry. *The Terror of Neoliberalism: Authoritarianism and the Eclipse of Democracy*. Boulder, CO: Paradigm, 2004.

Lenz Taguchi, Hillevi. *Going beyond the Theory/Practice Divide in Early Childhood Education: Introducing an Intra-active Pedagogy*. New York: Routledge, 2010.

Morin, Edgar. *Seven Complex Lessons in Education for the Future*. Paris: UNESCO, 1999.

Moss, Peter. "Power and Resistance in Early Childhood Education." *Journal of Pedagogy* 8, no. 1 (2017): 11–32. doi:10.1515/jped-2017-0001.

Readings, Bill. *The University in Ruins*. Cambridge, MA: Harvard University Press, 1996.

Rinaldi, Carla. *In Dialogue with Reggio Emilia: Listening, Research, and Learning*. New York: Routledge, 2002.

Rinaldi, Carla. "The Pedagogy of Listening: The Listening Perspective from Reggio Emilia." *Innovations in Early Childhood: The International Reggio Exchange* 8, no. 4 (2001): 1–4.

Schlechty, Phillip. *Schools for the 21st century*. San Francisco, CA: Jossey-Bass, 1990.

Vecchi, Vea. *Art and Creativity in Reggio Emilia: Exploring the Role and Potential of Ateliers in Early Childhood Education*. New York: Routledge, 2010.

18

Colaboring: Within Collaboration Degenerative Processes

Cristina D. Vintimilla and Iris Berger

We, Cristina and Iris, work within different early childhood contexts with researchers, educators and students in two universities on the west coast of Canada. Iris teaches and coordinates programs within a faculty of education and Cristina teaches future early childhood educators and is a pedagogista in the university's childcare program. Through our collaborative research projects with early childhood educators[1] and our discussions about preparing future early childhood educators, we have been paying attention to, and have been troubled by, the ways in which collaboration as an uncritical ideal without elaboration and/or question is absorbed into the early childhood education landscape. In this chapter we undo collaboration, employing what Reza Negarestani[2] calls a "positive degenerating process" in order to uncover collaboration's messy (co) laboring possibilities. We engage with collaboration through our particular histories, stories, and language games, layering within the chapter moments of practice-provoked thoughts and conceptual openings.

Collaboration: Between idealization and paradoxical potential

We are not so interested in defining collaboration. Rather, the everyday material and discursive practices around collaboration constitute our concerns. How do understandings and practices of collaboration coalesce and become given and stagnant? Through our practices we notice that we live within the material and discursive tensions in which collaboration exists. On the one hand we carry with us stories of collaboration as having the potential to create space for the emergence of new pedagogical compositions. On the other hand we carry stories about its homogenizing force, a force that works to normalize and conform by diffusing one's efforts to think and act differently.

Pedagogista note: It seems we are facing other moments of impasse. The beautiful desire of an educator to animate curriculum is juxtaposed with not wanting to say anything that might "shut down" her colleagues and her individual decisions about curriculum making. How can we encounter curriculum as a collective creation rather than a random creation based on our individual choices for how a day will unfold? Is the messiness of living together too much to bear neoliberal subjectivities?[3]

Collaboration has been co-opted as the concept par excellence for the corporate world, where, while it is flaunted as a more "humane" social practice of doing business, its aim remains, as one writer put it, creating a better kind of capitalism.[4] Within this discourse of collaboration, which is seeping into the early childhood landscape, its aim is preestablished in the name of accepting, unquestionably, the 21st century's social-economic order. Ironically, collaboration is made to look like a perfect fit for a world thriving on competition and global capitalism. For us it is a matter of concern to think of collaboration as a model to be pursued, as something that needs to be designed and built. It seems to us that when collaboration is thought in such ways, a predefined and fixed organization of how the collaborative should exist or manifest is present. Therefore we also question the metaphor of construction, that in collaboration we "build" meaningful relationships. Building, as the metaphor for what we do with relationships, requires the understanding that relations need a foundation and a permanent structure. Thinking with Martin Heidegger[5] and Tim Ingold,[6] perhaps we *dwell in* relationships rather than build them—a small difference on which so much hinges!

The corporate discourse of collaboration's danger is that under its name, collaboration is not only instrumentalized, it is also depoliticized, which may seduce us to assume that pedagogical decisions center on technical issues, leaving the highly politicized and conflictual nature of pedagogical engagements ignored. As we shared our stories of collaboration with each other, we noticed how many times we felt like paralyzed participants in what Cristina[7] refers to as the "politics of niceness." Collaboration here takes place within a politics underwritten by a commitment to social harmony. This politics often exists in the unsaid, in the hidden yet present, and therefore is more difficult to interrupt. This politics prescribes the privileging of certain ways of being, of certain feelings and the shattering of others.

By prescribing recognizable qualities to collaboration, a politics of niceness faithfully produces silence: the silence of those who don't fit in, those who don't conform to an obvious "common sense." The politics of niceness's troubling relations to neoliberal biopolitics and to the early childhood educator's image's historical legacy as the "good and caring teacher" are daunting for us, because the politics of niceness's another aspect is the reductive and moralistic understanding of relations in early childhood through the duality of respect/offense, where respect serves as the barrier to interrupting the "collaborative" enterprise's smooth functioning and its status quo maintenance. Troubled by these twists in the fate of collaboration, we were moved to ask: How might collaboration exist as a space for new pedagogical compositions to emerge and be animated? And while we don't know that we have any definite answers, this question opened for us, in a rather unpredictable way, a number of paths that we want to share.

Some collaborative trajectories: Undoing co-labor-ation

Language does. Living in translation exposes us to this doing in more intensive ways. But, we also do language. We have weaved our friendship in abundant common passions. Doing language is one. We turn it upside down, invent it, cut it, seduce it, reiterate it, disclose it, decompose it, chop it, put it back together and, as in a rupture, we discover it anew.

One of the unpredictable lively effects of our collaborative effort was born out of our living-in-translation existence. Since we both speak and think in more than one language, for the most part we become attentive to language in its defamiliarization potentialities. We catch ourselves carefully noticing what words can do or implicitly say. We experiment with language as a way to push the familiar boundaries of meaning. Living in translation allows us to experience language not as container but rather, and following Hélène Cixous, as that which "carries; it does not hold back, it makes possible."[8]

Cristina noted that in Spanish and Italian, collaboration, labor and laboratory (etymologically meaning a workshop) all have the Latin root *laborate*, which means to work, but also to start something. The laboratory is the place for "starting something." Iris realized that in Hebrew the word work, *Avoda*, and the word laboratory, *Ma-abada*, also share the same root. Yet, in Hebrew, collaboration is made of a compound—two words: *Sheetuf Peulah*—which, when linked, come to mean "to act together," to coparticipate in an action.

Through our translation engagement the word collaboration disassembled—fell apart—in front of our eyes, and we began to wonder what collaboration is quietly telling us when this word is punctured, or put through a degenerative process, as the one Negarestani[9] brings to our attention. In what follows we present a series of speculations, ideas that come out of the shadows once we undo collaboration and think of it in multiple conceptions, in relation to a rich group of considerations and practice-provoked thoughts about collaboration. In our undoing of this concept, we take this complex term to its inheritance in order to reengage/rearrange it, to deploy its consequences and practices otherwise. We present co-labor-a(c)tion, as a triplet: *co*, mutuality and relation; *labor*, work and the laboratory; and the suffix *ation*, which forms the *action* of a verb.

Co

The co evokes a mode of being together with others: a lively coexistence that is manifested in what Hannah Arendt[10] calls a "common world." Thus we pause to consider this mode of being. The co asks us to think about togetherness and what it means to live well with others. We realized how often we have entered collaborations with our own prejudices and assumptions of who the other is and how the other is going to appear. We asked: How often do we come with our webs of desire, our impassionate beliefs and also our frustrations, and who and what is left out? In this way, in our work, we find that collaborative encounters are often daunted by situations where educators, children, or, in Cristina's case, pedagogista are treated as fixed and determined subjectivities.

After all these years in the center I wonder if I am still perceived as the expert, the one that will fix things up or will tell how to proceed. And me? I left the room today asking myself, how can I keep open spaces of hospitality for educators who have been more reluctant to embark on these trajectories.

Just before leaving the center, two children and I pause and pay attention. They discuss; there is no agreement; one shouts; there is silence. An educator is walking towards them. I look at her, she pauses ... we give space. ... Another child comes and brings them a new problem. They work at it together. ... We give space. ... No one is invested in the ideas they have of each other. ... What a beautiful invitation to reencounter one another, to be exposed in the messiness of making a life.

Jean-Luc Nancy writes that to think *we* means to think of *being-with* (humans and nonhumans). Being-with, for Nancy, resists a shared identity, or a unified and preestablished grammar of existence (such as a politics of niceness or structural metaphor for relationships).[11] For Arendt our capacity to *experience* a world in common depends on an ongoing disruption of its commonalty.[12] Without these disruptions our sense of the world is reified; it automatically reproduces itself and we remain unresponsive to the ever-changing complexities of human and nonhuman plurality. The experience of a common world's main purpose is not to achieve agreement or consensus by homogenizing differences, but to sustain the tensions emanating from being-together-in-plurality in such a way that the unexpected or the new can emerge.

These invitations from Nancy and Arendt have influenced our collaborative projects because they invite us to think of collaboration as a relational performance that happens in moments of exposure. For Arendt these moments of exposure happen when we "venture into the public" with speech and action and signify not only the disclosure of a relation with the common world, but also a possibility to appear in the world in a new way, as a "newcomer." We understand such moments as intra-active[13] openings in our common lived-liveliness with the world.

Here we are shifting from thinking about the necessity of preexisting identities to recognizing the *relationship between* that emerges in moments of exposure and that cannot be delineated or predefined. Indeed what is emerging through this experience of collaboration is "uncodable, excessive, out-of-control, out-of-category."[14]

Action

In a nonlinear fashion we want to jump to the last part of co-labor-a(c)tion, which we are proposing as action. When we think collaboration as a harmonious social structure or as a practice conditioned by a consensus, it is difficult to imagine how it might exist as a space for action, the emergence of new configurations. But when we think collaboration as a relational performance and action as inserting something new into the world, we may begin to see the potentialities of collaboration differently.

Arendt conceptualized action as a beginning that is inserted into the world by an actor's words and deeds but is dependent, so to speak, for its existence on the responses of others.[15] She thought of action, in this sense, as the experience of freedom. This is not a "freedom from" or "freedom of the will," but an experience of initiation—bringing something into the world that did not exist before and setting something into motion without having the ability to control its end. Action is experienced as the gap between past and future, a moment in time, where resistance to what it ushers in might become possible. From this premise collaboration exists, not as a model or an object about which we can say "we know what it is" or how it is done. Rather it engages with a desire for a common project in which collaboration flows as a movement—of being something that is, at the same time, always already something else.

Labor

Labor, situated between co and action, is a word so abundant with meanings, connotations and contradictions that it presented us with a great challenge. Labor, which implicates the body in its engagement with the world, has suffered historically from being subordinated to thinking and theory.[16] Labor has an additional, particular meaning in relation to early childhood. We cannot help but notice how debates about the value of child care have become entangled with women progressively transformed into a strategic pool of labor. Nor can we ignore the historical and present predicament of "female labor" associated with precariousness, low pay, low status and the notion of "affective labor": the labor of human contact, whose products are relationships and emotional responsiveness.[17]

At the same time labor has come to signify the process of giving birth—bringing something new and unforeseen into the world. In our experience, when being in collaboration, it is the laboring part of collaboration that seems to us is avoided, tamed, or perhaps forgotten. In our work we have tried to dwell with the laboring processes of co-labor-a(c)tion and make them as visible as possible. These processes have shown us that collaboration is not a smooth project but something that intrinsically demands an effort in our coming together (i.e., it could be much easier, and perhaps efficient, to "just do it my way"). Laboring demands that we collectively experiment and work at it, as well as let ourselves be disappointed, troubled and even exhausted in the birthing of the multiple possibilities that a common project might bring.

The laboring processes and their demands that we are referring to here made us think about the etymological knot between labor and the laboratory. Here we want to think with Ingold of the laboratory's particular tradition: the alchemic laboratory. Ingold explains that alchemy is the old science of struggling with materials and not quite understanding what is happening. He adds that the alchemist laboratory "was not one of matter that might be described in terms of its molecular composition, but one of substances, which were known by what they look and feel like, and by following what happens to them as they are mixed, heated or cooled."[18] In other words the colaborers, or the "practitioners," to use Ingold's words, such as "the builder, the gardener, the cook, the alchemist and the painter are not so much imposing form on matter as bringing together diverse materials and combining or redirecting their flow in the anticipation of what might emerge."[19] This common, lively (re)search is always vibrant and unpredictable. Thus we came to see collaboration in its laboring, or colaboring: in the struggles with materials, questions, difficulties, frustrations and promises, as these are "mixed, heated, and cooled," flowing toward something that might emerge when it is not yet recognizable as such.

We are starting to have more intense conversations in the center about curriculum as collective laboring. Laboring because it asks us to work at it, to make decisions, to bring things together (masks, human, squirrel, music), to mix them up, to create new flows and see what happens. ... It seems hard to make this happen. ... Curriculum making: collectively charging curriculum with life. Why is this so difficult? What holds us back? How do we keep alive an idea?

The alchemist laboratory was also often depicted as the place where the heart is inflamed by love for the arts, beauty and knowledge. Bundling these ideas, we venture to say that the labor of collaboration can be the space where we fall in love with ideas, desires, materials and—why not?—also people. Thinking with Alain Badiou, love cannot be reduced to a feeling. Rather it is embarking on a common project, an "inauguration of innumerable common practices or shared investigations."[20] Yet this colaboring, we want to further argue, entails breakages and reassemblages, effort and endurance, not unlike Negarestani's notion of a "positive degenerating process."[21] In his musing about dust Negarestani writes, "Dust lives in an economy whose vehicles and systems never cease to degenerate themselves. For in this way they ensure their permanent molecular dynamism, their contagious distribution and diffusion."[22] Following dust, we were provoked to think about not only the shared investigations' generative forces we undertake, but also of such labor's "dustiness": the moments of dynamism and degeneration in the labor of collaboration. It is with the generative forces of colaboring, including its moments of degeneration—its dustiness—we hope this chapter leaves you as we come to a stop (letting the dust settle)—but certainly not to a closure.

Notes

1   Iris Berger, "Pedagogical Narrations and Leadership in Early Childhood Education as Thinking in Moments of Not Knowing," *Canadian Children* 40, no. 1 (2015): 130–147; Cristina D. Vintimilla, "Educators and Pedagogista: Encounters at the Intersection of History and Story," *Journal of Contemporary Issues in Early Childhood Education* 19, no. 1 (2016): 20–23.

2   Reza Negarestani, *Cyclonopedia: Complicity with Anonymous Materials* (Prahran: Re.Press, 2008).
3   Throughout the chapter, we have included excerpts from Cristina's daily notebook used in her work as pedagogista at Capilano University Children's Center. A pedagogista is someone who works collaboratively with all the protagonists within an educational endeavor to promote critical and dialogical encounters that consider the specificity of a pedagogical project as well as its relations with the broader philosophical vision and commitments of the early learning setting.
4   Charles Barthold, "Corporate Social Responsibility, Collaboration, and Depoliticisation," *Business Ethics: A European Review* 22, no. 4 (2013): 393–403.
5   Martin Heidegger, *What Is a Thing?* (Washington, DC: Gateway Editions, 1967).
6   Tim Ingold, *The Perception of the Environment: Essays on Livelihood, Dwelling, and Skill* (Hove: Psychology Press, 2000).
7   Cristina D. Vintimilla, "Neoliberal Fun and Happiness in Early Childhood Education," *Journal of Childhood Studies* 39, no. 1 (2014): 82.
8   Hélène Cixous, Keith Cohen, and Paula Cohen, "The Laugh of the Medusa," *Signs: Journal of Women in Culture and Society* 1, no. 4 (1976): 883.
9   Ibid.
10 Hannah Arendt, *The Human Condition* (Chicago, IL: University of Chicago Press, 1998, original publication 1958).
11 Jean-Luc Nancy, *The Inoperative Community*, vol. 76 (Minneapolis: University of Minnesota Press, 1991).
12 Arendt, *The Human Condition*.
13 Karen Barad, "Posthumanist Performativity: Toward an Understanding of How Matter Comes to Matter," *Signs: Journal of Women in Culture and Society* 28, no. 3 (2003): 801–831.
14 Elizabeth Adams St. Pierre, "Poststructural Feminism in Education: An Overview," *International Journal of Qualitative Studies in Education* 13, no. 5 (2000): 477–515.
15 Arendt, *The Human Condition*.
16 Ibid.
17 Johanna Oksala, "Affective Labor and Feminist Politics," *Signs: Journal of Women in Culture and Society* 41, no. 2 (2016): 281–303.
18 Tim Ingold, "The Textility of Making," *Cambridge Journal of Economics* 34, no. 1 (2009): 91–102.
19 Ibid., 94.
20 Alain Badiou and Nicolas Truong, *In Praise of Love* (London: Profile Books, 2012), 50.
21 Negarestani, *Cyclonopedia*, 91.
22 Ibid.

Bibliography

Arendt, Hannah. *The Human Condition*. Chicago, IL: University of Chicago Press, 1998 (original publication 1958).

Badiou, Alain, and Nicolas Truong. *In Praise of Love*. London: Profile Books, 2012.

Barad, Karen. "Posthumanist Performativity: Toward an Understanding of How Matter Comes to Matter." *Signs: Journal of Women in Culture and Society* 28, no. 3 (2003): 801–831.

Barthold, Charles. "Corporate Social Responsibility, Collaboration, and Depoliticisation." *Business Ethics: A European Review* 22, no. 4 (2013): 393–403.

Berger, Iris. "Pedagogical Narrations and Leadership in Early Childhood Education as Thinking in Moments of Not Knowing." *Canadian Children* 40, no.1 (2015): 130–147.

Cixous, Hélène, Keith Cohen, and Paula Cohen. "The Laugh of the Medusa." *Signs: Journal of Women in Culture and Society* 1, no. 4 (1976): 875–893.

Hard, Louise. "How Is Leadership Understood and Enacted within the Field of Early Childhood Education and Care?" PhD diss., Queensland University of Technology, 2006.

Heidegger, Martin. *What Is a Thing?* Washington, DC: Gateway Editions, 1967.

Ingold, Tim. *The Perception of the Environment: Essays on Livelihood, Dwelling, and Skill*. Hove: Psychology Press, 2000.

Ingold, Tim. "The Textility of Making." *Cambridge Journal of Economics* 34, no. 1 (2009): 91–102.

Latour, Bruno. "Why Has Critique Run Out of Steam? From Matters of Fact to Matters of Concern." *Critical Inquiry* 30, no. 2 (2004): 225–248.

Nancy, Jean-Luc. *The Inoperative Community*. Vol. 76. Minneapolis: University of Minnesota Press, 1991.

Negarestani, Reza. *Cyclonopedia: Complicity with Anonymous Materials*. Prahran: Re. Press, 2008.

Oksala, Johanna. "Affective Labor and Feminist Politics." *Signs: Journal of Women in Culture and Society* 41, no. 2 (2016): 281–303.

St. Pierre, Elizabeth Adams. "Poststructural Feminism in Education: An Overview." *International Journal of Qualitative Studies in Education* 13, no. 5 (2000): 477–515.

Vintimilla, Cristina D. "Educators and Pedagogista: Encounters at the Intersection of History and Story." *Journal of Contemporary Issues in Early Childhood Education* 19, no. 1 (2016): 20–23.

Vintimilla, Cristina D. "Neoliberal Fun and Happiness in Early Childhood Education." *Journal of Childhood Studies* 39, no. 1 (2014): 79–87.

19

Childing: A Different Sense of Time

Karin Murris and Cara Borcherds

The sciences and humanities' transformational agendas are not silent about gender or race as categories of exclusion, yet within them, *child* (childism or ageism) is still invisible. The identity prejudices involved in the concepts *child, children* and *childhood*[1] work in unexamined ways in all phases of education, even though for decades now, scholars in childhood studies and early education have argued that the normative knowing subject is assumed to be of a particular age (i.e., adult).[2] Children tend not to be listened to and taken seriously as knowers, because of their very *being* a child and therefore (it is claimed) being unable to make claims to knowledge. It is assumed they are (still) developing, innocent, fragile, immature, irrational and so forth.[3] Predominantly positioned as a knowledge *consumer*, not *producer*, child is denied epistemically on the basis of a certain ontology.[4] Entangled connections have been made among colonialism, imperialism, the institutionalization of childhood, capitalist discourses of progression and "natural" development.[5] Linear notions of progress and reason have colonized education through its curriculum construction that positions children as simple, concrete, immature thinkers who need age-appropriate interventions to mature into autonomous, rational, "fully human" beings.[6] Since ancient Greece Western education has been regarded as the formation of childhood, assuming the "natural" development of child as becoming-adult.[7]

    Critical posthumanism exposes how particular ways of thinking about the human and relationality have shaped these unequal adult-child relationships. In our work[8] and theorizing we focus in particular on child-adult relationality. Rosi Braidotti explains how the mature, white, able-bodied, heterosexual man of humanism[9] has been the yardstick in Western knowledge practices of what counts as "normal." This includes how "natural" child development is measured, with children at the patriarchal hierarchy's lowest level. What is urgently needed for justice is a reconfiguration of subjectivity, "a new starting place"[10] for theorizing how children grow, develop and learn.

Posthuman subjectivity: A different doing of identity

Dominant educational discourses both assume that individuation (subjectivity) involves psychological or sociological processes and equate child's *becoming* with the becoming *of* a being—a particular body located in space and time that can be measured at a distance. In contrast quantum physicist Karen Barad's feminist ontology assumes that relationality between human and nonhuman bodies ("entanglements") brings the individual into existence.[11] In other words, the ontological starting point is relationality, not individuality. This is not an epistemological matter, as would be the case if we claimed that we can only know a thing as part of relationships. For posthumanists a thing (body) is always ontologically part of entanglements that are in/determinate in space and time. So a child, call her Siobhan, is already entangled with what, for example, happens on Mars, and how a reading scheme measures reading abilities, and the fact that her parents moved from Ireland to South Africa in 1805, and the hurricane in Florida, and the ant crawling on the classroom floor, and the phone she is accessing WhatsApp messages with, and the chair she is sitting on, and ad infinitum. Hence it is impossible to trace all entanglements that are part of what makes Siobhan act the way she does. It is not that human bodies have performativity[12] but that human *and nonhuman entanglements* have performativity, which is a radical shift from thinking in terms of *individual agency*. Siobhan as a distinct entity does not exist prior to her interactions, but she e/merges through what Barad calls "intra-actions." And it is these intra-actions between the material and the discursive that constitute "the" subject Siobhan and "her" agency: cells, atoms, wind, fibers, dust, metal, skin, ant legs, soil, paper, government, concepts, policies, language, touch, atmosphere, etc. Now what evidence is there for such a radical shift in subjectivity?

Khronos and *aion*

Barad's scientific study of small organisms questions the individual/group binary and profoundly problematizes the nature of identity and individual existence. Things (including human bodies) *are* only because they are in relation to and influencing each other. Drawing on Niels Bohr's quantum physics, Barad proposes that relationalities are not just entanglements, but *quantum* entanglements. She explains: "Quantum entanglements are not the intertwining of two (or more) states/entities/events, but a calling into question of the very nature of twoness, and ultimately of one-ness as well."[13] This different *doing of identity* involves an ontological shift, in what we mean not only by space (and the bodies in it), but also by time. Therefore, differences are not about comparing "this" with "that" or "there" with "then," because this would prioritize *identity*, therefore individual existence. In a relational ontology, differences are always differences *within*, not *without*, thereby producing egalitarian, nonhierarchical relationality through disrupting binaries. Relevant for all phases of education is the power-producing adult/child binary and colonizing notions such as "development" and "progress." Development assumes that matter (here, human bodies) moves *in* time and *through* space, yet as quantum physics has shown empirically, time is never just here or now, but a dis/continuous movement.[14] A posthuman notion of progress and development "embraces mutuality, mess, multiplicity, and contradiction" in "continually emergent past-present-futures."[15]

Returning to Heraclitus, philosophers David Kennedy and Walter Kohan[16] argue that each conception of childhood presupposes a particular concept of time. Childhood conceptualized as the period at the start of a person's life presupposes a quantitative, chronological concept of time, thereby imposing an adult form of temporality (*khronos*), or linear and irreversible time. However, childhood is not just a period in a human life, but also a particular relationship with, and experience of, time (*aion*)—as associated with play—and "designates the intensity of time in human life—a destiny, a duration, an un-numbered movement, not successive, but intensive"[17]—a particularly forceful and intense experience of being-in-time: childlike. As such, the concept child shifts from noun to verb, something *all of us* can do: to child.[18] When childing, the ageless subject is always in process, always "on-the-way."[19] What are the decolonizing implications for pedagogy of a nonchronological experience of time? How does one prepare student teachers for posthuman pedagogical practices that posit a knowing subject that has little to do with age but more with a unbounded body's flux or intensity that continuously affects and is affected and e/merges relationally through intra-action and diffraction? How can educators be supported to foreground ontological relationality and posthuman subjectivity?

Image-nings

For one of our courses in teacher education, we use the textbook *The Posthuman Child*[20] and intragenerational and post-age pedagogies for students to experience this philosophical shift themselves. In this chapter we tell the story of the impact of this childhood studies course on Cara, one of the students, through images she made of Karin (the lecturer). The making of images in the university classroom by students alongside the lecturer (pedagogical documentation) was part of the course's ongoing formative assessment. What is particularly striking is how Cara's course "image-nings" (her journal documentation) express a shift in subjectivity, disrupting the lecturer/student binary through bodily *performances*. For example, in Figure 19.1, Cara, sitting on a low, comfy chair, made an image of Karin in the university classroom talking and directing students with her hand prior to the start of a lesson.

Deliberately showing only half of Karin's face, Cara's image shows she is aware of how Karin subconsciously disrupts the lecturer/student binary by sitting on the floor, lowering herself, making herself vulnerable. The two images prior to this one and the one after in Cara's camera roll show that Cara's image-nings

Figure 19.1 Karin in the university classroom.

were intentional and not a mistake or a badly taken photo. Cara's camera, Karin, the table, the carpet, the chairs and the human and more-than-human's positioning in the photo are all what Barad calls *apparatuses*, that is, "the material conditions of possibility and impossibility of mattering; they enact what matters and what is excluded from mattering."[21] In this case what matters is how Cara's making of images (pedagogical documentation) disrupted a humanist anthropocentric gaze. With her camera as apparatus, the chair she so often chose to sit in, her position, her gaze and what she as student-teacher-researcher brought to the moment are all part of the entanglement. In her image-nings, Cara's camera excluded Karin's face. Cara describes it as a particularly intense experience of being-in-time or always in process—a childing. As Barad points out, apparatuses (in this case Cara's camera) are open-ended practices without intrinsic boundaries, not "passive instruments for observations" but part of the world's ongoing intra-activity.[22] The apparatuses *produce* the phenomena, "real physical entities of beings."[23] Cara's camera brought this more egalitarian relationship between lecturer and student into existence, also when she shared the image with Karin. Importantly this was not an intentional act by Cara, as if she made the image to point out a changed relationality to Karin. Much could not, and still cannot, be articulated.

Entanglements are ontologically ad infinitum in space, and past, present and future are threaded through one another. After all any meaning the image has does not exist prior to the image's making and includes the observer and others—including the readers of this chapter. The image shows the quantum entanglement's political and pedagogical importance. What is brought into being is a power-disrupting, more egalitarian student-lecturer relationship through the material-discursive. Cara was fascinated by how Karin used her body to challenge power binaries. Cara played with the camera (and the camera played with her) without much concern for a particular product, for example, to make linear progress as a student teacher or to meet the course's assessment requirements. Absorbed in the moment and without intention, she played and experimented with the lecturer's subjectivity. She was childing.

Returning

Months go by. After qualifying as a teacher, Cara emails Karin. Working in a class in Papua New Guinea (on the left of Figure 19.2), she couldn't help thinking of the image she had made of Karin a year earlier (on the right of Figure 19.2).

Figure 19.2 Intra-action patterns: educator-students-newspaper-bird puppets-glass-tree-wind-waterbottles-tables-light.

Cara tells Karin why she sent the image:

There is a time of year the light in room 3.21 and the outside, not much noticed, has a beautiful glow. On this day, I don't think it was by chance that you chose to wear your grey jersey or to position yourself where you did. I couldn't help noticing the constructive intra-action pattern: you, the newspaper bird puppets (Jill's favorite), the outside, water bottles, tables. I have a vivid recollection of the moment.

When preparing the email, Cara simultaneously inserted another image (Figure 19.1) with one keystroke. What e/merged was a new image: two photos now touching vertically as one revealed in the email's body. The images, Cara's action and the technology all intra-acted to produce a new entanglement (Figure 19.3).

Cara wondered when sending the email whether this was an accidental juxtaposition or a diffraction. Barad's methodology of diffractively reading texts (in this case images) through one another is inspired by her diffractive reading of diffraction as understood by physics. Classical physics divides the world up into waves and particles. As Barad explains, "The quantum understanding of diffraction troubles the very notion of *dicho-tomy*—cutting into two—as a singular act of absolute differentiation."[24] Diffraction means "to break apart in different directions."[25] Diffraction patterns hold for water waves, as well as sound waves, or light waves[26]—and in this case, the images in Figures 19.1 and 19.2. It is where they interfere or overlap that the waves change in themselves in intra-action and create an interference pattern or "superposition."[27] The new pattern created in Figure 19.3 is the *effect* of difference and marks where learning has occurred. Always unpredictable and moving in indeterminate directions, the superposition or interference pattern is always ethical and political in that it queers identity-producing binaries (here, young/adult, student/lecturer, but also the binary between waves and particles, inanimate and animate). Diffraction

Figure 19.3 Diffracting two images.

attends to the relational nature of difference. Empirical evidence from quantum physics suggests that waves and particles are not bounded objects but disturbances, and their identity as either wave or particle is brought into existence through the apparatus that measures—even *after* the event.[28] In this case the apparatus (camera, theories, humans, university programs, etc.) disturbs the teacher/student binary by putting Karin physically above *and* under the table, which is more than simply *combining* the two images. Cara's un/intentional assemblage makes the observer and others, including the reader of this chapter, pay attention to the differences that matter—the power-producing binaries (in this case student/teacher) that include or exclude, thereby deterritorializing the educator's status (lecturer).

The diffractive methodology tries to break from the familiar habits of reflecting on the world from the outside toward a way of understanding the world from within and as part of it.[29] The de/colonizing move that diffraction affords researchers is to think with and through "differences across, among, and between genders, species, spaces, knowledges, sexualities, subjectivities, and temporalities ... differences that are not solidified as 'less than.'"[30] Barad states very clearly that the point is not that knowledge practices have material consequences, but that *"practices of knowing are specific material engagements that participate in (re)configuring the world.* Which practices we enact matter—in both senses of the word."[31] Making knowledge implies giving the world specific form (in this case through the image-nings), for which the authors here are also responsible and accountable by paying attention to accurate and fine details.[32]

Cara's camera images (image-nings) explore the educator's idea of the posthuman subjectivity. The two images in Figure 19.4 are striking examples of Cara's unbounded subjectivity as she visually and materially intra-acted with her apparatus. The first was created in the university classroom and the other during a field trip to the beach with what emerged as the educator's an almost-disappearance, closely resembling Umberto Boccioni's sculpture "Unique Forms of Continuity in Space."

They are both a powerful reminder that teaching without bodily boundaries as quantum entanglement is, as we have seen above, not a new unity, but it is like the sea that troubles the very nature of oneness, twoness, threeness and can bring about a different, more childlike, egalitarian way of being, doing, and thinking.

The verb *childing* expresses a notion of posthuman identity that is in/determinate, porous, with no fixed boundaries. Troubling age, development and progress, childing reminds us of a particularly forceful and intense experience of being in time, usually associated with childhood. Cara's camera creates a

Figure 19.4 Diffracting with the educator (top) and the educator's disappearance (bottom).

playful and intense engagement with posthuman subjectivity, with Karin as her example, but as her account testifies, much was coincidental. What is significant is that in the very process of Cara sharing the images with Karin and Karin responding as she did, the images disrupt the usual hierarchical relationship between lecturer and student. Being childlike, childing is and should not be reserved for the young.

For posthumanists the problem with the concept child is not that it is too abstract, but that it is not abstract enough. Each person is more than a body, always connected, embedded and embodied, dynamic and active. In contrast to the verb childing, the concept child suggests it is a sign for *an object in the world* (the fleshy child as a bounded unit in space and time), with adult as the transcendental signifier. What this chapter hopes to provoke is an image-ning of how relational childing practices, as seen in the images and through the use of childing as a verb, are a potent post-age and antichildist decolonizing strategy for the (university) classroom.

Notes

1. Karin Murris, "The Epistemic Challenge of Hearing Child's Voice," *Studies in Philosophy and Education* 32, no. 3 (2013): 245–259.
2. See, for example, Erica Burman, *Deconstructing Developmental Psychology* (London: Routledge, 1994); Gaile S. Cannella and Radhika Viruru, *Childhood and Postcolonization: Power, Education, and Contemporary Practice* (New York: RoutledgeFalmer, 2004); Valerie Walkerdine, "Developmental Psychology and the Child-Centred Pedagogy: The Insertion of Piaget into Early Education," in *Changing the Subject: Psychology, Social Regulation, and Subjectivity*, ed. Wendy Hollway, Couze Venn, Valerie Walkerdine, Julian Henriques, and Cathy Urwin (London: Routledge, 1984), 153–203.
3. Karin Murris, *The Posthuman Child: Educational Transformation through Philosophy with Picturebooks* (London: Routledge, 2016).
4. Ibid.
5. See Ashis Nandy, "Reconstructing Childhood: A Critique of the Ideology of Adulthood," in *Traditions, Tyranny, and Utopias: Essays in the Politics of Awareness* (Delhi: Oxford University Press, 1987), 41–56; Cannella and Viruru, *Childhood and Postcolonization*; Burman, *Deconstructing Developmental Psychology*; Veronica Pacini-Ketchabaw and Fikile Nxumalo, "Posthumanist Imaginaries for Decolonizing Early Childhood Praxis," in *Reconceptualizing Early Childhood Care and Education. A Reader*, ed. Marianne Bloch, Beth Blue Swadener, and Gaile S. Cannella (New York: Routledge, 2014), 131–142.
6. Cannella and Viruru, *Childhood and Postcolonization*, 109.
7. See Walter Kohan, *Childhood, Education, and Philosophy: New Ideas for an Old Relationship* (New York: Routledge, 2006); Andrew Stables, *Childhood and the Philosophy of Education: An Anti-Aristotelian Perspective* (London: Continuum Studies in Educational Research, 2008).
8. This work is based on research supported by the National Research Foundation of South Africa [grant number 98992].
9. Rosi Braidotti, *The Posthuman* (Cambridge: Polity Press, 2013).
10. Karen Barad, *Meeting the Universe Halfway: Quantum Physics and the Entanglement of Matter and Meaning* (Durham, NC: Duke University Press, 2007), 137.
11. Ibid., 139.
12. See, for example, Judith Butler, *Gender Trouble: Feminism and the Subversion of Identity* (New York: Routledge, 1990).
13. Karen Barad, "Diffracting Diffraction: Cutting Together-Apart," *Parallax* 20, no. 3 (2014): 178.
14. Ibid.
15. Pacini-Ketchabaw and Nxumalo, "Posthumanist Imaginaries," 134.

16 David Kennedy and Walter Kohan, "Childhood, Education, and Philosophy: A Matter of Time," in *The Routledge International Handbook of Philosophy for Children*, ed. Maughn Rollins Gregory, Joanna Haynes, and Karin Murris (London: Routledge, 2017), 46–53.
17 Ibid., 57.
18 David Kennedy and Walter Kohan, "Aión, Kairós, and Chrónos: Fragments of an Endless Conversation on Childhood, Philosophy, and Education," *Childhood & Philosophy* 4, no. 8 (2008).
19 David Kennedy, *Changing Conceptions of the Child from the Renaissance to Post-Modernity: A Philosophy of Childhood* (New York: Edwin Mellen Press, 2006), 10.
20 Murris, *The Posthuman Child*.
21 Barad, *Meeting the Universe Halfway*, 148.
22 Kit Stender Petersen, "Interviews as Intraviews: A Hand Puppet Approach to Studying Processes of Inclusion and Exclusion among Children in Kindergarten," *Reconceptualising Educational Research Methodology* 5, no. 1 (2014): 33.
23 Barad, *Meeting the Universe Halfway*, 129.
24 Barad, "Diffracting Diffraction," 168.
25 Ibid.
26 Barad, *Meeting the Universe Halfway*, 74.
27 Ibid., 76.
28 Ibid., chapter 2.
29 Ibid., 88.
30 Barad interviewed in Malou Juelskjaer and Nete Schwennesen, "Intra-active Entanglements: An Interview with Karen Barad," *Kvinder, Kon, & Forskning* 1–2 (2012): 16.
31 Barad, *Meeting the Universe Halfway*, 91, emphasis in the original.
32 Ibid., 91–93.

Bibliography

Barad, Karen. "Diffracting Diffraction: Cutting Together-Apart." *Parallax* 20, no. 3 (2014): 168–187.
Barad, Karen. "Intra-actions: An Interview with Karen Barad by Adam Kleinman." *Mousse* 34 (2012): 76–81.
Braidotti, Rosi. *The Posthuman*. Cambridge: Polity Press, 2013.
Burman, Erica. *Deconstructing Developmental Psychology*. London: Routledge, 1994.
Butler, Judith. *Gender Trouble: Feminism and the Subversion of Identity*. New York: Routledge, 2009.
Cannella, Gaile. S., and Radhika Viruru. *Childhood and Postcolonization: Power, Education, and Contemporary Practice*. New York: RoutledgeFalmer, 2004.

Juelskjaer, Malou, and Nete Schwennesen. "Intra-active Entanglements: An Interview with Karen Barad." *Kvinder, Kon, & Forskning* 1–2 (2012). https://tidsskrift.dk/index.php/KKF/article/view/51864/95447.

Kennedy, David. *Changing Conceptions of the Child from the Renaissance to Post-Modernity: A Philosophy of Childhood*. New York: Edwin Mellen Press, 2006.

Kennedy, David, and Walter Kohan. "Aión, Kairós, and Chrónos: Fragments of an Endless Conversation on Childhood, Philosophy, and Education." *Childhood & Philosophy* 4, no. 8 (2008). http://www.e-publicacoes.uerj.br/ojs/index.php/childhood/article/view/20524.

Kennedy, David, and Walter Kohan. "Childhood, Education, and Philosophy: A Matter of Time." In *The Routledge International Handbook of Philosophy for Children*, edited by Maughn Rollins Gregory, Joanna Haynes, and Karin Murris, 46–53. London: Routledge, 2017.

Kohan, Walter. *Childhood, Education, and Philosophy: New Ideas for an Old Relationship*. New York: Routledge, 2006.

Murris, Karin. "The Epistemic Challenge of Hearing Child's Voice." Child as Educator special issue. *Studies in Philosophy and Education* 32, no. 3 (2013): 245–259.

Murris, Karin. *The Posthuman Child: Educational Transformation through Philosophy with Picturebooks*. London: Routledge, 2016.

Nandy, Ashis. "Reconstructing Childhood: A Critique of the Ideology of Adulthood." In *Traditions, Tyranny, and Utopias: Essays in the Politics of Awareness*, 41–56. Delhi: Oxford University Press, 1987.

Pacini-Ketchabaw, Veronica, and Fikile Nxumalo. "Posthumanist Imaginaries for Decolonizing Early Childhood Praxis." In *Reconceptualizing Early Childhood Care and Education. A Reader*, edited by Marianne Bloch, Beth Blue Swadener, and Gaile S. Cannella, 131–142. New York: Routledge, 2014.

Petersen, Kit Stender. "Interviews as Intraviews: A Hand Puppet Approach to Studying Processes of Inclusion and Exclusion among Children in Kindergarten." *Reconceptualising Educational Research Methodology* 5, no. 1 (2014): 32–45.

Stables, Andrew. *Childhood and the Philosophy of Education: An Anti-Aristotelian Perspective*. London: Continuum Studies in Educational Research, 2008.

Walkerdine, Valerie. "Developmental Psychology and the Child-Centred Pedagogy: The Insertion of Piaget into Early Education." In *Changing the Subject: Psychology, Social Regulation, and Subjectivity*, ed. Wendy Hollway, Couze Venn, Valerie Walkerdine, Julian Henriques, and Cathy Urwin, 153–203. London: Routledge, 1984.

Index

Ahmed, Sara 43, 45
Alldred, Pam 151
Andrade, Fatima A. 29
Angell, Tony 85–6, 89
Anggard, Eva 152
animating stories
　linguistic imperialism 97–8
　writing strategies 98–9
Arendt, Hannah 190–1
art practice
　gathering 121–7
　learning 128
　place/space-time articulations 124–6
　renderings 122–3
　teaching 122–3, 127–8
artistic production or making 38–9

baby dolls 172–5
Badiou, Alain 193
Barad, Karen 54
　agential realism 8
　diffractive methodology 13, 202, 204
　dis/continuity concept 174
　on intra-action 198
　on "materiality" of bodies 63, 140, 198, 201
　ontological relation 2–3, 59, 197–8
Bastian, Michelle 88
Bateson, Gregory 182–3
Berger, Iris 13, 18
binary logics 2, 67, 93–4, 114, 123, 171, 174, 198–200, 202, 204
　human/animal 140
Blaise, Mindy 9, 10, 89, 93, 105
Bonilauri, Simona 183
Braidotti, Rosi 68, 197

camera 11, 75, 77, 123, 132–4, 150, 153
　durable action 132, 150
　mobile 11, 131
Cameron, Jenny 106, 153
care/caring

act of dis/connection 175–6
clay/claying 25–32
concepts 171–2, 174, 176
dictionary definitions 173–4
gender and 171, 176, 178
obligation vs 172–3
childhood education
　child-animal relations 102–7
　childing 197–205
　clay practices 27–32
　collaboration 187–93
　crowing 85–90
　fabric and studio practices 37–41
　literacying 53–9
　muscle performances 73–9
　neoliberal approaches 181–2
　practices of collaboration 187–9
　rabbiting tales 112–16
　refiguring presences 31–2, 160–5
　shimmering 93–9
　sticks 43–9
　urban play spaces 141–2
　use of cameras 11, 75, 77, 123, 132–4, 150, 153, 155
　with digital tools 63, 65, 134, 152
childing
　diffractive methodology 204
　image-nings 200–1
　ontological relationality 197–8
　posthuman subjectivity 198–205.
　(See also Barad, Karen)
choreographies 38, 41
Cixous, Hélène 189
classic curriculum theory on
　commonplaces 67–8
classroom 7–9, 28, 56–8, 90, 171, 173, 175
　curricula 67–71, 132–3, 188, 193
clay/claying
　childhood education 7
　Dja Dja Wurrung 27
　ecological memory 27–8
　gifting 30–1

in early childhood education 32
projects 31
Wadawurrung 27
Clement, Susannah 11, 12, 149
Clifford, Rachelle 123
co-inhabit/co-inhabitants 10, 12, 164
coevolution 85–6, 89
colaboring 193. *See also* collaboration
collaboration 13, 31
    action and 191–2
    co, notion of 190–1
    concept 187–9
    laboring as part of 192–3
    living-in-translation 189–90
colonialism 16, 21, 162, 164, 197
colonization 1, 17, 19, 93, 111, 114, 176
common worlds 4, 9, 13, 85, 87–8, 90, 98, 190–1
communities 13, 21, 68, 122, 127, 131, 134, 136
creativity 2, 140, 147
crows/crowing 103–5
    coevolution 85–6
    companion call 87–8
    cultural relationship with humans and 85–9
    food droppings by children 88–9
    in education research 85, 89–90
    matters of fact and matters of concern 89
curriculum 67–71, 132–3, 188, 193
    embodied visions 132–3
    science and technology 132
    wearable cameras, use of 131–5

Dahlberg, Gunilla 183
de Finney, Sandrina 105
death 47, 63–5, 71, 105, 110, 136, 164
Deleuze, Gilles 2, 7, 54, 58–9, 151
Despret, Vinciane 107
dis/connections 172–6
dispossession 125, 159

early childhood educators 8, 12–13, 64, 73, 93, 121, 164–5, 171, 187
ecology of intimacy. *See* clay/claying
Egyptian pyramid game board 53–8
    cardboard slide 56–8
emotion 92, 152, 154, 180
entangled relations

21st-century life worlds 1–2, 4–7, 13, 182
camera-body-image 131, 135, 141, 201–2
children and materials 8–9, 48, 57
emotional and coercive activities 152
fabric and bodies 37, 39–40
gender and care 175–6
human body 73, 79
laboring processes 192
literacying 53
neoliberal pedagogies 184
post-theories 54, 63, 143–4, 197–8
quantum theories 199, 204
situated contexts 90, 164, 173
species diversity 88, 114
ethics 2, 5, 10–11, 50, 106, 124, 127–8, 136–9, 142–4, 154, 171, 184
Euro-Western research paradigms 3–4, 6
Evers, Clifton 152–3

fabrics
    choreographies 41
    fluidities 38–40
    hockey game 39–41
    in early childhood education 37–8
    making 38–9
    materials 36–7
    as play thing 37–8
    studio 35–6, 39
    translucent quality 35
families 11, 58, 65, 105, 131, 149–52, 154
Filippini, Tiziana 183
forest 73, 86–8, 124–5, 160–1, 163–4, 182
Fox, Nick J. 151

gathering
    art practice 121–7
    rebodying through 127–8
    teaching as 127–8
gender 15, 21, 171, 176, 178
gesture 4, 30–1, 37, 40, 141
gifting 27, 30–2
GoProing
    affects and emotion 152–3
    participant and researcher subjectivities 151–2
    uncomfortable encounters 153–4
    video methods 150–1
    walking practices 149–54

grappling 114–16
Guattari, Felix 2, 54, 58–9, 151

Hamm, Catherine 9, 10, 89, 93
Haran, Joan 6
Haraway, Donna 6, 76, 87, 104, 115
  on caring 171–2
  on collective thoughts 131–2
  on endurance 136
  on response-abilities. 175
  on rules of play 140
Heidegger, Martin 188
Heydon, Rachel 8, 63
hockey game 39–41
Hodgins, B. Denise 1, 12, 171
human bodies 8, 31, 73, 75, 78, 87, 198–9

Indigenous knowledge 2–4, 7, 9–10, 162, 164
Indigenous peoples 17, 21, 121, 125, 160–2, 165
Ingold, Tim 38, 188, 192
Instone, Lesley 8, 48, 87
interactions 7, 43–4, 48, 102, 134, 139, 141–2
intergenerational learning 63–8
  children and elders 63–8
  classroom curricula 63–8
  intra-relations effects 64, 67–8
intra-actions 20, 56, 67, 198–9
Iorio, Jeanne M. 89

Kennedy, David 199
Kimmerer, Robin Wall 97–8
Kind, Sylvia 7, 29–30, 35, 46, 122
Knight, Linda 11, 139, 143–4
knowing
  aesthetics 182
  logics of walking 127
  pedagogical practice 197, 199
  sensorial modes of 133
  thinking and 98
  of world 93
Kocher, Laurie 46
Kohan, Walter 199
Kuby, Candace R. 8, 53, 57–9
Kummen, Kathleen 9, 85

Landau, Ben 31
Lather, Patti 1, 6, 14

Latour, Bruno 85, 89, 93
Law, John 123
learningliving 179, 181–4
Lee, Damien 164
Lenz Taguchi, Hillevi 5, 36, 59
literacy artifacts 56
literacy desiring 8, 53–7, 59
literacying 8, 53–5, 57, 59

MacLure, Maggie 59
Manning, Erin 37–8, 41
Marzluff, John 85–6, 89
mashing 131
  creative practices 135–6
  students' engagement 134–5
Massumi, Brian 41
materiality 8, 58, 63, 79, 132–3, 164
meaning making, situated stories 179–80
metaphor 21, 122, 131, 188
Meuret, Michel 107
more-than-human 4, 8, 12, 45, 48, 57, 87, 90, 94, 98, 115, 117–18, 137, 171
Morrill, Angie 159
Mukherjee, Swapna 28
multiplicity 2, 135, 183, 199
multispecies relations 9, 44, 48, 93–5, 98
  human exceptionsim and 93–5
  language of animacy 97–8
  matters of fact and matters of concern 93
  shimmering 94–5
Murris, Karin 13, 197
muscles
  in education research 79
  physiological understanding 73–9
Myers, Misha 102

Nancy, Jean-Luc 190–1
Negarestani, Reza 187, 189, 193
nonhumans 56, 98–9, 143, 190
  animals 139–40, 143
Nxumalo, Fikile 12, 159

O'Sullivan, Simon 38
Obrist, Hans-Ulrich 35

Pacini-Ketchabaw, Veronica 7, 25, 27–8, 46, 105
pedagogies 4, 7–8, 11, 13, 20, 54, 73, 89–90, 184, 186

play
    concepts 139–41
    human vs nonhuman contexts 139–44
    in urban spaces 141–2
    inefficient mapping 142–4
Plumwood, Val 113
politics 5, 19, 30, 58, 133–4, 184, 188–9
postqualitative research 1, 5, 13, 171–2, 176
provocations 5, 11, 39, 64, 85, 132
Puig de la Bellacasa, María 6
    concept of *touching visions* 11, 131, 133–4
    on matters of care 12, 27–8, 171–2, 174–6

qualitative research. *See* childhood education

rabbits/rabbiting
    Australian context. 112–15
    child-rabbit relations 114–16
    colonization narrative 114–15
    grappling 114–15
Rautio, Pauliina 44
Readings, Bill 13, 180
reclaiming 131, 135
reconfiguring 12, 110, 148
refiguring presences 12, 160, 165
Rooney, Tonya 7, 8, 43
Rose, Deborah Bird 9, 89, 94–5, 98, 104, 113, 115
Rotas, Nikki 11, 131

Schwab, Joseph 67
Sciallano, Lucile 31
settler colonialism 3, 121–2, 160
settlers 3, 7, 27, 102, 115, 124, 161
shimmering
    Creek-egretta-child-yabbie relations 95–7
    multispecies world 94–5
Simpson, Leanne Betasamosake 5, 159
    on ecology of intimacy 27
    on indigenous relationalities 160
situating knowledges
    forest discovery 161–4
    Indigenous land 160–1
    settler colonialism 160–5

Smith, Linda Tuhiwai 123–4
Springgay, Stephanie 122
sticking/sticks
    children's risky encounter 48–9
    in early childhood education 44–6
    lively materiality 46–8
    meaning 43
subjectivity 1, 5, 11, 131, 138, 198

TallBear, Kim 3
Taylor, Affrica 10, 44, 105, 111
Todd, Zoe 3
touch/touching
    affective dimensions 133–4
    hot compost 131–2, 135–6
Tsing, Anna Lowenhaupt 78, 101, 104
Tuck, Eve 3, 123–4, 159, 160
21st century children. *See also* childhood education
    child-animal relations 101
    entangled legacies 1–3
    place fidelity 104–7
    postqualitative research 1–3, 5–6, 13–14, 64, 131, 139, 143, 150–1, 171–2, 176
    tracking engagements 102–4, 107
    tracking engagements with animals 101–7

urban play spaces 141–2

van Dooren, Thom 89, 104–5, 115, 159
    Flight Ways 104
Vecchi, Vea 182
video methods. *See* GoProing
Vintimilla, Cristina D 13, 187
vision 133–5. *See also* mashing; touch/touching

walking 11, 44, 102–3, 121, 123–4, 127, 149–50, 152, 154, 163
Watts, Vanessa 3
wearable cameras 133–5, 152
Wood, Dennis 142
Wright, Kate 113
Writers' Studio. 53, 58–9

Yang, K. Wayne 123, 160
Yeomans, Julia M. 141